A
FLYING
LIFE

A
FLYING
LIFE

AN ENTHUSIAST'S PHOTOGRAPHIC RECORD
OF BRITISH AVIATION IN THE 1930s

RICHARD RIDING

FONTHILL

Dedication

This book is affectionately dedicated to my father E. J. 'Eddie' Riding (1916-50) and his pal J. G. 'Jimmy' Ellison (1919-94), whose joint enthusiasm for everything aeronautical, coupled with their meticulous recording of the aviation scene in Britain during the 1930s, made this book possible.

Fonthill Media Limited
Fonthill Media LLC
www.fonthillmedia.com
office@fonthillmedia.com

Published in 2013

British Library Cataloguing in Publication Data:
A catalogue record for this book is available from the British Library

ISBN 978-1-78155-087-8

Typeset in 9pt on 12pt Sabon LT
Printed and bound in England

Connect with us
 facebook.com/fonthillmedia twitter.com/fonthillmedia

Contents

Acknowledgements

Although the work of writing and collating this book has been a solitary journey, I was conscious that both my father and his pal Jimmy Ellison were somehow looking over my shoulder as I scanned hundreds of negatives from their collections and thumbed through their collective records. On occasions, particularly working in the quiet of the night, so deeply did I get involved that I felt I was a third member of their expeditions. Had they lived, I like to think that they would have been chuffed to see their collections combined in this way. I sincerely hope that I have done them justice.

I am grateful to Carol Agius, Jimmy's daughter, for her help and enthusiasm throughout the project. I am also indebted to my old friend Ray Hankin, a staff member of *The Aeroplane* during its final years in the 1960s, for running his critical eye over the text and captions. Any errors or howlers are of my own making.

I am particularly grateful to Jay Slater, senior commissioning editor of Fonthill Media, for giving me the opportunity of sharing this collection of photographs with a wider audience.

Preface

Much of E. J. Riding's life up until the outbreak of the Second World War is the subject of this book, but briefly, Edwin James Riding was born 1 February 1916 in Charlton, London. When war was declared in September 1939, E. J. R. was working for the Aeronautical Inspection Directorate (AID), and was attached to the Fairey Aviation Company Ltd at Hayes. He was transferred to the company's Great West Aerodrome in October 1941, where most of his time was spent inspecting Fairey Albacores. This involved a certain amount of flying, and he made forty or so flights as an 'observer' for test pilot F. C. Dixon. In April 1942, he was transferred to A. E. Opperman & Company Ltd, at Borehamwood, Hertfordshire, where he was promoted to senior examiner, responsible for the inspection of Short Stirling undercarriage assemblies and gearboxes. Next, he was posted to London Aircraft Production's flight shed at Leavesden in September 1943, where his inspection skills were focused on Handley Page Halifax IIs and IIIs. In June 1944, he moved to the other side of the aerodrome to the de Havilland Aircraft Company's Mosquito flight shed, where he was responsible for signing out Mosquito Marks III, 33, and 36, during which time he enjoyed seventy or so test flights; the pilots were only too delighted that the man who signed out the aircraft wanted to accompany them!

E. J. R. left the AID in February 1946 and joined the Harborough Publishing Company, based at Eaton Bray and run by Douglas A. Russell. Here, he worked as a photographer and journalist for the company's *Air Review* and *Aeromodeller* publications, in addition to working on a number of books, including Volume VII of *Aircraft of the Fighting Powers,* for which he produced all the three-view drawings. His articles on full-size aircraft, for which he also took the accompanying photographs and produced magnificent 1/72-scale drawings, are still well-regarded to this day. He also built beautiful scale models and produced plans for *Aeromodeller*. As a tribute to his model making, the E. J. Riding Memorial Trophy for flying scale models is eagerly contested to this day.

In March 1949, E. J. R. finally learnt to fly, and for a year spent many happy hours at the controls of a Piper Cub flying from Elstree, generously giving flights to family and friends, or popping into Eaton Bray on some errand or other. But this was all brought to a sudden halt at Easter the following year.

On 7 April 1950, Good Friday, he took off from Elstree in Auster Autocar G-AJYM, piloted by Stanley Orton Bradshaw, to cover the opening of the Boston Aero Club in Lincolnshire for *The Aeroplane*. After the ceremony, they left for the return to Elstree in a strong wind that provided the ideal opportunity to show those on the ground the Auster's slow-flying capabilities. At an altitude of about 700 feet, and flying very slowly, the aircraft suddenly dropped a wing and entered a spin. Although recovery action was taken immediately, the aircraft hit a dyke bordering the airfield and all three occupants died instantly. Death by misadventure was the coroner's verdict at the subsequent enquiry. E. J. R.'s death robbed his three children of a father, his wife of a husband, and hundreds of aviation enthusiasts of a man who had dedicated his life to aviation.

E. J. 'Eddie' Riding, 1916-50.

Introduction

Nerds, anoraks, or worse? Every so often these days, the activities of aircraft/reggie spotters give rise to the kind of jibes traditionally aimed at train spotters. Sometimes, they make the headlines by getting into trouble while indulging in their hobby, particularly when falling foul of officials at foreign airports who have no understanding of such activities and treat 'offenders' as spies. In Britain, aircraft spotters have been around since the end of the First World War, and possibly earlier, and to many, the pastime would appear as pointless as collecting car numbers; an activity I shamefully admit to taking part in with an equally deranged friend for a whole morning in the 1950s by the side of the A41 at Hendon. By lunchtime, we had filled our notebooks and were suffering from writer's cramp. We looked at each other, realised how pointless it all was, and the next day started train spotting. But what if we each had owned a camera and photographed even 1 per cent of the cars that we spotted? Imagine how interesting those photographs would be today, sixty years later.

From 1929, my late father not only noted the registrations of every aeroplane that passed over the family home at Chorlton-cum-Hardy, Manchester, he also recorded its type, owner, the direction in which it was flying, height, and colour scheme. The most worthwhile information recorded was colour schemes; today, such information on pre-war civil aeroplanes is scarce. After two or three years, E. J. R. came to realise that there was more to just spotting and recording the passing of aircraft. He later wrote to aviation author A. J. Jackson, 'I can't understand anybody being satisfied with just *seeing* a machine. If I couldn't take a camera, I'd prefer not to go.'

And so in 1932, he started visiting local Manchester aerodromes with a very second-hand camera. Over the ensuing years, and with better cameras, he built up an enviable collection of photographs, mostly taken in the north-west and south of England. Initially, he worked alone, but from mid-1934 until August 1939, often in the company of his aero modelling friend Jimmy Ellison (J. G. E.). During the war, they went their separate ways; E. J. R. worked in the aviation industry in Middlesex and Hertfordshire as an inspector for the Aeronautical Inspection Directorate (AID), while J. G. E. found employment with the joinery firm of F. Hills & Sons in Manchester, which later constructed aircraft.

Sadly, my father was killed in an aircraft accident in April 1950. Fortunately, rather than dispose of his photographic collection, and knowing my interest, my mother entrusted it to me, even though I was aged only eight at the time of my father's death. J. G. E. died in 1994, but we had kept in contact sporadically over the ensuing years. Some while ago, I acquired both Jimmy's negative collection and records of his outings with my father.

Although I now had both collections in my possession, I had never come across any record of E. J. R.'s negative collection, giving dates and locations of his visits to aerodromes. Knowing how meticulous he was with such things, I knew that he must have kept a record, but as time passed I forgot about it. In 1982, E. J. R.'s close friend A. J. Jackson (A. J. J.) died. He of course

This amazing assortment of mostly non-flying scale models was produced by members of the Chorlton-cum-Hardy Model Club. Interestingly, Westland Widgeon G-EBRO and the D.H.53 Humming Bird are the only monoplanes amongst this collection. How many types can you recognise?

is known universally as the author of the three-volume *British Civil Aircraft 1919-59*, first published by Putnam in 1959 and dedicated to 'Eddie Riding'. They had met during the war at RAF Colerne, where A. J. J. was running a Spitfire maintenance unit. E. J. R. occasionally dropped in as 'test observer' passenger in D.H.98 Mosquitoes, on delivery from Leavesden, where in his AID capacity, he had cleared them for flight. The two men soon discovered their shared obsession for photographs of British civil-registered aircraft, which they had each been collecting for many years. Between March 1943 and March 1950, they exchanged more than 100 letters, the contents of which would make a fascinating book in its own right, crammed as they are with information pertaining to their hobby. Each chapter heading in this book is sub-headed with a quote from E. J. R., taken from letters he wrote to A. J. J. in 1943.

Today, the A. J. Jackson Photographic Collection is one of the largest of its type, and after A. J. J.'s death, it was administered by his younger son Roger. Tragically, Roger died in 2004, and the collection is currently curated by his brother Wg Cdr David Jackson. Shortly after Roger's funeral, the Jackson family presented me with a parcel. On opening it, I was overjoyed to discover that not only did it contain all my father letters to A. J. J., but the long-lost book containing E. J. R.'s personal record of every aircraft photograph he had taken since 1929. Shortly before his death, my father had obviously lent A. J. J. the book, and it had gathered dust for almost sixty years. So, armed with E. J. R.'s and J. G. E.'s negative collections, together with detailed records of when and where photographs were taken, there was no longer anything preventing me from producing this book.

In a long wartime letter to A. J. J., in which he reminisced about his spotting adventures, my father wrote, 'Blimey, fifth page already. Why don't we write a book and be done with it? Something like *Airdays*, the best book on aviation ever published.' (Written by John F. Leeming and published in 1936 by George G. Harrap & Company Ltd.) There is little doubt in my mind that had E. J. R. lived, *British Civil Aircraft 1919-1959* would have been a joint effort – certainly much of the information contained within its volumes came from E. J. R. via the aforementioned letters.

Shortly before he died, I gave J. G. E. a blank audio tape and asked him to recall what he could about my father during their friendship of the 1930s. A few months later, the tape arrived, and the following is an edited transcript:

Your father was in many ways my mentor and master, not only in our common interest in aircraft, photography, cars, and DIY [that was before DIY was invented], but in many aspects of my life. Remember, he was some four years older than me, and in teen years this can be a great age difference in some areas. I think I first met him in about 1934 when he was at the Manchester College of Technology, not at that time a faculty of the university. I was just leaving school at about fifteen-years-old, and we were introduced by a mutual friend, Eric Daniels, who with myself ran a model aero club, the one you have a picture of taken in a cellar (see page 12). Somehow, we heard of your father's interest in aircraft. At about that time, he was building a full-size aeroplane with an ex-Manchester Grammar School colleague, a fellow called Fred Sunter. It was never finished, partly because Fred's interest was diverted to a rather beautiful female, and partly because we became more interested in scale models, usually of about one twelfth scale.

When I first met your father, he used to ride a Rudge bicycle with a three-speed box and an enormous armchair saddle. I, like a good scholar, also bought a Rudge and demanded a wide saddle be fitted so that for the next few years, that is until the Austin Seven era, we pedalled the south Manchester area, regularly visiting Barton, then the Manchester Airport, and Woodford, which was the home of the Lancashire Aero Club and also the airfield from which A. V. Roe flew test flights. We also visited Hooton Park across on the Wirral peninsula, where the Liverpool Aero Club had an annexe and hangared two or three smaller aircraft, particularly Tigers and D.H.60 Moths. Most of these visits were recorded on film, and we each kept log books indicating where we'd been and what aircraft we had seen. We also used to record all the aircraft flying over our homes and could recognise individual local aircraft at distances of perhaps 5-6 miles, because we each had a telescope mounted at our respective bedroom windows. I still have some of the log books from the years of '34, '35, and '36. They make interesting reading now because of the aircraft that were spotted in those days.

The aircraft modelling business went on quite a pace. In fact, we ran two clubs at that stage, and probably had fifteen to twenty members in each, the main object of which was to make models and visit local airfields and generally record information that was available on aircraft. Eventually, your pa and I split off to form the Northern Model Aircraft Club because we were more interested in scale models, a few of which were elastic-powered flying models; this was before the age of petrol engines. And for some reason, we also had an interest in gliders. Each year, we exhibited at the Manchester Hobbies and Models Exhibition and managed to pull off a few certificates of merit in competition with our previous colleagues, which was great fun at the time.

Our visits to the airfields, or aerodromes as we used to say in those days, were improved when we acquired an Austin Seven open-tourer at a cost of £5 from a man who pocketed the money and left us to push the car home, as neither of us could drive! I recollect that we both knew there was such a thing as a clutch and it probably had a brake as well, and a handle to start it. We turned the Austin on its side and looked underneath and worked out how everything worked, and within a couple of days your father was driving it; I wasn't old enough to get a licence at the time. Three weeks later, he passed his test, which had then not long been introduced, and from then on we were mobile. So for about the next two years, that must have been the 1936-38 period, we spent all our spare cash on film and petrol, the latter being 1s 5d a gallon for Shell Mex in those days, or 1s 7½d if you could afford Cleveland Discall! Hence the magnificent collection of photographs he has of that period.

E. J. R., far left, pictured in friend Bob Purdy's cellar in December 1934, working on his model of Avro 504K G-EBKX, with other members of the Chorlton-cum-Hardy Model Club. Second from right is J. G. E., E. J. R.'s close friend and companion on many of the trips recorded in this book.

In 1937, we did a tour of airfields and cathedrals. This turned out to be an epic occasion and we covered about 1,300 miles in his Austin open tourer BU5575, known as 'Busby'. There were many incidents, and according to my notes, sixteen punctures! Your father drove the whole of the trip, as I had no licence, and there must be many photographs in the collection of various incidents that occurred during the tour. We tented all the way, though we did once stay with an aunt of his in Woolwich, I remember, and then went onto our first cathedral, which was Canterbury. From there we drove along the South Coast; Southampton, Salisbury Plain up into and across Wales, and eventually returned through Chester to Manchester. We had an excellent time.

Shortly after this tour, your father took a job with A. V. Roe, where he was employed as an inspector of incoming aircraft materials. This was his first step on the ladder towards getting his ground engineer's ticket. Shortly after that, he went to Hooton Park Airfield and worked for 'Pop' Rimmer, who ran an air circus visiting fairly remote towns in Lancashire with two Avro 504s, an Avro Tutor, and a Tiger Moth. Your father acted as ground engineer until the following year when he took his ground engineer's ticket. In fact in those days, he lived at Hooton, either on the airfield or in local digs. He used to spend the winter overhauling the aircraft; it was pretty cold in that hangar too. In the spring and/or summer he would go out on tour, and occasionally I would join him at the weekends, or we would meet up at our parents' homes where we both had our rooms literally papered with fabric panels from aircraft, as per some of the photographs you have.

During all this, I was influenced greatly by Ed, and in retrospect, he gave me a great deal, which I didn't fully appreciate at the time. You will remember that Rupert Moore

J. G. 'Jimmy' Ellison accompanied
E. J. Riding on many tours and visits to
aerodromes during the 1930s. After his
death in 1994, J. G. E.'s negative collection
and meticulous records were combined
with those of his former friend and form an
integral part of this book.

(the aviation artist and E. J. R.'s friend) once said, 'He was a man of most even temper, a modest man and one of great intensity.' I think that sums him up fairly well in many ways because he was interested not only in aircraft but also music. He had a great interest in the countryside for instance, and there was a period when his mother and father had a long-term arrangement with a cottage at Church Stretton near Shrewsbury. I can remember strolling the moor-tops with Ed on many occasions. An added interest there of course was the gliding camp, where we used go along and help with the gliders, though in those days we weren't allowed to fly them. It was a pleasant interlude going to Church Stretton and seeing the Welsh countryside, an area we both loved very much.

In about 1939, Ed's parents moved to Wimborne, in Dorset, and shortly after, in July 1939, Ed got married to Marjorie. A few days after they were married I went on a tour to Cornwall with them. I had an old Austin Ten at that time, and as it was a considerable improvement on Ed's Austin Seven, we took my car as well. I suppose it was an extension of their honeymoon really, and we spent a very pleasant time together. We hadn't been as far west as that before, and obviously we called at one or two airfields along the way and took a few photographs. And then shortly after, in early September, war put paid to any further tours together.

A few words about J. G. E.: born 28 September 1919, James G. Ellison spent most of his working life with F. Hills & Sons Ltd, a company formed by Francis Hills in 1849 as a one-man joinery company in Yarm on Tees. Cooper and Walter Hills (grandsons of Francis) took over in 1907, and during the First World War, the company made ammunition boxes and joinery for the Forces. In 1921, Hills became a limited company, and in 1933, moved to larger premises in

Stockton. The company turned its hand to making aeroplanes after Managing Director W. R. Chown, who was interested in aircraft development, visited Prague, Czechoslovakia, to obtain a licence for the manufacture of the Praga Air Baby two-seat light aircraft. Following this, he purchased the old Ford Motor Company premises in Trafford Park, Manchester, for joinery and aircraft production.

The first aircraft built by Hills was a Pou du Ciel, an H.M.14 Flying Flea designed for homebuilders by Frenchman Henri Mignet. The aircraft was registered G-ADOU in October 1935, and test flown at nearby Barton Aerodrome. The first licence-built Praga E.114 was sold to Australia, and the second registered G-AEEU became the company's demonstrator in April 1936. Total production by Hills amounted to twenty-eight aircraft, plus seven uncompleted. There followed two one-off Hillson light aircraft, both designed by Norman Sykes: the Pennine, a two-seat, side-by-side, high-wing monoplane, not dissimilar to the Praga, registered G-AFBX; the Helvellyn G-AFKT, an open cockpit, tandem, two-seater, low-wing monoplane. During 1938-39, Hills built Anson wings and laminated spars for Airspeed Oxfords. During the war, the company produced no fewer than 480,000 JABLO propeller blades and 10 million square feet of aeronautical plywood for Mosquito and other aircraft. In addition, the company produced more than 800 Percival Proctors and the extraordinary slip-wing Hawker Hurricane I, after first building and testing a research aircraft called the Hillson Bi-mono. An expendable slip-wing was mounted above the fuselage in order to obtain more lift for operating out of small fields. Once the aircraft was airborne, the slip-wing could be released by the pilot.

After the war, Hills returned to manufacturing for the building trade, and also developing interests overseas. In 1969, Hills became part of the Bowater Corporation, and in the mid-1980s, Bowaters sold to the company to Sarek of Sweden, becoming Crosby Sarek in 1990.

With Hills overseas interests, J. G. E. travelled extensively with his job, often to Germany, Sweden, Holland, and Saudi Arabia, as well as making several trips to Africa, some lasting several months, to Takoradi, Ghana, (then called the Gold Coast), and to Libreville, Gabon.

Apart from his interest in aero modelling and aeroplanes, all his life J. G. E. was a fly fishing enthusiast, tying his own flies, making rods, and organising casting competitions at local country shows. His interest in sailing probably started in the late 1950s when he and Bill Precious, a work colleague and family friend, bought an Enterprise sailing dinghy together, which was kept at Runswick Bay Sailing Club and called *Joca* after Ellison's daughters Joan and Carol. They raced together for a couple of years before Jimmy bought out Bill, and daughter Carol crewed for him until her impending 'A' levels took precedence. He said that in any case, she wasn't growing into the 6-foot hunchback needed! He always enjoyed walking, especially on the North Yorkshire moors and in Teesdale.

After his wife Freda died, Jimmy fished and went walking in Scotland each year with his friend Bill Moonie. He also enjoyed playing cricket for an F. Hills & Sons team, taking part in an annual match against CIBA in Cambridge, which was also a social event for wives and families. Jimmy also enjoyed music and loved listening to his wife playing the piano.

J. G. E. was a man with enthusiasm, humour, courage, and enormous patience. He always had time for his family, and throughout his life, gave them his utmost support. His friendship with Eddie Riding was enormously important to him, and to lose his brother Jack and Eddie within three years of each other must have been hard for him. When he died on 20 November 1994, J. G. E. had outlived his friend Eddie by forty-four years.

CHAPTER ONE

An Eye on the Sky (1916-29)

We also collected relics and draped our bedroom walls with them – fabric side panels plus registration numbers … Amongst them were two genuine black crosses from an LVG and Fokker DVIII (Hendon 1936 plus scissors) a D.H.6 prop and 'Southern Sun' torn off Kingsford Smith's Xmas Mail from Australia. Vandalism is not a hobby of mine!

Letter from E. J. Riding to A. J. Jackson in 1943

During the evening of Monday 31 January 1916, nine German naval Zeppelins crossed the North Sea into eastern England with orders to bomb targets over a larger area than on any previous occasion, taking in southern and central England, and Liverpool especially. Leading the attack was Fregattenkapitan Peter Strasser, the head of German airships, in Zeppelin L.11. As the airships passed over the English coast, the weather was abysmal, with fog over the sea, and rain and snow. Later, with ice forming on their gas bags and visibility obscured by cloud, the raiders dropped bombs on what they thought was Liverpool. In fact, they never reached the North West, but instead put the fear of God into Midland towns, including Burton-on-Trent, Walsall, and the outskirts of Birmingham. Bombs were also dropped in Norfolk, Suffolk, Lincolnshire, Leicestershire, Staffordshire, and Derbyshire. The death toll was heavy; 61 dead and around 100 injured. The Zeppelins had suffered engine failures, and one, L.19, came down in the North Sea. The raid was front page news in the evening papers of 1 February.

A few hours after the raid, on Tuesday 1 February, at 26 Little Heath, Charlton, London, Vera Amor Riding gave birth to her second child Edwin James Riding, a brother to Elvina, who had been born the day before Christmas Day 1914. Vera's husband Leonard, formerly a cable station manager with the Indo European Telegraph Company in Tehran and Tabriz, had returned from a four-year posting to Persia at the end of 1913. The couple married at Marylebone in January 1914.

The Riding family moved to Manchester in 1920, and settled at South Drive in the smart suburb of Chorlton-cum-Hardy, to the south-west of the city. E J. R. first attended South Manchester School, and in 1929, entered Manchester Grammar School. It was around this time that his interest in aviation took off, so to speak. Various school text books were enhanced, or mutilated, depending on one's point of view, by nicely sketched ink drawings of aircraft in combat and witty alterations to otherwise pedestrian illustrations. E. J. R.'s copy of *Horace Odes III,* for example, was definitely made more interesting by his artistic prowess!

At home, E. J. R.'s bedroom walls were covered with fabric panels and other artefacts liberated from wrecked aircraft, including rudder bars, windscreens, and control columns. A modelling board, balsa wood, and tissue were always on hand, with various model aircraft in the process of being built. Right from an early age, E. J. R. was interested only in building scale models, and he and a number of like-minded friends formed the Chorlton-cum-Hardy Model Club, meeting in a member's parents' cellar. Much later, during the Second World War and up

Above left: E. J. R. sitting on the roof of the garden shed at the family home in South Drive, Chorlton-cum-Hardy, Manchester, *c.* 1929. This was a favourite vantage point for recording the passage of aircraft overhead to and from the airfields at nearby Wythenshawe, and later, Barton and Woodford.

Above right: E. J. R. freshly scrubbed up and wearing the uniform of Manchester Grammar School, *c.* 1932.

until his death in 1950, E. J. R. was to make a name for himself as the designer and builder of flying scale models for *Aeromodeller* magazine. He also kept a large scrapbook of newspaper reports of aircraft accidents, running from 1929 until the late 1940s; a useful record of all-too-frequent occurrences in the those days, but invariably containing very dodgy and inaccurate accounts from so called eyewitnesses.

The nearest aerodrome to the Riding home was Wythenshawe, known locally as Rackhouse Aerodrome, located in the fork of Sale Road and Wythenshawe Road on an area that originally embraced fields and for which a new housing estate was planned. Opened in April 1929, Wythenshawe served briefly as Manchester's municipal aerodrome while construction of a permanent one was taking place at nearby Barton, alongside the Manchester Ship Canal. Wythenshawe Aerodrome was very basic, and although there was provision for fuel, there were no radio or lighting facilities. The field was identifiable from the air by the letters M/C encircled on the ground. A small barn was converted into a hangar, providing accommodation for just one aircraft, and a farmhouse served as an office. Wythenshawe was granted an 'all-purpose' licence by the Air Ministry, and Manchester became the first municipality in Great Britain to possess its own airport.

In his youth, E. J. R literally collected, with prior permission, aeroplane serial numbers and registration letters. This view of E. J. R.'s bedroom at the family home features the fabric covering from the rudder of Avro 504K F9844. Let it be said that the aircraft was long dead when it was skinned!

A later view of E. J. R.'s bedroom showing the addition of an RAF serial number cut from deceased D.H.60M Gipsy Moth K1206. This aeroplane was unusual in that after delivery to the Station Flight at RAF Upavon, it was returned to de Havilland for conversion for inverted flying before service with the Central Flying School. It crashed after a forced landing in bad weather in January 1935, and the wreckage taken to Castle Bromwich aerodrome, where subsequently, trophy hunter E. J. R. got his hands on it. A rudder bar and joystick from an Avro 504K are seen hanging on the wall.

An aerial view of Chorlton-cum-Hardy, with South Drive running along the bottom of the photograph. The Riding family home is just visible bottom left.

South Drive, Chorlton-cum-Hardy, in the late 1920s.

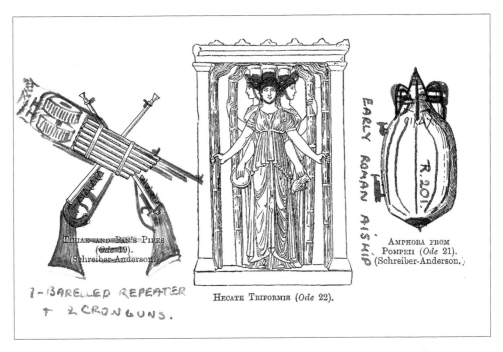

THIIAE AND PAN'S PIPES
(*Ode* 19).
(Schreiber-Anderson.)

HECATE TRIFORMIS (*Ode* 22).

EARLY ROMAN AIRSHIP

AMPHORA FROM
POMPEII (*Ode* 21).
(Schreiber-Anderson.)

1-BARELLED REPEATER
+ 2 CRONGUNS.

Above and below: At Manchester Grammar School, E. J. R. had little time for Latin lessons, and these mutilated pages taken from his copy of *Horace Odes III* by T. E. Page bear testament to his level of boredom! E. J. R.'s thoughts were literally in the clouds.

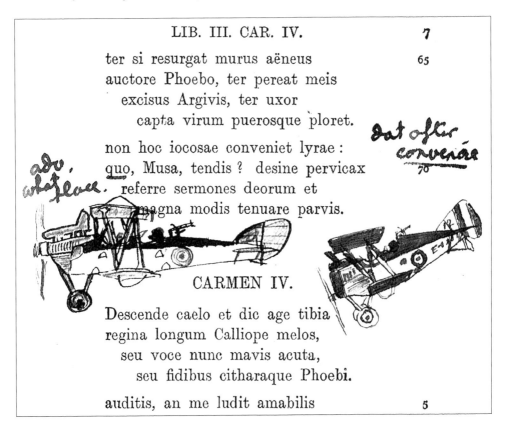

LIB. III. CAR. IV.　　　　7

ter si resurgat murus aëneus　　　　65
auctore Phoebo, ter pereat meis
　　excisus Argivis, ter uxor
　　　capta virum puerosque ploret.

non hoc iocosae conveniet lyrae :
　quo, Musa, tendis ? desine pervicax
　　referre sermones deorum et
　　magna modis tenuare parvis.

CARMEN IV.

Descende caelo et dic age tibia
regina longum Calliope melos,
　　seu voce nunc mavis acuta,
　　　seu fidibus citharaque Phoebi.

auditis, an me ludit amabilis　　　5

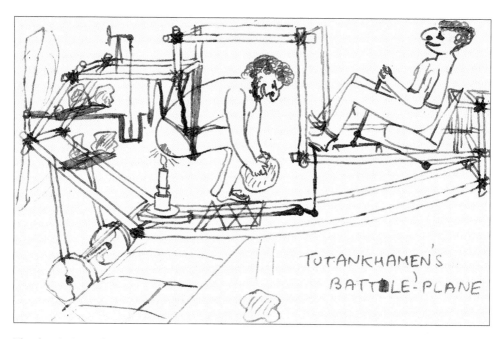

TUTANKHAMEN'S
BATTLE-PLANE

The frontispiece of E. J. R.'s Latin text book was greatly enhanced by his inventive depiction of 'Tutankhamen's Battle Plane'.

But the small size of Wythenshawe made it unsuitable for anything larger than single-engine club and private aircraft; it was the base for the blue and silver D.H.60 Moths and Avro 504Ks of Northern Air Lines (Manchester), used for joyriding and charter work. Visiting aircraft included Avro Avians of the Lancashire Aero Club from nearby Woodford Aerodrome. Despite its modest dimensions, aircraft as large as the Ford Tri-motor and Fokker Universal nonetheless landed at Wythenshawe without any problem.

Air traffic from Wythenshawe passed over the Riding household in South Drive, Chorlton-cum-Hardy, and E. J. R. started making a note of everything that flew overhead. His personal air log begins on Saturday 27 July 1929, and the first entry is the Avro 504K G-EASF. Frequent visits to Wythenshawe followed, on his Rudge bicycle, with its strange 'armchair' saddle. There, with his film pack Brownie, he took his first photographs of aeroplanes – the Genet-engined Avro Avian IV G-AACF and D.H. 9C G-EBIG, both belonging to Northern Air Lines (Manchester) Ltd. The following month, on 3 September, E. J. R. and his family were on holiday in the Whitby area in Yorkshire and came across the barnstorming Avro 504K G-EBVW in the blue, white, and silver colours of Berkshire Aviation Tours Ltd. The ensuing 5-minute flight, with A. N. Kingwell, costing 5 bob (5s), was E. J. R.'s first experience of flight. He loved it, and the first seed of his affection for the Avro 504K was sown. This first flight was later the subject of a watercolour painting by E. J. R.'s close friend aeronautical artist Stanley Orton Bradshaw. Commissioned by E. J. R., the painting was completed a year or two before both men were killed together in an air crash in April 1950.

In a letter written to A. J. Jackson in April 1943, E. J. R. wrote:

One of the finest sights I ever saw was from the top of Filey cliffs in August 1929 and consisted of two Avros following each other down the sands towards Flamborough. The leading one was old friend G-EBKB [red, white, and silver], and the other G-AAAF [red all over]. It seemed funny to look down on them, and I remember them climbing to get over

Above and below: E. J. R.'s first flight was from Whitby Moor on 3 September 1929. This was a five-minute 'five bob flip' in Avro 504K G-EBVW of Berkshire Aviation Tours Ltd, flown by A. N. Kingwell. The Avro 504K soon became E. J. R.'s favourite aeroplane, and such was the impact of that first time aloft that after the war he commissioned aviation artist Stanley Orton Bradshaw to record the thrill of it all in a watercolour painting. E. J. R. was to enjoy this painting for less than two years; both he and Stanley were killed in an air crash at Boston Aerodrome on 7 April 1950.

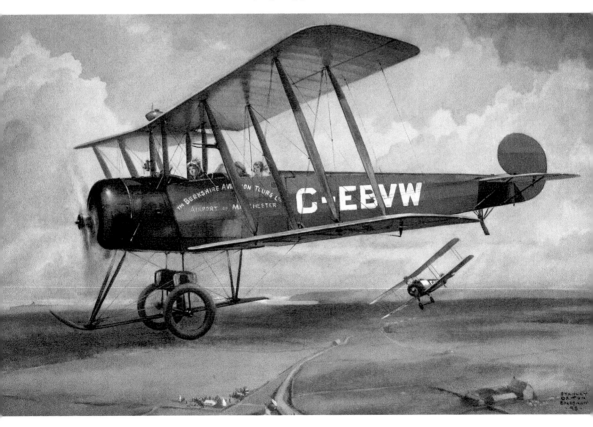

the headland and then disappearing over the other side. Since then, I have flown down the same stretch of sand in the Hull Club's Swallow G-AEVZ and Moth G-AAMS and seen people looking down on us. (see page 171)

The visit to Wythenshawe in August 1929, and E. J. R.'s first flight the following month, appear to be the only contact he had with aeroplanes in 1929. But via the aeronautical press, and the weeklies *Flight* and *The Aeroplane*, he was undoubtedly aware that in June, the RAF began equipping with the Bristol Bulldog fighter, entering service with No. 3 Squadron at RAF Upavon. In that same month, Imperial Airways introduced 30-minute 'tea flights' over London with Armstrong Whitworth Argosies, priced at £2. 2s per person. During August, the world marvelled when Germany's *Graf Zeppelin*, captained by Dr Hugo Eckener, carried out the first round the world flight by an airship, flying east from Lakehurst, New Jersey, via Tokyo and Los Angeles.

British pride rose to a high when in September, the Schneider Trophy was won by Flt Lt H. R. D. Waghorn flying Supermarine S. 6 N247 at an average speed of 328.6 mph. Days later, Sqn Ldr A. H. Orelbar broke the world's speed record in N247 at 358 mph. Earlier, on 1 September, former First World War Hanworth Aerodrome was officially re-opened as London Air Park, soon becoming the equivalent of an aviation country club and the base for National

Flying Services' orange and black training aircraft. On 10 October, HRH Prince George opened Hull's Hedon Aerodrome, the country's second municipal airport, Hull being renowned as the birthplace of Amy Johnson, although she learned to fly with the London Aeroplane Club at Stag Lane in July 1929.

A few days after the opening of Hedon, the ill-fated R-101 airship made its first flight from the Royal Airship Works at Cardington, and on 28 October, there was a sharp fall on the London Stock Exchange as the effects of the Wall Street Crash in the USA sent shock waves around the world. On 16 December, the R-100 airship G-FAAV made its first flight, from Howden, Yorkshire, travelling south to Cardington. Just before Christmas, at Hooton Park, the diminutive prototype Comper Swift G-AARX took to the sky for the first time in the hands of its designer Nicholas Comper. Hooton Park was an aerodrome at which E. J. R. was destined to spend many happy months.

E. J. R. about to hand launch a scale model of Avro 504K G-EBKX, *c.* 1931. The full-sized aircraft crashed at Crosby in Lancashire in July 1934, and owner Lancelot 'Pop' Rimmer gave E. J. R. the portion of fuselage fabric bearing the registration letters to adorn his bedroom wall!

Opposite: In 1929, E. J. R. began saving newspaper cuttings reporting air accidents in Britain in a large scrapbook. The book covers the period 1929-39, and has been an invaluable record, though some of the 'eye-witness' statements are laughable and must have been unhelpful to accident investigators.

Above: E. J. R. often photographed his models in realistic settings, even going to the trouble of trimming the grass in the immediate vicinity. Depth of field was always a problem, and this is illustrated here by the slightly out of focus tail of the model.

Below left: Of course, everyone interested in flying during the 1930s spent *6d* every month on the latest issue of W. E. Johns' *Popular Flying* magazine. Better known as the creator of 'Biggles', Johns was editor from 1932-39, after which time, the magazine's name was changed to *Aeronautics* and edited by Maj. Oliver Stewart until its closure in 1961.

Below right: As a teenager, E. J. R. kept copious records of aeroplanes that over flew the family home in Chorlton-cum-Hardy; initially, everything was recorded in this *Flying Log Book* produced by W. E. Johns. In addition to being used for recording aircraft details, there was plenty of gen for the young aero-spotter to digest.

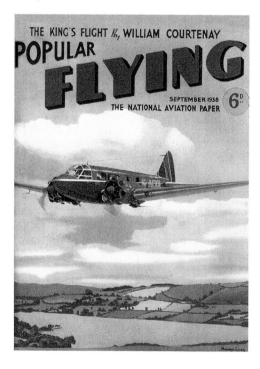

1929.

PLACE	DATE & TIME	MACHINE	NUMBER.	HEIGHT	COURSE	OWNER.	COLOUR
Wythenshawe	July 27 Sat	Auro 504K	G-EASF.		JOY RIDING.	NORTHERN AIR LINES LTD.	BLUE & SILVER.
Chorlton.	July 27.	D.H. MOTH.	G-EBZU.	1,200ft	S.E.	NORTHERN AIR LINES LTD.	BLUE & SILVER.
Chorltonville *West Dids.*	July 27.	Auro Avian GENET.	G-AACF.	—	N.W. or to S.	NORTHERN AIR LINES LTD.	BLUE & SILVER
Chorltonville	July 27.	Auro Avian IV.	G-AABX.	1,000ft	N.W. then S.	P.T. ECKERSEY.	SILVER & RED TOP.
Wythenshawe	July 28	Auro Avian II.	G-EBQL.	—	N.W S.	LANCASHIRE AERO CLUB.	SILVER, BLUE TOP.
Sale.	Jul. 28. Sun	D.H. MOTH.	G-EBZU.	1,500 ft.	S.	NORTHERN AIR LINES.	BLUE & SILVER
Chorltonville	July 28	Auro Avian IV.	G-AABX.	1,200ft.	N.W. S.	P.T. ECKERSLY.	SILVER. RED TOP.
West Didsbury.	July 28.	Auro Avian GENET.	G-AACF	AEROBATICS		NORTHERN AIR LINES LTD.	BLUE, SILVER NOSE, SILVE
Sale.	July 30. Tues	Auro Avian GENET.	G-AACF.	1,000ft.	W. then S.	NORTHERN AIR LINES LTD.	BLUE & SILVER.
Wythenshawe	July 30.	Auro Avian IV.	G-AABX.	—	S.	P.T. ECKERSLY.	SILVER & RED TOP.
Chorlton. W.	Aug. 3. Sat	D.H. 61.	G-AAAN.	950ft.	S.E.	DAILY MAIL.	SILVER RED TOP.
Wythenshawe	Aug. 4. Sun	Auro 504K.	G-EBVW	—	E.	BERKSHIRE AIR TOURS LTD.	SILVER ALL OVER.
Wythenshaw	Aug. 4th	D.H. MOTH.	G-EBZU.	—	E.	NORTHERN AIR LINES LTD.	BLUE & SILVER
Sale.	Aug. 4.	D.H. 61.	G-AAAN.	1,200ft.	S.	DAILY MAIL.	SILVER, RED TOP.
Wythenshaw	Aug. 4.	Auro Avian G.	G-AACF.	CIRCLING		NORTHERN AIR LINES LTD.	BLUE & SILVER.
Wythenshaw	Aug. 5. Mon	Auro. Avian II.	G-AAAD.	LANDED.	—		SILVER,
Chorltonville	Aug. 5.	Auro Avian GYPSY.	G-AAHK.	20ft.	N. then S.	J.C. CANTRILL	BLACK. & SILVER
Wythenshaw	Aug. 5. Tues	Auro Avian GENET.	G-AACF.	—	—	NORTHERN AIR LINES.	BLUE & SILVER.
Wythenshaw	Aug. 8.	2 Auro 504N 1 Bristol 89A.	J. ....J..... J.	—	W.	NO. S.T.S. SEALAND.	SILVER RAF.
Wythenshaw	Aug. 8.	Auro Avian III	G-EBXY	—	W.	LIVERPOOL, A.C	SILVER.
Wythenshawe	Aug. 9.	D.H. MOTH.	G-EBZU.	—	—	NORTHERN AIR LINES	BLUE & SILVER
Wythenshaw	Aug. 9.	Auro Avian III A.	G-EBVZ	—	—	W. S. BROWN	SILVER & RED TOP.
Wythenshaw	Aug. 9.	Auro 504N	J-9432.	CIRCLING		NO S. T. S. SEALAND.	SILVER RAF

From 1929, E. J. R. kept his own record of aircraft flying in the vicinity of his home and elsewhere. Details recorded include: location, date and time, aircraft type, identification letters or serial numbers, height and direction of flight, colour scheme, and owner. The colour schemes of civil aircraft of this period are rarely recorded, so data of this kind is particularly invaluable to aero modellers. This is the first page of his first air log; it records details of aircraft passing over the local area between 27 June and 9 August 1929.

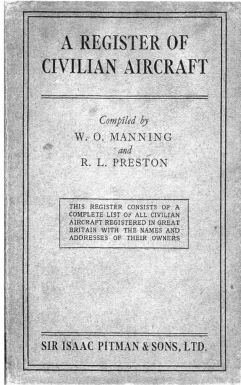

A REGISTER OF
CIVILIAN AIRCRAFT

Compiled by
W. O. MANNING
and
R. L. PRESTON

THIS REGISTER CONSISTS OF A
COMPLETE LIST OF ALL CIVILIAN
AIRCRAFT REGISTERED IN GREAT
BRITAIN WITH THE NAMES AND
ADDRESSES OF THEIR OWNERS

SIR ISAAC PITMAN & SONS, LTD.

Above: From 1930, E. J. R. embarked upon photography in a big way. He acquired this Goerz Roll-Tenax camera, probably second-hand. Made in Berlin by the C. P. Goerz Optical Works Company, *c.* 1926, the camera took 116-size film; the 115 mm x 69 mm format negatives were ideal for photographing aeroplanes. This camera was still being used by the author well into the 1960s.

Left: Sir Isaac Pitman & Sons Ltd produced this pocket-sized register of civilian aircraft, which E. J. R. carried with him everywhere. Compiled by W. O. Manning and Col. R. L. 'Mossy' Preston, and first published in 1931, this alphabetically listed all aircraft currently airworthy and the owners' addresses. Rupert Preston, born in 1902 and formerly of the Coldstream Guards, was later to become a very popular Secretary General of the Royal Aero Club. William Manning, born in 1879, was an aircraft designer with English Electric and had served in the Royal Naval Air Service during the First World War.

A typical double-page of E. J. R.'s copy of *A Register of Civilian Aircraft*, copiously annotated. Aircraft that he had seen were underlined, those he had photographed were marked (P), and those in which he had flown were marked (F). This particular edition's listing opened with G-EAAC, a D.H. 9J; the last entry was G-ABMS, a D.H.80A Puss Moth.

E. J. R's first serious attempt at aircraft photography; Avro 594 Avian IV G-AACF is seen at Manchester's Wythenshawe Aerodrome in August 1929. Doped blue and silver, the aircraft was owned by Northern Air Lines (Manchester) Ltd and based at Wythenshawe. After suffering damage in a gale on Guernsey in November 1935, the aircraft was shipped to Germany in March 1941 during the German occupation of the Channel Islands.

The subject of E. J. R.'s second aircraft photograph, also at Wythenshawe in August 1929, was Northern Air Lines' D.H. 9C G-EBIG. The aircraft began life with the RAF as H5886. It was first registered to William Beardmore and Company Ltd in October 1923, and operated as a Reserve School trainer. Later, it was converted to a D.H.9C, and based at Barton until scrapped in 1931.

CHAPTER TWO

First Photographs and
First Flights (1930-31)

My mother always used to curse because on returning from photographing, I would insist on developing the films first before grub, which after all makes sense, because you enjoy food far more on an easy mind.

Letter from E. J. Riding to A. J. Jackson in 1943

On 1 June 1930, Barton Airport was opened officially, and Wythenshawe became redundant almost overnight. Flying continued, albeit spasmodically; the last recorded flight took place on 19 June, although E. J. R., in his air log, recorded the blue and silver Fokker Universal G-EBUT of Air Taxis Ltd landing there on the afternoon of 17 August.

Barton was built on unsuitable ground; much of it was peat and subject to frequent waterlogging, and so extensive drainage was put in place. A large, brick-walled hangar was erected, and later, in 1933, an ultra-modern control tower, built to a design by Manchester Corporation architect G. Noel Hill; it was the first control tower to be constructed outside London. It is now Grade II listed and believed to be the oldest control tower in Europe still being used for the purpose for which it was designed. After Barton was officially opened, the D.H.60s and Avro 504Ks of Northern Air Transport, embracing both Northern Air Lines and Berkshire Aviation Tours, transferred from Wythenshawe, although the first aircraft to land there was Avro Avian G-AADL.

During 1930, E. J. R. photographed aircraft on just two occasions, during the family holiday in September. On 9 September, he and his sister Elvina took a 5-minute, 5-bob (5s) flip from Holyhead in Berkshire Aviation Tours' Avro 504K G-ABAV, flown by E. W. 'Jock' Bonar. It was E. J. R.'s second flight.

Opportunities to photograph aircraft that year were few and far between, although E. J. R. continued to record details of aircraft that passed over South Drive. Most sightings were of locally-based Avro 504Ks, de Havilland Moths, and Avro Avians from newly-opened Barton and Woodford. Exceptions were the enormous Beardmore Inflexible, spotted on 5 June, and several sightings of Imperial Airways' Handley Page H.P. W.10 G-EBMR in June, July, and August. During that year, his log recorded thirty-five different aircraft of fourteen types.

On one occasion, a local incident made the headlines. On 13 April, the silver and blue Avro Avian IV G-AAEC of the Lancashire Aero Club crashed at Woodford. Flown by Marcos Lacayo, the aircraft failed to recover from an intentional spin and crashed into a marsh near the aerodrome. Although Lacayo and his female passenger survived, they were badly injured. He was not so lucky in February 1946, when he was killed testing a D.H.98 Mosquito.

E. J. R. was an avid reader of the weekly aeronautical journals *Flight* and *The Aeroplane*, which would have made him aware of the following events in 1930.

Between 5 and 24 May, plucky Amy Johnson left Croydon in D.H.60G Moth G-AAAH to make the first solo flight by a woman from Britain to Australia, less than a year after obtaining

Left: A Berkshire Aviation Tours Ltd flyer advertising 5s passenger flights in the Holyhead area during the early part of September 1930. Two tickets were purchased by E. J. R. and his sister Elvina for their flight in Avro 504K G-ABAV on 9 September.

Opposite: On 9 September 1930, E. J. R. took to the air for a second time, flying from Holyhead in Berkshire Aviation Tours' Avro 504K G-ABAV. The pilot was Eric 'Jock' Bonar, born in 1899, who later became a test pilot with Rolls-Royce and D. Napier & Sons. The photograph shows E. J. R., wearing his Manchester Grammar School cap, striding away in the slipstream of the departing 504K. In the rear cockpit, his sister Elvina and a friend prepare for the thrill of their first flying experience. G-ABAV, registered to National Aviation Tours only a few weeks earlier, crashed at Holyhead shortly after this photograph was taken.

her 'A' licence. Her steed, named *Jason*, perhaps the most famous Moth of all, can be seen today in the London Science Museum. A few days later, on 31 May, Bristol Whitchurch Airport was opened officially by HRH Prince George, and during June, the prototype Handley Page Heyford J9130 took to the air for the first time from Radlett.

Also during June, Heath Row, separate words in those days and also known as Fairey's Great West Aerodrome, came into use after the company's move there from Northolt, where for many years, testing of its aircraft had been carried out. On the last Saturday of June, at the eleventh RAF Display at Hendon, the R-101 airship made its stately passage over proud, upturned faces, but with only three of its five engines running. More impressively, between 29 July and 1 August, the R-100 airship travelled from Britain to Montreal, Canada, returning to Cardington during 13 to 16 August in just over 57 hours. On 4 October, R-101 crashed near Beauvais, France, on its journey to India via Egypt, killing Maj.-Gen. Sir Sefton Branker, the popular and effective Director of Civil Aviation, and Lord Thompson, Secretary of State for Air. This tragedy also effectively killed off the British Government's airship programme. On 14 November, the prototype Handley Page H.P. 42 G-AAGX was first flown after assembly at Radlett. Such was the extensive usage of these stately, galleon-like biplanes on European and Empire routes, it is hard to believe that only eight examples were built.

E. J. R. took very few photographs of aircraft during 1931, apart from four Avro 504Ks he came across barnstorming in Rochdale in October. There, he met and photographed Capt. 'Jimmy' Orrell, later to make his name as a test pilot for A. V. Roe, and E. W. 'Jock' Bonar, famous aviator and later a test pilot for Napier, with whom E. J. R. had flown at Holyhead the previous year.

E. J. R.'s air log for 1931 covers ten pages and records sightings of the Duchess of Bedford's Fokker F.VII G-EBTS *The Spider*, flown by C. D. Barnard, among the dozens of D.H.60 Moths and Avro 504Ks of Northern Air Lines, Avro Avians and D.H.60 Moths of the Lancashire Aero Club, RAF Armstrong Whitworth Siskins from nearby RAF Sealand, and the odd Westland Wapiti. During the year, E. J. R. recorded seeing fifty-four different aircraft of fourteen types.

In addition to recording aircraft sightings in his own log book, E. J. R. also possessed *A Register of Civilian Aircraft* compiled by W. O. Manning and R. L. Preston, published by Sir

Isaac Pitman & Sons Ltd in 1931, and the equivalent of today's *ABC Civil Aircraft Markings*, still published by Ian Allan and in its sixty-fourth edition in 2013. The little, sixty-two-page Pitman book consisted of a complete list of all civilian aircraft registered in Great Britain, with the names and addresses of their owners. The register listed all extant aircraft from G-EAAC, a D.H.9J, to G-ABMS, a D.H.80A Puss Moth. One of the last aircraft listed was G-ABML, an Avro 504k owned by the Calder Valley Aero Club at Todmorden, Yorkshire.

In a wartime letter to A. J. Jackson, E. J. R. referred to this aircraft with some passion:

> Ever hear of the Calder Valley Aero Club? My feet feel instinctively sore when I hear that name. I tramped for miles an' miles looking for their besotted G-ABML, but to use their vernacular, no-one knew fook-orl abaht it! Still, these few failures don't compare with the feeling you get when after a hard days 'sport' chasing some fictitious Avro, Widgeon, or what have you, you sink back into the cushions (!) of a third class carriage mentally adding up all the exposures you've got in your rucksack, or the suspense in the darkroom when you get home. My mother always used to curse because on returning from photographing, I would insist on developing the films first before grub, which after all, is only sense because you enjoy food far more on an easy mind.

Despite the fact that there was very little activity with the camera, E. J. R. kept an eye on the aviation events of that year. On 25 March, the beautiful prototype Hawker Fury I biplane fighter K1926, with 'George' Bulman in charge, first took to the air from Brooklands. Entering RAF service in May and June, the Fury remained in front-line service until it was superseded by its stable mate, the immortal Hawker Hurricane. On 1 April, C. W. A. Scott departed Lympne for a flight to Australia in D.H.60M Moth G-ABHY, arriving at Darwin on the 9 April, having flown 10,500 miles in 9 days, 4 hours, and 11 minutes. Between 26 May and 5 June, Scott made the return flight to the UK in D.H.60M VH-UQA. Also on 1 April, the Air Ministry introduced a new scheme for affording financial assistance to approved UK flying clubs, of which there were about fifty in operation.

Eric 'Jock' Bonar at Milnrow, Rochdale, in October 1931. He is about to take off in D.H.60X Moth G-EBZU of Northern Air Transport (Manchester) Ltd. On 24 May 1932, Bonar saved the life of the instructor pilot of an RAF Armstrong Whitworth Siskin trainer from No. 5 FTS, at nearby RAF Sealand, after he crashed just outside the boundary of Barton Aerodrome. The Siskin immediately burst into flames, and the pupil occupying the front cockpit died instantly. Despite the obvious danger, Bonar, wrapped in asbestos, managed to extricate the pilot from the burning wreck.

On 2 June, Stanley Park Aerodrome at Blackpool was officially opened by Prime Minister Rt Hon. J. Ramsay MacDonald, and a few days later, the thirty-eight-seat Imperial Airways' Handley Page H.P. 42W G-AAGX *Hannibal* operated a proving flight on the London–Paris route.

On 14 June, Broxbourne Aerodrome, on the borders of Essex and Hertfordshire, was declared opened by Jim and Amy Mollison, assisted by comedian Will Hay. The twelfth annual RAF Display held at Hendon on 27 June featured in-flight refuelling of a Vickers Virginia and the launching of another Virginia by catapult. 'The most thrilling spectacle ever seen in exhibition flying', according to *The Aeroplane*, was provided by Flt Lt Harry Day and one Flg Off. Douglas Bader, each flying a Gloster Gamecock single-seat fighter. During June, the world was enthralled by the progress of the one-eyed American Wiley Post and co-pilot Harold Gatty as they flew round the world in the Lockheed Vega *Winnie May*, covering 15,474 miles in 8 days, 15 hours, and 51 minutes. Three weeks after the return of the Americans, Alan Cobham was making a 12,000-mile survey flight to explore a new route to Central Africa for the Air Ministry in Short S.11 Valetta G-AAJY.

On 13 September, Britain won the Schneider Trophy outright. The British team was the only entrant, because for one reason or another, teams from France, Italy, and America pulled out. Flt Lt J. N. Boothman, flying Supermarine S.6B S1595, recorded an average speed of 341 mph. On the same day, Flt Lt G. H. Stainforth of the RAF's High Speed Flight broke the world's speed record by averaging 379 mph when flying over the Solent in S.6B S1596.

Later, between 27 and 28 October, Sqn Ldr O. R. Gayford and Flt Lt D. L. G. Bett flew the Fairey Long-Range Monoplane on the first non-stop flight to Egypt, covering the 2,857 miles from RAF Cranwell in 31 hours and 30 minutes. In the meantime, Yeadon, the municipal airport for Leeds and Bradford, was opened officially on 17 October. On 26 October 1931, the prototype D.H.82 Tiger Moth E.6/G-ABRC made its first flight at Stag Lane, and a day later, plucky Bert Hinkler set off on a solo flight from New York to London via Central America, during which he made a 22-hour crossing of the South Atlantic in D.H.80 Puss Moth CF-APK, arriving at Hanworth on 7 December. On 10 December, another important training aircraft made its first flight when the side-by-side prototype Blackburn B-2 G-ABUW took to the air from Brough, East Yorkshire.

CHAPTER THREE

Mostly Manchester (1932)

In the Manchester District, it was a real achievement to 'bum' a ride, even in 1939, to anywhere but within the vicinity.

Letter from E. J. Riding to A. J. Jackson in 1943

E. J. R. really got into aircraft photography from April 1932, at the age of sixteen. He was still keeping extensive records of flights passing over the family home in Chorlton-cum-Hardy, but the urge to photograph aeroplanes was growing. Years later, he wrote to A. J. Jackson:

I can't understand anybody being satisfied with just *seeing* a machine. If I couldn't take a camera, I'd prefer not to go. I went to the opening of Speke in July 1933 without a camera and have never ceased to regret it. Seeing G-EAUM [Avro 543 Baby], G-EBRQ [Westland Widgeon III], and sundry others without getting a picture have been my waking nightmares for many a year.

During 1932, he began paying irregular visits to Barton Aerodrome, photographing locally-based Le Rhone-engined Avro 504Ks and Cirrus-engined D.H.60 Moths of Northern Air Transport and Northern Aircraft (G-EBZU, G-EBWA, and G-EBST). His air log for 1932 records the daily passage of Moths, Avians, and Avro 504Ks over the house, but now and then, something more interesting would hove into view, such as the distinctive orange and black Desoutter G-AATJ of National Flying Services. Among other rarer types were the all-silver Isle of Man Services' Saro A.21 Windhover G-ABJP on 1 June; the all-silver Spartan A.24 Mailplane G-ABLI on 12 June; Campbell-Black's silver Waco CSO two-seater VP-KAP on 17 June and 10 July; several brand new D.H.80A Puss Moths; Marcos Lacayo in the Comper Swift demonstrator G-ABUU on 22 July; the silver, black-nosed Junker F.13 G-ABDC on 18 September; and Edgar Percival's silver and black Percival Gull G-ABUR on 27 September. Viewed through E. J.R.'s telescope, 1932 was a good year. No fewer than sixty-two aircraft, comprising eighteen different types, had passed overhead, the majority being Northern Air Transport and Lancashire Aero Club aircraft.

Of wider interest during 1932, E. J. R. was aware of the accidental sinking of the Royal Navy's submarine M.2, originally the K.19, off Weymouth, Dorset, on 26 January. Carrying the experimental Parnall Peto N255 floatplane in its tiny, ship-borne hangar, it is generally accepted that an order was given to open the hangar door as the submarine submerged, resulting in the drowning of sixty crew members. During March, Jim Mollison flew his long-range D.H.80A Puss Moth G-ABKG solo from Lympne to Cape Town, South Africa, in 4 days 17 hours, and 19 minutes. During the same month, the prototype of the remarkable D.H.83 Fox Moth G-ABUO made its first flight from Stag Lane, Edgware, North London. Designed by Arthur Hagg, it was remarkable, because although having only a 120-hp Gipsy III engine, the Fox Moth could carry four passengers and a pilot, although subsequent versions were powered by Gipsy engines of slightly more power.

The official programme for the Great Air Pageant held at Barton Aerodrome in 1932 contained the chance to win a free flight in one of Northern Air Transport's aircraft.

On 1 April, a new Air Ministry scheme for providing financial assistance to approved flying clubs was inaugurated, continuing until March 1937. Under the new arrangement, clubs would be paid a grant of £25 for each club member qualifying for an 'A' or 'B' pilot's licence, and £10 for every licence renewal. Total membership of approved flying clubs at the time was 6,161, of which 1,675 members held pilots' licences. The total number of light aeroplane clubs in operation in the UK was fifty. The most popular aircraft types registered were the D.H.60 Moth (31 per cent) and the D.H.80A Puss Moth (11 per cent).

The year 1932 will be remembered for the introduction of Sir Alan Cobham's National Aviation Day displays, known more popularly as Cobham's Circus. Until 1935, this organisation gave hundreds of thousands of people there first taste of flying, and many men who fought in the RAF and Fleet Air Arm during the Second World War received their aerial baptism from Cobham and his pilots. During the first season, from April to October, the 'circus' appeared at 170 towns, flew on 168 consecutive days, and clocked up other impressive statistics. The distance flown between towns exceeded 145,000 miles, and 190,000 fare-paying passengers were flown, plus 10,000 civic guests besides.

During 19 to 28 April, C. W. A. Scott broke the England–Australia record in D.H.60M Moth G-ACOA, flying from Lympne to Darwin in 8 days, 20 hours, and 47 minutes. A local incident that made national news on 24 May concerned an RAF Armstrong Whitworth Siskin from No. 5 FTS, RAF Sealand. The biplane trainer fell out of an attempted low-level roll and spun in at nearby Barton Aerodrome, trapping the two occupants in the ensuing fire. Eric 'Jock' Bonar, Chief Flying Instructor of Northern Air Transport Ltd, wrapped himself in an asbestos blanket and plunged into the flames to extricate the pilot from the wreckage, who denied later that

D.H.60X, operated by Northern Air Transport (Manchester) Ltd, at Barton in September 1932. A few days later, on 9 October, the blue and silver biplane was written off at Irlam, Greater Manchester, after spinning into a council house garden shortly after taking off from Barton. Passenger Mrs Olga Homewood lost her life, and husband Leslie, the pilot, was badly injured. Commenting on the accident, chief flying instructor Eric 'Jock' Bonar said that G-EBZU was his favourite machine; the one he preferred to use for flying instruction.

he was stunting. The pupil occupying the front cockpit was killed. For his bravery, Bonar was awarded the George Cross. It was Barton Aerodrome's first fatality.

The four-engine Armstrong Whitworth AW.XV airliner was already in production when the prototype G-ABPI *Atalanta* made its first flight on 6 June from Whitley Abbey, Coventry. Thousands of people converged on Hendon Aerodrome on Saturday 26 June for the thirteenth annual RAF Display. One of the more light-hearted events was a slow-flying race for D.H.82 Tiger Moths. A shape of the future appeared in the form of the tailless, swept-wing, three-seat Westland-Hill Pterodactyl IV K1947, painted as a toothed monster and causing much amusement when it 'attacked' a hippopotamus-shaped balloon. A couple of days later, the world's first trade flying display was staged at Hendon by the Society of British Aircraft Constructors (SBAC), with the support and assistance of the Air Ministry. Thirty-five different types of civil and military aircraft were demonstrated before nearly 1,000 invited guests, who represented the world's military and civil air services.

On 1 July, German airship *Graf Zeppelin* flew over Hanworth from Brooklands, and on the following day, the Secretary of State for Air Lord Londonderry officially opened Portsmouth Airport. The eleventh annual King's Cup air race was held on 8 to 9 July, starting and finishing at Brooklands. The 1,220-mile course embraced most of England. One of the stages passed through the Manchester area, from where it was watched by E. J. R. and a friend via the former's telescope. A photograph of them was published in the *Daily Dispatch* newspaper a day later. The race was won by Wally Hope flying D.H.83 Fox Moth G-ABUT, entered by Arthur E. Hagg, its designer.

On 18 to 19 August, courageous Jim Mollison made the first solo east–west crossing of the Atlantic in D.H. 80A Puss Moth G-ABXY *Heart's Content*. Fitted with a massive fuel tank

This *Daily Dispatch* photograph shows E. J. R. and his friend Wilmer Townend near Woodford watching the 1932 King's Cup air race held on 8-9 July. The 1,223-mile, round-Britain race started and ended at Brooklands, passing over Woodford and Hooton Park in the process.

The silver and red Avro 504K G-ABHJ, pictured at Barton in September 1932, was delivered to the RFC/RAF as J8343, and took up civilian registration in December 1930. First owned by Northern Air Transport (Manchester) Ltd, and based at Barton, it was later acquired by Lancelot Rimmer and William 'Jock' Mackay. In June 1933, it was destroyed in a crash at Hooton Park.

The handsome chocolate and silver Avro 504K G-AAEZ at Barton in September 1932. First owned by Aeroplane Services Ltd at Croydon, it was purchased by Northern Air Transport Ltd and based at Barton. The 504K later passed to Lancelot Rimmer and William 'Jock' Mackay, and remained at Hooton Park until withdrawn from use in December 1934.

giving a range of 3,000 miles (cynics said the tank was full of brandy), the Puss Moth took off from Portmarnock, Dublin, and landed at New Brunswick 31 hours and 20 minutes later.

On 16 September, the world's altitude record was raised by Capt. Cyril Uwins when he coaxed a Vickers Vespa up to 43,976 feet. The following month, on 12 October, Gravesend Airport was opened officially during a visit by Cobham's National Aviation Day display. A few days earlier, on 9 October, tragedy struck again at Barton when a young married couple took off in D.H.60 Moth G-EBZU destined for Hooton Park, where they planned to have tea. A few seconds into the flight, the Moth crashed into the garden of a house at Irlam, about 1 mile away. Although the pilot survived the crash, his passenger was killed.

On 12 November, the D.H.84 Dragon prototype E.9/G-ACAN made its first flight from Stag Lane, and during 14 to 18 November, Amy Mollison flew from Lympne to Cape Town in 4 days, 6 hours, and 54 minutes in D.H.80A Puss Moth G-ACAB; she bettered husband Jim's flight time by more than 10 hours.

1932 also saw the introduction of the first direct-control Autogiro. Tilting the rotor about its axis led to shorter take-off runs, a steeper angle of climb, and improved control at slow speeds near the ground. The Cierva C.19 was the most common Autogiro in use at the time.

CHAPTER FOUR

The Circus Comes to Town (1933)

I've cycled from Manchester through heat, winds of appalling ferocity (It's always blowing a gale along the Ormskirk Road, even if it's foggy), flies (yes, plagues of 'em), and hunger and thirst (only one who has cycled along the East Lancashire Road knows what real thirst is), only to find the hangars locked and no flying.

Letter from E. J. Riding to A. J. Jackson in 1943

In March 1933, seventeen-year-old E. J. R. cycled to Woodford, the busy aerodrome from where A. V. Roe and Co. Ltd had been test-flying its aircraft since 1925. He photographed several Avro Avians (G-EBQL, G-EBXD, G-AAEC, G-AAYV, and G-ABEE), Avro 632 Cadet G-ABWJ, and the Avro 640 K-11. He made another visit on 10 June during the stopover by No. 1 Tour of Alan Cobham's National Aviation Day display team on arrival from Bawtry.

E. J. R. took photographs of the Handley Page W.10 G-EBMM both on the ground and flying low across the aerodrome, with the pilot of the airline sitting exposed in his open cockpit. In complete contrast was the diminutive, single-seat Blackburn Lincock G-AALH, painted orange, being put through a programme of aerobatics. Also being turned inside out was D.H.82 Tiger Moth G-ABUL with its front cockpit faired over and flown by aerobatic wizard Charles Turner-Hughes, universally known as 'Toc-H'. The following day, the 'circus' travelled on to Leeds. During the 1933 season (April–October), Cobham's National Aviation Day displays, divided into two separate tours, visited 306 towns, and more than 800,000 people paid admission to displays. The number of people taking passenger flights totalled 194,000, and the 18-aircraft NAD fleet flew approximately 700,000 miles.

For the remaining months of that year, E. J. R. mostly confined his visits to local aerodromes; Hooton Park and Barton, as well as Woodford, although he strayed as far as Blackpool's Squires Gate on one occasion in September. One day in July, he arrived at Barton to be confronted by the sight of one of Maj. Savage's S.E.5a skywriters, G-EBVB, doped silver overall and featuring fuselage-length exhaust pipes.

Throughout the year, E. J. R. continued recording activity over the Riding home, even though most of the aircraft were the Moths, Avians, and 504Ks of Northern Air Transport and the Lancashire Aero Club. Exceptions included Spartan Aircraft's Simmonds Spartan G-ABLJ, the all-silver Monospar S.T.4 G-ABVP, D.H.83 Fox Moth G-ACBZ of Scottish & Midland Air Transport, another Fox Moth in Hillman's livery, and several privately-owned D.H.80A Puss Moths. He also logged the Shell company's cream, grey, and brown Comper Swift G-ABUS, Cobham's silver and green Airspeed A.S.4 Ferry G-ABSI, M. L. Bramson's yellow and green Southern Martlet G-ABBN, Edgar Percival's yellow and green Gull Four G-ACLG. and D.H.84s G-ACAO and G-ACCE. The aforementioned S.E.5a flew over on 22 July. On 27 July, aircraft of Cobham's 'circus', including the three Avro 504Ns, flew over; they were appearing at nearby Altrincham and Redditch. On 3 September, the silver and red Avro 618 Ten VH-UXX of Capt.

Being manhandled into its hangar at Barton in April 1933, following a C of A test flight in April 1933, is Avro 504K G-AAEZ. Formerly of Northern Air Transport Ltd, it was sold in 1933 to Lancelot Rimmer and William 'Jock' Mackay. It was withdrawn from use after Mackay was killed in Avro 504N G-ACRS in June that year.

Ulm twice passed overhead. Probably the most exciting sighting was that of the Bristol 89 Fighter G-ABYE on 8 August.

E. J. R.'s only flight that year was on 17 September, when he took himself to Squires Gate, Blackpool, and paid 5 bob for a flight in Blackpool & West Coast Air Services purple, cream, and silver D.H.84 Dragon G-ACGU, piloted by J. Higgins.

For the aviation world at large, the death of thirty-two-year-old Winifred Spooner in January 1933 was a sad start to the year. Ill from influenza for only one day, and despite injections of strychnine being tried, Britain mourned the premature passing of its only female professional pilot. Another death in January was that of Bert Hinkler, killed when his D.H.80 Puss Moth CF-APK crashed in the Bernese Oberland while on his way to Australia. His body was not discovered until 27 April.

During 6 February, Sqn Ldr O. R. Gayford and Flt Lt G. E. Nicholetts set out from RAF Cranwell in Fairey Long-Range Monoplane K1991 on an attempt at the Cape Town record, landing instead at Walvis Bay (in what was then south-west Africa, and now Namibia) on 8 February. The flight was 5,341 miles, and was covered in 57 hours and 25 minutes, thereby securing the world distance record and achieving the first non-stop flight from England to South Africa.

Imperial Airways completed its first 10 million miles of flying in February, and on 29 March, the Miles M.2 Hawk prototype G-ACGH made its first flight, from Woodley, Reading. During April, two Everest flights were carried out in Westland Wallace G-ACBA and Houston-Westland P.V.3 G-ACAZ; the first on 3 April and the second on 19 April. A height of 30,000 feet was reached, 1,000 feet higher than Everest's summit. The flights were of added importance because they represented the first attempt at aerial survey from this altitude.

The Airspeed Courier prototype G-ABXN made its first flight on 10 April, and likewise, on 27 May, the prototype D.H.85 Leopard Moth E.1/G-ACHD from Stag Lane. On 21 June, the prototype Supermarine Walrus (Seagull V) K4797 was first flown, and two days later, Stapleford Tawney Aerodrome in Essex was officially opened.

On 10 June 1933, Sir Alan Cobham's National Aviation Day display fleet visited Woodford, where several of the aircraft were photographed by E. J. R., among them Handley Page W 10 G-EBMM, about to take off with a full load of passengers. Initially delivered to Imperial Airways in 1926, and named *City of Melbourne,* it passed to NAD and was based at Ford in Sussex. It was later converted to a tanker for use with Cobham's flight refuelling experiments, and crashed at Aston Clinton, Buckinghamshire, in September 1934; a tailplane bracing bolt fractured, causing the pilot to lose control with fatal results.

Handley Page W 10 G-EBMM airborne over Woodford.

The following day, Saturday 24 June, the fourteenth annual display of the RAF was held at Hendon. Despite pouring with rain all day, only one event was cancelled. One of the highlights was a flypast by three large flying boats in the shapes of a Supermarine Southampton, Supermarine Singapore II, and a Short Sarafand. The display ended with the traditional 'bombing' of the set piece, which that year was in the shape of a coastal military base 'attacked' by Handley Page Hinaidis. Two days later, Hendon Aerodrome played host to the second SBAC exhibition. The exhibition was larger than the previous year's event, with forty-six aircraft, comprising practically every type of modern British aircraft, with the unavoidable exception of seaplanes.

That year's King's Cup air race was held on 8 July, and took the form of a knock-out competition with a series of heats and a final, starting and finishing at Hatfield Aerodrome. The total distance of the several courses amounted to 831 miles, and Captain Geoffrey de Havilland, on D.H.85 Leopard Moth G-ACHD, was declared the winner, carrying away the cup on home ground. Later that year, Geoffrey de Havilland would have been pleased to learn that an analysis of aircraft types registered in Great Britain during 1933 revealed 27 per cent were D.H.60 Moths, 9 per cent were D.H.80 Puss Moths, 3.5 per cent were D.H.83 Fox Moths, and 3 per cent were D.H.82A Tiger Moths. In all, de Havilland types occupied four of the top ten places.

On 1 July, Liverpool Airport (Speke) was opened by Lord Londonderry, and on 22 July, Jim and Amy Mollison left Pendine Sands in D.H.84 Dragon I G-ACCV *Seafarer*, arriving at Bridgeport, Connecticut, USA, on 24 July, having flown approximately 3,000 miles in 39 hours.

The prototype Short S.16 Scion G-ACJI made its first flight on 18 August from the company's airfield at Rochester, Kent, while on 4 October, Sir Charles Kingsford Smith left Lympne in Percival Gull G-ACJV, arriving at Wyndham Australia after flying approximately 10,000 miles in 7 days, 4 hours, and 44 minutes.

One local near-tragedy that made the national press occurred on 18 November. Avro 594 G-EBQL was taking part in a three-aircraft formation flypast at a meeting arranged by the Lancashire Aero Club when it stalled and spun into Barton Aerodrome and caught fire. The pilot managed to stagger out of the burning wreckage and was only slightly injured.

G-AALH was an all-metal version of the Blackburn Lincock I; a wooden, single-seat, light fighter of only 22-feet, 6-inch wingspan, first flown in 1928. This Mk II civil version was powered by a 255-hp Armstrong Siddeley geared Lynx IV, and after evaluation by the Royal Canadian Air Force at Camp Borden, was used by Cobham's National Aviation Day display team for aerobatic routines until it was dismantled in March 1935. At Woodford, it was in an overall orange colour scheme.

National Aviation Day displays was the first civil organisation to take delivery of the limited number of D.H.82 Tiger Moths available in 1932. Seen at Woodford is G-ABUL with the front cockpit faired over. It was invariably flown by Turner-Hughes, known as the Tiger Moth maestro, who perfected a crowd-rousing, crazy flying routine. G-ABUL was still going strong at the outbreak of the Second World War, and was impressed into RAF service as BB792 in September 1940. On 23 June 1944, it struck a cyclist at Wollaston, Northamptonshire, when the pilot was indulging in low flying.

It is interesting to note that by December 1933, membership of Air Ministry approved flying clubs totalled 4,931, of whom 1,569 held pilots' 'A' licences. Corresponding figures for the previous year were 4,750 and 1,106 respectively. The latter figures did not include members of clubs affiliated to National Flying Services Ltd, which did not receive Government assistance after July 1932.

Typical flying rates at this time were: £2 an hour; solo flying, £1 5s an hour; and the average cost of trial flights, 15s.

By the end of 1933, there were seventy-nine licensed permanent aerodromes or landing grounds and seaplane stations in the UK, compared to sixty-eight the previous year. This number included sixteen licensed municipal aerodromes, of which there were none in 1928, and thirteen in 1932.

In 1933, a British Aircraft Mark was established for the purpose of distinguishing aircraft of British construction in possession of a Certificate of Airworthiness granted under the Air Navigation (Consolidation) Order 1923. The mark consisted of a lion rampant in gold within three rings of red, white, and blue, with the words 'British Certificate of Airworthiness' inscribed in the white ring.

During 1933, there were sixty-five accidents in the UK that required notification under the Air Navigation Regulations. Twelve resulted in losses of life, seven caused serious, but not fatal injuries to persons, and the remaining forty-eight had no serious consequences beyond structural damage to the aircraft. No foreign aircraft met with a serious accident in Britain that year. Nearly 60 per cent of the accidents were caused by errors of judgement. Engine failure was responsible for one fatal and five minor crashes. Club and private pilots accounted for more than forty of the accidents.

A gathering of National Aviation Day display aircraft at Woodford on 11 June 1933, before they moved on to the next show at Middleton Park in Leeds. In the background is Handley Page W 10 G-EBMM and Avro 504Ns G-ACCX and G-ABVY.

The Barton-based Avro 638 Club Cadet G-ACGY of Light Planes (Lancs) Ltd at Woodford in July 1933. Delivered to the club the previous month, this Cadet was sold to the Aero Club de Mozambique in February 1939, and became CR-AAS.

Reckless flying has often been a cause of fatal accidents, and this anonymous account is typical: 'In an attempt to take off in a spectacular manner, that is to say, by "zooming" off the ground, the pilot stalled the aeroplane at a height of 150 feet. The machine nosedived to the ground and burst into flames on impact. The pilot and passenger were instantly killed.'

Parked by the petrol pumps at Hooton Park on 9 August 1933 is Avro 616 Avian IVM G-ABMO of Merseyside Aero & Sports Ltd, delivered to the club brand new a few days earlier. This Avian was impressed into the RAF in January 1940 as 2070M.

Avro 594 Avian IIIA G-EBXY at Squires Gate, Blackpool, on 17 September 1933. It was owned originally by the Liverpool and District Aero Club Ltd, but when this photograph was taken, it was registered to Blackpool and West Coast Air Services Ltd, also based at Squires Gate. In December 1939, it was impressed into the RAF as 2078M.

Rollason Aviation's Spartan Three Seater II G-ABWV at Stretford on 25 August 1933 during a visit by the British Hospitals Air Pageant. The port wing is folded back while work is carried out on the aircraft prior to departure for Sheffield the next day. The following month, on 26 September, the aircraft crashed and caught fire at Grantham.

D.H.84 Dragon I G-ACGU of Blackpool and West Coast Air Services Ltd, about to taxi out for take-off from Squires Gate, Blackpool, on 17 September 1933. This Dragon was destroyed on 16 July 1935 when it crashed while taking off from Heston. The slightly overloaded aircraft was taking a party to see the Royal Review at Spithead, but stalled just after take-off. Two passengers died, while five others, including the pilot, survived.

Stinson Junior S G-ABTZ at Woodley in October 1933, almost certainly photographed by E. J. R.'s sister Elvina, who at the time was attending Reading University. In a letter to his sister asking her to go to nearby Woodley and take photographs, with strict instructions that they be side views so that the registration letters were clearly visible, E. J. R. at least had the decency to include a roll of film. Built at Wayne in 1931, and registered NC10879, this aircraft was imported into the UK in 1932, and was flown usually from Hanworth until scrapped in 1940.

Opposite above: Savage Skywriting Company's S.E.5a G-EBVB, powered by a 250-hp Wolseley Viper, visiting Barton in August 1933. At the time, it was attached to Cobham's National Aviation displays and flown by W. Ogden. The aircraft was withdrawn from use in April 1934, and scrapped at Hendon.

Opposite below: Southern Martlet G-ABBN at Woodford on 19 September 1933. Completed in 1930, this neat little single-seater was sold to the Marquis of Douglas and Clydesdale, and based at Hamble. It was acquired by National Aviation Day displays in January 1932, and flew one season with A. C. Rawson, giving aerobatic displays, for which it was ideally suited. Powered by an 80-hp Armstrong Siddeley Genet II engine, the 25-feet biplane cruised at 95 mph and had a range of 280 miles. When this photograph was taken, G-ABBN had a yellow fuselage with green registration letters and stripes on the fin and rudder. This beautiful little biplane was scrapped in 1937.

CHAPTER FIVE

Wings of One's Own (1934)

> I once cycled 95 miles to get a picture of S.E.5a G-ABIB – probably do it again tomorrow in spite of the pain it would cause.
>
> Letter from E. J. Riding to A. J. Jackson in 1943

During the winter of 1933-34, E. J. R. and a school friend by the name of Fred Sunter decided to build an aeroplane to their own design. Calling themselves the Cheshire Aero Club, its headquarters was dubbed the 'Airport of Timperley', otherwise known as Fred's home in Wood Lane in the town of the same name.

The R-S 1 (Riding-Sunter 1) was a low-wing, single-seat monoplane designed around a two-cylinder Douglas, horizontally-opposed, motorcycle engine, allegedly capable of delivering 2.5-hp. The design was somewhat dependent on what could be cannibalised from crashed or redundant aircraft discarded at local aerodromes; in the quest for which, both lads had befriended people useful to their cause.

The following excerpts from some of the correspondence between E. J. R. and Fred Sunter throw some light on their endeavours:

22 January 1934

Eddie,

I have done great things since you were here on Sunday. Firstly, I have completed the airframe, and secondly, I have swept the workshop out and cleaned up all the tools. I am looking forward to seeing you on Wednesday about 6.15, or thereabouts. Have you secured the wire yet? The work was finished last night at 9.45 and I cut the wood up in about 30 minutes, and it was tough work.

Yours truly, till pigs fly,

Fred

22 February 1934

Eddie,

The airman friend visited us last night and the only remark he passed was; 'Don't forget the camber on the tail plane,' otherwise he thought it was great. P.s. I have a proposal to make re the engine and where to get it.

Fred

Not dated

During late 1933, E. J. R. and friend Fred Sunter embarked upon building a full-size aeroplane. Named the Riding-Sunter 1 (RS-1), it was a single-seat, low-wing monoplane designed around a two-cylinder, horizontally-opposed Douglas motorcycle engine, allegedly capable of producing 2.5-hp. This first photograph of the fuselage structure shows Fred Sunter trying the cockpit for size.

Dear Fritz, [the nickname Fred used occasionally for E. J. R.]

I have secured a tin of signal red paint and spent last Friday working on the 'plane. I was nearly weeping over your absence, but I pulled myself together and worked. Herr Hillick visited the 'aerodrome' this afternoon, but was not admitted to the 'hangar'. I have been wondering whether or not we should start the wings to save time later, so that one day for covering will be sufficient for the whole 'plane without covering the fuselage, and then the wings later. Don't you think so? Did you get any wreckage for the bus? The engine goes on Monday night for decarbonising. I have been thinking – if he is going to decarbonise it for us and he wants the gearbox, we might consider giving it to him – what say you brother? The next item on the programme is to fix the undercarriage and get the wheels on. We shall have to have a dinnertime in search for the wheels. I have instructed a greaseball to come and fix the engine at his earliest convenience.

    Fred

The last surviving piece of correspondence on the subject reads:

26 July 1936

Dear Fritz,

Now with regard to the flying machine: Father wants it either taken to pieces or removing from the garage. Will you let me know if you or any of your friends would like the machine. If not, perhaps you would like me to take same to pieces and let you have your share of the concern. Anyway, which ever you decided to do will, I can assure you, be in agreement with me.

    Fred

A later view of the RS-1, with tailplane added, propped up in Fred Sunter's parents' garden at Timperley in early 1934.

Fred Sunter looks on as 6-feet 3-inch E. J. R., complete with goggles, tries the RS-1's cockpit for size. The rudder cables are connected, but the fuselage structure looks on the light side.

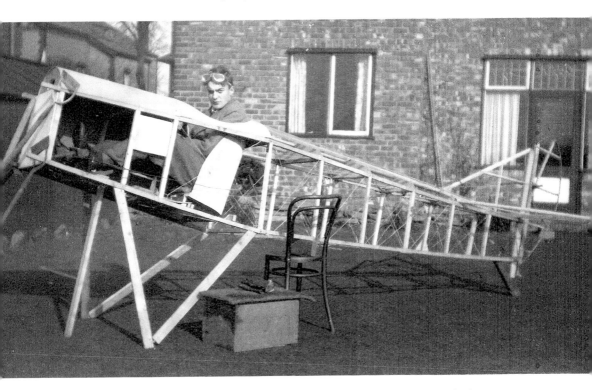

E. J. R. sitting in the uncovered fuselage of the RS-1 in Fred Sunter's garden at Timperley, Cheshire.

Sitting on an interesting set of wheels, the RS-1 after having been manoeuvred into Fred Sunter's father's garage in early 1934. The fuselage covering is obviously temporary, and except for the over-sized wheels, the aeroplane displays quite pleasing lines.

Another view of the RS-1 at Fred Sunter's father's Timperley garage. This is the last known photograph of the aeroplane, as construction was abandoned shortly after. Had the project been finished, the Douglas engine would undoubtedly have proved grossly underpowered.

Fortunately, the Douglas-engine proved to be woefully underpowered, and it is doubtful that the RS-1 proceeded any further than the stage in which it is seen in the last of the accompanying photographs. By 1936, E. J. R.'s time was taken up with real aeroplanes, and Fred was otherwise gainfully employed, and also involved with girls. The ultimate fate of the RS-1 is not recorded.

During 1934, E. J. R. spent more and more time on his Rudge cycling to local aerodromes and even to Hooton Park, some 45-miles distant. The following is a brief résumé of his visits, interspersed with events occurring beyond the confines of Manchester.

Despite Stag Lane Aerodrome's licence being cancelled on 5 January prior to the de Havilland Company's move to newly built Hatfield, the unnamed D.H.86 prototype G-ACPL made its maiden flight from there on the 14 January in the hands of Hubert Broad. On 21 March, Railway Air Services Ltd was registered, formed by the four main railway companies: London Midland and Scottish Railway, London and North-Eastern Railway, Great Western Railway and Southern Railway, and Imperial Airways.

The prototype Fairey Swordfish (TSR.II) K4190 first flew on 17 April, and on the same day, the prototype D.H.89 Dragon Six, soon to be re-named the Dragon Rapide, and destined for Switzerland, made its first flight from Stag Lane.

On 7 May, Railway Air Services Ltd opened its first route with D.H.84 Dragon G-ACPX, and two days later, the prototype D.H.87A Hornet Moth E.6/G-ACTA was first flown at newly opened Hatfield.

E. J. R. visited Croydon (London) Airport on 11 May and photographed Armstrong Whitworth Argosy G-AAEJ and G-AACJ, in addition to an Air France Fokker F.VII3m and a Short Scylla. He called in at Heston the following day and photographed a new resident: Ford 5-AT-E Tri-motor G-ABHO, owned by the British Air Navigation Company.

Between 8 and 23 May, Jean Batten flew from England to Port Darwin (10,500 miles) in D.H.60M Moth G-AARB in 14 days, 23 hours, and 25 minutes, thus beating Amy Mollison's (nee Johnson) record of 1930 by 4 days, and thereby obtaining the women's solo record.

Avro 618 Ten G-ACGF at Hooton Park in March 1934. This tri-motor was a licence-built version of the Fokker F.VIIB/3m and featured a one-piece, plywood-covered cantilever wing. The Ten was so named because it carried eight passengers and two crew; a smaller version, the Five, carried four passengers and a pilot. G-ACGF was built to the order of John Sword for service with Midland and Scottish Air Ferries Ltd, and was based at Renfrew for several years. The warning, 'Keep clear of propellers' can be seen aft of the front engine.

Avro 616 Avian IVM G-ACIF at Hooton Park in March 1934. At the time it was owned by Merseyside Aero & Sports Ltd. Following ownership by private individuals at Woodley and Doncaster, G-ACIF's registration was cancelled in 1946.

Avro 504N G-ACOK at Lymm, near Warrington, on 24 April 1934. Previously F2588 with the RAF, this Mongoose-powered 504N was first registered in April 1934, and straight away embarked upon a tour with National Aviation Day displays, when this photograph was taken. In March 1936, the aircraft was acquired by Lancelot 'Pop' Rimmer, who used it for barnstorming until a crash at Rhyl on 14 August 1938 brought this activity to an abrupt halt.

Surrey Flying Services Ltd was still using an Avro 504K for pleasure flying in the mid-1930s. G-AAAF seen here at Croydon on 11 May 1934. Once a familiar sight in the all red livery of the Cornwall Aviation company, 'AF was first registered in September 1928, and passed to Surrey Flying Service Ltd in August 1933, which continued using it for pleasure flights until it was sold to a private owner in June 1935. The old stager was burned at Gatwick in 1939.

The prototype Fokker F. VII first flew in 1921, and production aircraft in various forms flew with most European airlines, some even going to the USA. Normal accommodation was for two crew and eight passengers. Fokker F. VIIb.3m F-AJC? of Air France is seen at Croydon on 11 May 1934.

The Klemm I..26 was a larger version of the popular L.25 produced by Leichtflugzeugbau Klemm GmbH, Berlin, from 1927. Photographed at Croydon on 11 May 1934, G-ABOJ was one of six imported into the UK during 1930-31. Powered by a 90-hp ADC Cirrus engine, the 42-foot-span aircraft was scrapped at Knowle, Birmingham, in 1945.

The first Ford Tri-Motors were produced in the USA in 1926, and soon appealed to commercial operators because of their rugged, all-metal construction and ability to operate from almost anywhere. In 1926, two demonstrators came to the UK, but only two sales resulted. One of these aircraft was G-ABHO, a Ford 5-AT-E registered to Lord Lovelace, who took it to his estates in Tanganyika. G-ABHO is pictured later at Heston on 12 May 1934, when it was owned by British Air Navigation Company Ltd and named *Voyager*. A year later, the Tri-Motor went to New Guinea Airways and became VH-UBI.

The first Empire Air Day was held on 24 May. The Air League had suggested the idea to the Air Ministry in order to bring the public into closer contact with aviation, and they also wanted charities to benefit in the event of any profit being made. Until that date, the opportunities for public access to aviation were restricted to RAF displays at Hendon, or flying 'circus' visits to their locality. RAF aerodromes were 'no-go' areas for anyone not calling on business, and flying clubs hardly encouraged the curious unless they were potential members with convincing credentials or introductions. This first Empire Day was successful, and thirty-nine service stations were open to the public, attracting 82,000 people. The RAF Benevolent Fund benefited to the tune of £2,564. And it was not only service aerodromes that opened their gates; Croydon alone attracted 4,000 visitors, where Surrey Flying Services were busy with 5s joyriding trips.

On the same day, E. J. R. took himself to Lymm, near Warrington, Cheshire, where Cobham's National Aviation Day display had just arrived from Birmingham. There, he bagged various 'circus' aircraft, including the Handley Page Clive G-ABYX and the diminutive Blackburn Lincock, before the 'circus' moved to the next town – Bolton.

On 2 June, E. J. R. paid 5s for a flight in the silver and brown Bellanca Pacemaker G-ABNW from Barton to Stockport return, with pilot A. Weedon. A few days later, on 8 June, a visit to Woodford to take photographs was probably the first occasion on which E. J. R. was accompanied by his fourteen-year-old pal Jimmy Ellison (J. G. E.). They were to be inseparable for the next five years.

E. J. R. and J. G. E. flew together from Barton to the Woodford Air Display on 23 June in the same Bellanca Pacemaker, chartered by Windsor & District M. A. S., where they photographed a couple of RAF Bristol Bulldogs, including a two-seat trainer and the Airspeed A.S.5 G-ABXN Courier. The return flight cost 10s each, and they arrived back at Barton at 8.45 p.m.

Looking more like a product from the USA, the four-seat D.H. 75 was first flown in December 1928, and found to be underpowered. G-AAUZ, the fifth production aircraft, is seen at Barton on 24 May 1934 in the all red livery of Air Taxis Ltd, powered by either a 240-hp Armstrong Siddeley Lynx or a 300-hp Wright Whirlwind. Following a period in storage at Heston, G-AAUZ was sold abroad in January 1936.

D.H.84 Dragon 2 G-ACMO at Barton on 24 May 1934. Named *St Ouen's Bay*, it was first registered to Jersey Airways Ltd in January 1934, and in July 1935, passed to Northern and Scottish Airways Ltd at Renfrew. In March 1938, the Dragon was shipped to Australia, where it became VH-ABK.

First registered in November 1930, this smart D.H.80A Puss Moth, with non-standard rear windows, at Woodford on 8 June 1934. Its colour scheme was blue, with silver nose and wings. In May 1938, G-ABEM was sold to Holland and became PH-ATL. Its Certificate of Registration lapsed in May 1941.

The blue and silver Avro 594 Avian III G-EBXD at Barton on 12 June 1934. First registered to the manufacturer in April 1928, 'XD soon passed to the Lancashire Aero Club and was based at Woodford. It was last registered to Woodford private owner Richard Davies and withdrawn from use in 1937.

Avro 621 Tutor K3244 of No. 5 FTS at the Lancashire Aero Club's annual air pageant at Woodford on 23 June 1934. K3244 was part of a batch of 288 Tutors delivered to the RAF between March 1933 and December 193. It served with No. 5 FTS, No. 23 ERFTS, and No. 2 Flying Instructors School. In June 1941, it was damaged at Lundy and struck off RAF charge in July that year.

Also at the Woodford pageant on 23 June 1934 was Bristol Bulldog TM K3181, a two-seat training version of the fighter, powered by a 450-hp Bristol Jupiter VI FH engine. This aircraft was delivered to 19 Squadron in 1933, and also saw service with 56 Squadron before being struck off RAF charge in 1937.

The fifteenth annual display of the RAF at Hendon on Saturday 30 June was marred by the death of the Lord Mayor of London's son Sqn Ldr Stanley Collett, who was killed after the Hawker Hart in which he was flying had engine failure and crashed when it undershot the aerodrome while trying to land. The pilot survived. A couple of days later, on 2 July, the third SBAC Display was staged at Hendon, with more than 40 aircraft and 1,500 invited guests attending in brilliant sunshine.

On that same day, a Hooton pilot, the inimitable William 'Jock' Mackay, was killed while performing a crazy flying demonstration at Farnborough in Avro 504N G-ACRS. During his routine, he would be seen to chuck what appeared to be the control column out of the aircraft and then proceed to fly the 504N from outside of the cockpit while the real control column was held in place by a length of rubber bungee. According to the official report of the accident, the pilot unwittingly fouled the throttle control bracket on the side of the cockpit during a steeply banked turn near the ground, causing the aircraft to crash in spectacular fashion. Mackay was able to recount what happened before he died of his injuries. During his flying career, he had taken part in no fewer than 600 displays all over the country.

The thirteenth King's Cup air race started in rain and finished in sunshine at Hatfield Aerodrome during 13 to 14 July, having been staged over several courses totalling 801 miles, with 43 entrants. Flt Lt H. M Schofield in Monospar ST-10 G-ACTS, with the aircraft's designer H. J. Stieger beside him, took the cup, achieving an average speed of 134 mph in the final race.

During 8 to 9 August, Captain L. Reid and J. R. Ayling flew D.H.84 Dragon G-ACJM *Trail of Caribou* from Canada non-stop to Heston; a distance of 3,000 miles was covered in 30 hours and 50 minutes.

With Bristol Jupiter engines running, these Bristol Bulldog IIAs are about to take off from Woodford on 23 June 1934 during the Lancashire Aero Club's annual air pageant. Nearest is K1665, one of a batch of ninety-two Bulldogs delivered to the RAF between October 1930 and May 1931. K1665 flew with Nos 32 and 56 Squadrons before being relegated to instructional airframe 1129M in September 1938. The Bulldogs put up a notable aerobatic display, much to the delight of the 30,000 spectators. In its report on the display, *Flight* magazine described Woodford as, 'One of the prettiest aerodromes in the country, but the only access for motor traffic is by a long and narrow approach road.'

Originally designed as a Hinaidi replacement for service in India, the Handley Page H.P. 33 Clive J9126 was later modified and furnished to carry sixteen passengers. It was first flown in this configuration in September 1932 and was sold to Sir Alan Cobham the following year. Named *Youth of Australia,* it toured Britain with Cobham's National Aviation Day display organisation, giving joyrides to thousands. In 1933 alone, G-ABYX carried 120,000 passengers. The Clive was also used by Sir Alan for in-flight refuelling trials, and was renamed *Astra.* 'YX is seen here at Woodford on 23 June 1934. It was scrapped in 1935.

Shell Mex & BP's D.H.85 Leopard Moth G-ACLY during a visit to Woodford for the 23 June air pageant. Registered to the company in December 1932 and kept at Heston, G-ACLY passed to Rollason Aircraft Services Ltd at Croydon, and spent the last three years of peace with Southend Flying Services Ltd before being impressed into RAF service as AW166 in July 1940 and employed on Army cooperation work. During such a flight on 9 November 1940, engine problems forced the pilot to ditch in the Bristol Channel. Both pilot and aircraft were rescued, but the Leopard was taken off RAF charge in February 1941.

Fokker F. XII PH-AIE at Liverpool Speke on 23 July 1934. Powered by three 420-hp Pratt & Whitney Wasp C radial engines, the Fokker F. XII carried eighteen passengers. PH-AIE flew originally with KLM and when the type was disposed of in favour of DC-2s, four of the Dutch airline's F. XIIs were sold to Crilly Airways Ltd; 'AIE became G-ADZJ in January 1936. Crilly was soon absorbed by British Airways, and on 15 August that year, 'ZJ and three other British Airways F. XIIs flew from Gatwick to take part in the Spanish Civil War.

Hearing that an S.E.5a was at Hooton Park, E. J. R. cycled the 45 or so miles from Chorlton-cum-Hardy on 4 September to photograph Savage Skywriting's S.E.5a G-EBIB, arriving just as Sidney St Barbe was about to take off. St Barbe was one of the most colourful characters of the time, and a brilliant pilot, but he sadly lost his life in an Avro 504N G-ADEI while taking off from Hanworth on 16 May 1939, towing a banner. The Lynx-engine packed up, and though he walked away from the crash, St Barbe died shortly after from an internal haemorrhage.

During September, the prototype Gloster Gladiator (S.S. 37) K5200 made its first flight, and on the 9 September, the first D.H.88 Comet prototype E.1 / G-ACSP flew for the first time in the capable hands of Hubert Broad at Hatfield. With the MacRobertson England–Australia air race only weeks away, for which G-ACSS and two other Comets were entered, the de Havilland company was cutting things a bit fine. A few days later, on 12 September, the prototype two-seat Hawker Hind bomber K2915 flew for the first time.

RAF Mildenhall was the focus of the aviation world on 20 October for the dawn start of what was regarded as the most important aviation contest of the time; the MacRobertson Mildenhall–Melbourne, a distance of 11,300 miles. Originally, there were sixty-four entries, but on the day, twenty started, of which only nine completed the distance. The red and white D.H.88 Comet G-ACSS *Grosvenor House*, flown by Tom Campbell Black and C. W. A. Scott, won the speed race in a time of 70 hours and 54 minutes, and pocketed the £10,000 prize. The handicap race was won by a more or less standard KLM Douglas DC-2 airliner, piloted by Capt. K. D. Parmentier and J. J. Moll, in an elapsed time of 90 hours and 13 minutes. Owen Cathcart-Jones and Ken Waller, flying D.H.88 Comet G-ACSR, flew back from Melbourne to Lympne in 6 days, 16 hours, and 10 minutes. The total Mildenhall–Melbourne–Lympne journey of 23,000 miles was achieved in 13 days, 6 hours, and 43 minutes.

Designed as a twin-engine equivalent of the highly successful and economical D.H.83 Fox Moth, the six-passenger D.H.84 Dragon, powered by two 130-hp de Havilland Gipsy Major engines, was first flown in November 1932 and soon went into production. An improved version, the Dragon 2, with faired-in undercarriage struts and individually-framed windows, followed in 1933. Railway Air Services' D.H.84 Dragon 2 G-ACPX is seen at Speke also on July 23 1934. At the outbreak of war, this Dragon was flying for Western Airways Ltd, and in April 1940, was impressed into RAF service as X9399. After only a few days, the Dragon crashed at Castle Bromwich while assigned to an anti-aircraft cooperation unit.

Avro 504K G-ABLL was built in 1927 as J8333 for the RAF, and received its first C of A in June 1931, while first placed on the civil register with Northern Air Transport and based at Barton. The Avro passed to Lancelot 'Pop' Rimmer in August 1933 and was used for joyriding, plying its trade when this photograph was taken at Ashton-in-Makerfield on 7 August 1934. A few days later, the aircraft was lost after a crash at Lowton Moor, Manchester.

Avro 504K G-EBGZ at Hooton Park in August 1934. First registered in July 1923 to William Beardmore & Company Ltd and used as a reserve school trainer, this 504K was sold to Lancelot 'Pop' Rimmer's North British Aviation Company in February 1929 and based at Hooton Park. When this photograph was taken, the 504K was being dismantled after its C of A had expired several months earlier.

D.H.83 Fox Moth G-ACFC at Speke on 8 August 1934. Completed at Stag Lane in 1933, 'FC was first sold to Blackpool & West Coast Air Services Ltd, in whose black and white livery the aircraft is pictured. Note the name *Progress* on the engine cowling. It remained in service with this company until sold to Olley Air Services Ltd in January 1936, and operated from Croydon. In September 1938, the Fox moved still further south to Shoreham to be flown by Great Western & Southern Air Lines Ltd. After impressment into the RAF as AX859 in May 1940, the Fox became instructional airframe 2583M.

Desoutter I G-AAPU at Speke on 8 August 1934. Built at Croydon in 1929, 'PU joined the fleet of National Flying Services at Heston. At the time of its visit to Speke, it was operated by the Staverton-based Cotswold Aero Club, and later passed into the hands of Norman A. de Bruyne of Aero Research fame, and based at Duxford from mid-1938. The following year, 'PU was put into storage at Marshall's Aerodrome at nearby Cambridge, but was impressed into RAF service with No. 41 Group in September 1940. The requisition order was subsequently cancelled and the Desoutter scrapped before the war's end.

Avro 504K began life as E9353 with the RAF, and received its first C of A and registration G-ABWK in June 1932. Operated for a while by the Essex Flying Club at Abridge, it passed to Kinmel Bay Air Services in August the following year. For a while, it flew holidaymakers from the beach at Rhyl, Wales, where it is pictured returning from such a flight on September 1 1934. In December 1935, it was sold abroad. In a letter to A. J. Jackson, E. J. R. wrote: 'Your account of G-ABWK is interesting since we "collected" this aircraft, together with G-EBYW, at Rhyl in August 1934. In that month during my holidays, I did a sweep of the Atlantic sea board from Blackpool to Aberystwyth by bike. It took a fortnight, but was worth the trouble. 'WK and 'YW belonged to a joint called Kinmel Bay Air Services and I believe 'WK went up north somewhere afterwards. Marcus Brunton was one of the pilots – he drank himself out of quite a number of good jobs and ended up as a railway porter at Paddington Station.'

Also pictured on the beach at Rhyl on the same day is Kinmel Bay Air Services' Avro 504K G-EBYW, initially registered to Surrey Flying Service in September 1928 and based at Croydon. After service with Kinmel Bay Air Services, the aircraft passed to local man Edward Clerk in 1934, but was not flown after its C of A expired in June the following year.

S.E.5a G-EBIB outside No. 7 hangar at Hooton Park on 4 September 1934, with Sidney St Barbe sitting smoking in the cockpit. This is probably the occasion when E. J. R. made a 95-mile return cycle trip from Manchester just to photograph this aircraft. The S.E.5a was doped silver overall with black lettering. One of nearly thirty S.E.5as of the type owned by Maj. Jack Savage's Hendon-based skywriting concern between 1922-29, 'IB was built by Wolseley Motors Ltd in Birmingham and converted for skywriting at Hendon. All Savage's SE5as were purchased new, and although 'IB previously carried the serial number F938, it never saw military service. This S.E.5a continued to fly until the C of A expired in August 1935. In July 1939, the aircraft was presented to the Science Museum in London and exhibited for a while bearing the serial number F937 (actually allocated to G-EBIC). In recent years, the aircraft was restored to its skywriting configuration, complete with extended skywriting exhaust pipes, and continues on display at the Science Museum.

During the autumn and winter of 1934, E. J. R. and J. G. E. restricted themselves to visiting local aerodromes; one highlight was the sight of Bristol F.2b Fighter G-ACAC at Hooton Park, belonging to W. L. Handley. It was based there until scrapped in January 1936. He later recalled in a letter to A. J. Jackson, 'We used to have lunch in an old Bristol Fighter G-ACAC up at Hooton in 1934. This used to vary according to the mood. Sometimes it would be the luxurious Avro 642 G-ACFV, and in times of sentiment, poor old Avro 504K G-EASF. Happy Days!'

There was great sadness on 31 December, when Edward Hillman, former farmer's boy and motor coach operator, who successfully turned his hand to forming and running Hillman's Airways, died from a coronary, presumably as a result of overwork.

The year was not particularly a good one for aviation accidents. During 1934, there were ninety accidents involving British registered civil aircraft, of which twenty-five had fatal consequences; figures that were much higher than the previous year. Of this total, private and club flying accounted for sixty-nine accidents. Error of judgement or faulty airmanship were regarded as the sole cause of 50 per cent, and as ever, the worst accidents were the result of showing off. In one particular case, a pilot performed a high-speed dive towards the clubhouse at a low altitude, followed by a 'zoom' and climbing turn; the aeroplane stalled and fell in a spinning nosedive to the ground. The passenger, who was in the front cockpit, was killed instantly; the pilot was seriously injured. Also, shortly after the start of an instructional flight, the pupil was acting as though physically or mentally deranged; he refused to respond to the instructor's orders, and held persistently on to the flying and engine controls. Having tried in vain to obtain control of the aeroplane, the instructor switched off the engine and attempted to land in a large field, but owing to the pupil's interference, the aircraft bounced heavily and turned over. The instructor escaped serious injury, but the pupil, who had joined the club and started to fly only that day, was severely injured.

The ST-3, first flown in 1931, was the first General Aircraft Monospar aircraft to feature the Monospar method of construction, in which the wing consisted of a single-spar duralumin Warren girder spar brace with a pyramidal system of tie rods. There followed a series of ST types, culminating with the ST-25 Jubilee, De Luxe, and Universal. Seen here is ST-6 G-ACIC at Hooton Park on 9 September 1934. The ST-6 was the second British aircraft to feature a manually-retracted undercarriage and its redesigned fuselage enabled, at a pinch, a fifth person to be carried. Only four examples were built. G-ACIC was registered in July 1933 and passed through the hands of several private owners before ending up with the Romford Flying Club at Maylands in August 1938. It was lost in a disastrous hangar fire that wiped out several aircraft at Maylands on 6 February 1940.

After the First World War, a few Avro 504Ks were converted to Avro 548s; their rotary engines were exchanged for in-line 80-hp Renault or 120-hp Airdisco powerplants. One such conversion was G-EBOK, first registered in July 1926 to Light Planes (Lancashire) Ltd and based at Woodford. It was later sold to the Lancashire School of Flying Ltd at Squires Gate, Blackpool, but by the end of 1936 was no longer airworthy. It is seen here at Barton on 9 September 1934.

Nicholas Comper's sprightly single-seat Comper CLA.7 Swift was first flown in December 1929, and over the ensuing four years, forty-one examples were built, first at Hooton Park and latterly at brand new premises at Heston. Comper Swift G-ABWE was built in 1932 and was first owned by Richard Shuttleworth, who was also a director of Comper Aircraft Ltd. He sold it to Stan Lowe, who faired-in the lift struts and fitted a hideous engine cowling to enhance the Swift's performance for air racing. After being based at Gravesend by owner C. H. Tutt, the Swift was sold abroad in February 1940. On 2 December 1934, G-ABWE was photographed in one of the hangars at Hooton Park.

The Avro 642/2m was a Fokker derivative built by A. V. Roe & Company Ltd in 1934. In 1928, A. V. Roe acquired a licence to build the Fokker F. VIIB/3m, which featured a one-piece, ply-covered cantilever wing. The company produced several aircraft based on the Fokker design, including the Avro Ten and the Avro Five. The Avro 642/2m was the last of these developments, featuring a shoulder-positioned wing with integral engines. It was much larger than its predecessors and carried eighteen passengers. Two examples were built; one went to India, and G-ACFV, seen here at Hooton Park on 2 December 1934, was delivered to Midland and Scottish Air Ferries Ltd based at Renfrew. In September 1936, it was sold in New Guinea as VH-UXD, and destroyed by enemy action in March 1942.

Avro 504 G-EBIS was first registered in 1924 to William Beardmore & Company Ltd and used as a Reserve School trainer. It was sold to the North British Aviation Company Ltd at Hooton Park in 1929, and remained there until its C of A expired in May 1935. It was still airworthy when this photograph was taken at Hooton Park on 9 December 1934, though the tyres look as though they could do with some air.

CHAPTER SIX

Fresh Fields (1935)

The Blackburn Darts G-AAAX and G-EBWB used to be in a junkyard at Leeds. Blackburn Velos G-AAAW came to Hooton and belonged to a bloke called Parker, but he soon tired of the aircraft's petrol consumption of his £15 aeroplane.

Letter from E. J. Riding to A. J. Jackson in 1943

The new year began with a visit to Hooton Park on 20 January to photograph Bristol F.2b G-ACAC lurking in a hangar, and Avro 504K G-EBKX. A week later, E. J. R. called into Southport where the Renault-engined Avro 548A G-EAFH and the dismantled fuselage of D.H.6 G-EBWG were photographed.

During February, J. G. E. wrote to Lewis's Ltd of Market Street, Manchester, asking if he and E. J. R. could visit the store where D.H.88 Comet G-ACSS *Grosvenor House*, winner of the MacRobertson England–Australia race the previous October, was being exhibited. The store's publicity manager arranged this, and though the lighting was poor, E. J. R. managed to secure a photograph.

A visit to Woodford on 24 March was rewarded with a photograph of the Avro 652A prototype K4771, forerunner of thousands of Avro Anson Is. It had made its first flight that very day. Also seen was the Lancashire Aero Club's D.H.60 Moth G-EBLV, still airworthy more than seventy-five years later and flown from Old Warden, Bedfordshire, by the Shuttleworth Collection. Also present at Woodford was Lancashire county cricket captain Peter Eckersley's smart Avro Avian IVH G-AABX.

The following month, E. J. R. journeyed south, calling at Croydon on 11 April, where he photographed Handley Page H.P. 42 G-AAXD *Horatius* and D.H.84 Dragon G-ACCR, undergoing a C of A renewal. Amy Mollison's Beechcraft B17L G-ADDH was also there. Brooklands was visited the following day, and Vickers Vincent K4140 was photographed while having its compass swung before being crated for shipment to No. 8 Squadron in Aden. On 13 April, E. J. R. looked around Hanworth, photographing Bristol F.2b Fighter G-ACPE, Monospar S.T.12 G-ADDY, and Cierva C.18 Autogiro G-ABXG. At nearby Heston the day after, pictures were taken of Junkers F.13 G-EBZV, Airspeed AS.6J Envoy I G-ADAZ, and Airspeed AS.5A Courier G-ADAX. Back north again, E. J. R. was on Southport sands on 27 April taking more photographs of Avro 548A G-EAFH.

During 12 to 29 April, Jean Batten flew from Darwin to Croydon in her D.H.60G Moth G-AARB, a distance of around 9,000 miles in 17 days, 16 hours, and 15 minutes; she become the first woman to fly solo from Australia to the UK. Another woman who made headlines was fifty-four-year-old grandmother Mrs. G. E. Alington when she became the first woman in Britain to make a parachute jump, over Brooklands on 4 May. Two days later, the country celebrated the silver jubilee of HM King George V. On 22 May, the British Government announced plans to triple the size of the RAF during the following two years.

Looking not unlike an American Waco cabin biplane of the period, the 1934 Avro 641 Commodore appeared at about the same time as the D.H.87 Hornet Moth. Although both were cabin biplanes, the Avro 641 accommodated five people, the Hornet Moth only two. Powered by a 215-hp Armstrong Siddeley Lynx, only five of the metal-structured Commodores were produced, of which G-ACNT, seen here at its Woodford birthplace on 6 March 1935, was the prototype. It was owned by the maker for most of its life, was dismantled at Woodford in October 1939, and is believed to have been scrapped in 1950.

D.H.88 Comet G-ACSS was exhibited in the Manchester store Lewis's Ltd in February 1935. In October 1934, the red and white Comet, named *Grosvenor House* and flown by Charles W. Scott and Tom Campbell Black, won the MacRobertson England–Australia race with a time of 70 hours and 54 minutes. During 1935-36, the Comet was flown by the RAF as K5084, and afterwards restored to the civil register, flown as *The Orphan* and then *The Burberry*. It was later stored at Gravesend, subsequently at Leavesden, and after a very lengthy restoration to airworthy condition, currently resides at Old Warden with the Shuttleworth Collection.

LEWIS
CENTRAL BUYING OFFICE
47, GRESHAM ST
LONDON
E.C.2
Telephone
NATIONAL 1414

LEWIS
ROYAL POLYTECHNIC OR
GLASGOW
· · ·
LEWISS
·LEEDS·
LTD

LEWIS'S Ltd.
LIVERPOOL · MANCHESTER · BIRMINGHAM

CENTRAL 3200
Telephone
Telegrams: LEWISS
MANCHESTER

PLEASE REPLY TO

MARKET STREET
MANCHESTER 1

J.G. Ellison, Esq.,
16, Bentley Road,
Chorlton-cum-Hardy,
MANCHESTER.

4th
February
1935.

Dear Sir,

    I cannot definitely promise that you will get a
photograph of the "COMET", but if you care to call in and
see me one afternoon I will try and make arrangements
whereby you can get a nice photograph. Somehow I don't
think the light is too good and the only time you could
get a photograph would be round about 6-30 p.m. or this
Wednesday afternoon.

        Yours faithfully,
        for LEWIS'S Ltd.,

T.H. GRENFELL.
Manchester Publicity Manager.

On 4 February 1935, J. G. E. wrote to Lewis' and asked for permission to photograph the D.H.88 Comet in the company's Manchester Market Street store.

Avro Avian IVH G-AABX at Woodford on 24 March 1935. Completed in late 1928, this red and silver Avian was first sold to former Lancashire County Cricket Club captain Peter T. Eckersley (1904-40) and named Comette. The Avian later passed to the Lancashire Aero Club, and at the outbreak of war, was owned by Herbert Armstrong and based at Stanley Park Aerodrome in Blackpool. Unusually for a civil registered aeroplane, the C of A was renewed in February 1940. Following impressment into the RAF, the Avian was used as instructional airframe 2080M until scrapped at RAF Morecambe in May 1944. Peter Eckersley was killed near Eastleigh in 1940 in a flying accident while serving in the Fleet Air Arm.

E. J. R. and J. G. E. ventured to Leeds and Yeadon Aerodrome on 26 May and photographed Arrow Active II G-ABVE in a hangar. More interesting still was a scrapyard in York Road, Leeds, where they came across a couple of leviathans in the forms of Blackburn Velos G-EBWB and the equally unlovely Blackburn T. 3 Velos torpedo bomber G-AAAX. Both were complete with their Napier Lion engines, and surrounded by derelict cars and engines.

Back at Woodford on 30 May, the Airspeed A.S.4 G-ABSI tri-motor was photographed with Mongoose-engined Avro 504N G-ADBD and Lynx-engined Avro 504N G-ACLV. Railway Air Services D.H.84 Dragon 2 G-ADED and D.H.86 G-ACVY were photographed while being refuelled at Barton in June.

On 4 June, the prototype Armstrong Whitworth Whitley long-range, night-bomber prototype K3585 made its maiden flight, followed by that of the prototype Vickers Wellesley two-seat, general-purpose bomber K7556 on 19 June. A few days later, on 23 June, K3583, the prototype Bristol 130, later named *the Bombay*, made its first flight.

The sixteenth RAF Display was held at Hendon on 29 June, of which C. G. Grey, editor of *The Aeroplane* commented, 'There was nothing new or startling among the machines.' Unscheduled excitement was provided by a demonstration flying lesson by instructor and 'pupil'. During the landing, things went badly wrong; the Avro Tutor hit the ground and slid along in a collapsed state. Fortunately, the occupants escaped unharmed, and the fire crew were only too happy to leap into action and spray the aircraft in foam. Two days later, the SBAC Display was staged at Hendon.

Miles M.2 Hawk G-ACYA photographed at Barton on 29 March 1935. Registered in October 1934 to H. J. Hardy and kept at Barton, this pretty little aeroplane was sold to S. B. Wilmot in April 1938 and kept at Steventon strip, Ludlow. On 8 July 1940, the Hawk was destroyed in a hangar fire at Hooton Park.

Seen in a hangar at Croydon on 11 April 1935 is D.H.84 Dragon 1 G-ACCR. It is undergoing a C of A renewal, although the absence of people would suggest that it was a lunch break. This was an early production aircraft registered in 1933, first to W. A. Rollason and then to Barnstaple & North Devon Air Services. The following year, it was sold to Commercial Air Hire Ltd, but on 22 January 1936, was lost in the channel off the French coast. The aircraft was carrying about £80,000 in gold bars when static electricity caused by a hail storm forced a landing in shallow water off Ault. The three occupants climbed out and managed to wade ashore, only to have to climb cliffs to avoid the incoming tide. Note the D.H.60 Moth fuselage turned on its side to the right of the photograph.

The popular press made much of the first flight on 14 July of the first British-built H.M.14 Pou du Ciel, which in the UK was called the Flying Flea. It was flown at Heston by its builder Stephen Appleby. Registered G-ADMH, it was powered by a 30-hp Carden Ford. In 1934, the Air League of the British Empire translated Henri Mignet's book *The Flying Flea: How to Build It;* the first edition of 6,000 copies sold out in a couple of months. Due to Mignet's slightly misleading claim that anyone who could make a packing case could build a Pou *and* teach themselves to fly it, frenetic activity began in hundreds of garages and garden sheds throughout the land. Following several fatalities less than a year later, after more than eighty examples had been granted Authorisations to Fly, a simple design fault became apparent. The Flea's subsequent adverse publicity, plus a loss of confidence in the design by its builders, both amateur and professional, virtually killed it on the spot, despite the introduction of subsequent modifications to remedy the design fault. The Air Ministry did not ban the Flea, but chose to refuse to issue unmodified Fleas an Authorisation to Fly from October 1936.

On 7 July, E. J. R. was back at Heston, where he photographed Short S.16 Scion G-ACUZ, Miles M.4A Merlin G-ADFE, and visiting Koolhoven F.K.41 PH-ATE. Calling in to Hanworth an hour or so later, Bristol F.2b Fighter G-ACPE, Breda 13 G-AAVL, and Southern Martlet G-AAII received his attention. The following day, a visit to Croydon revealed Boulton Paul Mailplane G-ACOY, Caudron Phalene F-AMZB, and Avro 652A G-ACRN. He also photographed Sabena Fokker F.VII 3m OO-AIS. Reward for a return visit to Hanworth on 13 July was the presence of a couple of Hendy aircraft: 302 G-AAVT and Heck G-ACTC. Viper-engined Avro 552 G-ACAW and Southern Martlet G-AAYZ were also recorded.

Lympne was visited on 17 July, where the ancient Bristol F.2b Fighter G-ABYT was photographed, together with Klemm L.25 G-AATD and Miles M.3 Falcon G-ACTM. En route back to London, E. J. R. looked through the hedgerows surrounding RAF Hawkinge and RAF Manston, and took some distant shots of Vickers Virginias and a Handley Page Hinaidi.

Back home, a visit was paid to a field at Stretford on 27 July, where Avro 504Ns G-ADBO 'R and 'S of Jubilee Air Displays were plying their trade. E. J. R. twice spent 3s 6d on two 4-minute flights in G-ADBS with Leslie Anderson; his aircraft was strikingly doped yellow all over with black lettering. Anderson was killed in the same aircraft on Bodmin Moor on 15 August.

E. J. R. called in at RAF Sealand, home of No. 5 FTS, on 30 July, and photographed three or four Armstrong Whitworth Atlas trainers, including K2523, about to set off on an instructional flight. Calling in at Hooton Park on the way home, he came across the prototype Short S.16 Scion G-ACJI. On 1 August, he was at a field at Lowton, Lancashire, taking several photographs of old favourite Avro 504K G-EASF, plus another photograph of Scion G-ACJI. At Reddish on 6 August, E. J. R. came across Westland Wessex G-EBXK, in service with Cobham's National Aviation Day displays, giving countless members of the public their first taste of flying.

The first flight of the prototype D.H.90 Dragonfly took place from Hatfield on 12 August. Six days later, the Heston Phoenix prototype made its maiden flight from Heston.

As well as for de Havilland with the first flight of the Dragonfly, 12 August was a red letter day for E. J. R. That day, he began an apprenticeship with A. V. Roe & Company Ltd at Newton Heath, Manchester. His notebook for the following period records: instruction in welding and alignment of Avro Cadet and 621 fuselages; repairs to bottom longerons and Certificate of Airworthiness renewal on D.H.53 Humming Bird G-EBXN; repairs carried out on Avro Avian G-ACKE following crash landing; renewal of Certificate of Airworthiness on Avro Commodore VT-AFN; servicing and maintenance of Lancashire Aero Club aircraft for ten days.

His notes continue: transferred to Inspection Department at Newton Heath where time was spent in Bond Store inspection – tubes, bars and sheets, free issue etc. This was followed by a period inspecting Avro Anson spars. On the day after his arrival at Newton Heath, back at Hooton Park, a serious fire destroyed one of the hangars. Luckily, it was practically empty;

Handley Page H.P.42s were such a regular sight at Croydon it was hard to believe that only eight of these archaic airliners were built, all for Imperial Airways Ltd. The prototype flew for the first time on 11 November 1930 from Radlett. Two versions were built: the H.P.42E Eastern was for use on European routes; the 42W Western for Empire routes. H.P.42W G-AAXD is seen here between flights at Croydon on 11 April 1935. Named *Horatius*, it served with Imperial Airways from 1931 until wrecked while attempting a forced landing on a golf course at Tiverton, Devon, on 1 March 1940.

Vickers Vincent K4140 having its compass swung at Brooklands on 12 April 1934. A few days later, it was packed into a crate for shipment to No. 8 Squadron in Aden. On 3 March 1939, the Vincent flew into a hill while flying in cloud near Mukeiras.

Cierva C.19 Mk. IV Autogiro G-ABXG was operated by the manufacturer at Hanworth from 1932 until sold in April 1935 to a couple of private owners, one of whom was aged sixty-nine. It remained based at Hanworth where this photograph was taken on 15 April, and was destroyed in a crash there on 25 April 1937.

The sole British-registered example of a Junker F.13fe was imported into the UK in 1928 and sold to Rt Hon. F. E. Guest, who kept it at Hanworth, where it was seen on 17 April 1935. G-ABZV had an open cockpit for a crew of two; four passengers were carried in cabin comfort. The original 385-hp Junkers L. 5 engine was replaced with a 450-hp Bristol Jupiter VI in 1930, and in this configuration, the F. 13 passed to Lord Semphill. In April 1937, the aircraft was sold to Sweden; it became SE-AFW and was based at Stockholm, only to crash shortly after.

the only casualties were a few wings. The fourteenth King's Cup air race was staged during 6 to 7 September; an eliminating contest was held over a course of 953 miles, and a final course of 350 miles. It was won by popular Tommy Rose, flying Gipsy Six-engined Miles M.3B Falcon Six G-ADLC at an average speed of 176.4 mph.

At Woodford on 7 September, E. J. R. came across the one-off T.K.II, built by de Havilland Technical School students, British Klemm Eagle's G-ACPU and G-ACRG, and two D.H.85 Leopard Moths, prototypes G-ACHC and G-ACUO. Miles M.2H Hawk Majors G-ADLA and G-ADLB were also bagged. Two further visits to Woodford that month were rewarded with photographs of the Jaguar-engined Avro 636 A.14, destined for the Irish Army Air Corps, and Swedish-registered Avro Avian IVM SE-ACP.

E. J. R. had 5 minutes with H. A. Crommelin in the Lancashire Aero Club's Avro 631 on its daily test flight from Woodford on 14 September. On the same day with the same pilot, he made a similar test flight in the club's blue and silver Avro Avian G-EBXD.

On 27 October, E. J. R. lugged his half-plate camera to Castle Bromwich and photographed Hawker Tomtit G-ABAX, D.H.60 Moth Major G-ACNR, and Klemm L.25 G-ABCY.

The merger of United Airways, Hillman's Airways, Spartan Airways, Highland Airways, and Scottish Airways into Allied British Airways Ltd occurred on 30 September; the word 'Allied' being dropped from the title on 29 October.

During 2 to 9 November, H. L. Brook flew his Percival Gull from Croydon to Port Darwin, a distance of around 9,000 miles, in 6 days, 21 hours, and 19 minutes, beating C. W. A. Scott's time from 1932. While Brook was heading for the Antipodes, the prototype Hawker Hurricane K5083 was first flown from Brooklands on 6 November.

Avro 548 G-EAFH on the beach at Southport on 27 April 1935. Originally an Avro 504K and registered K-147 in the first system of British civil registry, 'FH was converted to an Avro 548, and as such first flew in June 1920. It spent many years owned by the Giro Aviation Company Ltd, flying from Southport sands and based at Hesketh Park. On 31 March 1935, the aircraft was destroyed when it crashed while performing low-level aerobatics over the sands. The pilot John Houson died later in hospital, but the mechanic, though badly shocked, survived.

Of the four Miles M.4A Merlins built, one was delivered to Birkett Air Services Ltd at Heston in mid-1935. It flew many long distance charter flights, in particular to Abyssinia to take press reporters to cover the war with Italy. The aircraft's ultimate fate is not known, although it may have been destroyed in bombing during 1940. G-ADFE is seen at Heston on 7 May 1935.

D.H.60M Moth G-ABTF of the Leicester Flying Club at Woodford on 22 May 1935. Note the 'fox' motif on the rudder. First registered in March 1932, its last pre-war owner was the Strathtay Aero Club. On the outbreak of war, the Moth was impressed into RAF service as BK829. It was shuttled around various maintenance units before being taken off RAF charge in April 1942.

Not the winner of a spot landing contest, but Blackburn Velos G-EBWB in a scrapyard in York Road, Leeds, on 26 May 1935. Built in 1926 as a seaplane for an abortive sales tour of South America, the Velos was converted into a seaplane trainer on return to the UK, and in 1928, was registered to North Sea Aerial & Transport Company Ltd, Brough. Powered by a 450-hp Napier Lion, the vast 48-foot, 6-inch-span Velos was costly to run, and was withdrawn from service in 1933, ending its days as scrap.

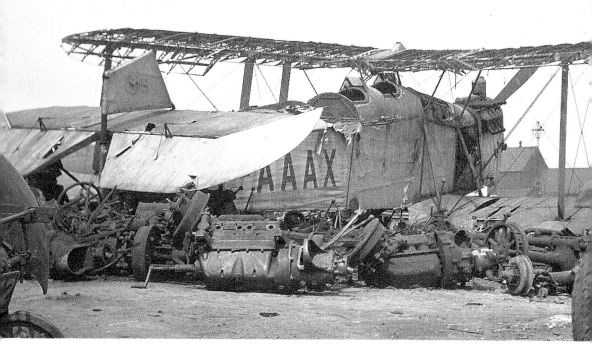

The equally unlovely Blackburn T.3 Velos torpedo bomber was developed from the company's Swift and Dart for the Greek Navy. Powered by a single 450-hp Napier Lion V, on a good day the two-seater cruised at about 100 mph. In 1929, four Velos, G-AAAX among them, were delivered to North Sea Aerial & General Transport Co. Ltd at Brough, and flown as trainers with interchangeable wheel and float undercarriages. Decidedly uneconomical to operate, once their training days were finished, they were sold for scrap to the same Leeds yard as G-EBWB.

The heavy half-plate was used again when E. J. R. journeyed south to Hendon Aerodrome on 6 December. A few days earlier, he had written to Maj. Jack Savage, asking permission to take further photographs of the Major's skywriting aircraft. He set up his tripod in one of the hangars, now housing part of the RAF Museum's collection, and exposed several plates of G-EBIB, G-EBIC, and G-EBVB. The lighting in the hangar was not good, and exposure times for each were 3 minutes. The following day, E. J. R. nipped over to Heston and photographed D.H.87A Hornet Moth G-ADJX, with tapered wings, Parnall Elf G-AAIN (now part of the Shuttleworth Collection), and the Mignet HM.14 Pou du Ciel G-ADPY.

By December 1935, there were around seventy light aeroplane clubs in the UK, of which forty-two were participating in the Air Ministry scheme for providing financial assistance. Total membership of these clubs was 9,112, of which 2,489 held 'A' licences. The previous year's figures were 5,814 and 1,823 respectively.

Licensed municipal aerodromes totalled twenty-seven, an increase of six on the previous year. There were ninety-five permanent licensed aerodromes by December, compared with ninety the previous year.

During 1935, records show that there were sixty-one accidents, of which twenty-two had fatal consequences; fewer than the previous year. Errors of judgement accounted for 58 per cent of them. One accident was due to the control column coming out of its socket while the pilot was performing aerobatics; another was caused by the passenger interfering with the controls while the pilot was trying to land.

In 1931, Arrow Aircraft Ltd of Leeds built a nifty little single-seat biplane powered by a 115-hp Cirrus Hermes. The Arrow Active was registered G-ABIX in May that year and its performance so impressed Alex Henshaw that he purchased the aeroplane in May 1935. While performing aerobatics in December 1935, the engine caught fire and Henshaw was forced to leave the aircraft in a hurry, parachuting to safety. The Active crashed at Markschapel, Lincolnshire, and burnt out. The Active 2 followed in 1932, and featured various refinements. By raising the upper wing on struts rather than mounting it directly to the fuselage, the pilot's forward vision was improved. The more powerful 120-hp de Havilland Gipsy engine enhanced performance, and G-ABVE was raced in the 1932 and 1933 King's Cup events. The silver and red trimmed Active 2 is pictured at Yeadon on 26 May 1935 with port wings folded. During the 1950s, the Active 2 was rebuilt and re-engined with a 145-hp de Havilland Gipsy 1C, and flown by the Tiger Club. After many years under the ownership of Desmond Penrose, the aircraft continues to fly from Breighton with the Real Aeroplane Company.

The silver and green Airspeed A.S.4 Ferry G-ABSI airborne at Woodford on 30 May 1935 during a National Aviation Day display appearance. The three-engined Ferry carried ten passengers and made its name as a safe mode of transport, giving countless thousands their first taste of flying. 'SI was operated by Cobham from 1932 until it passed to C. W. A. Scott for similar passenger work in March 1936. Following a period of use by Air Publicity Ltd, the Ferry operated occasionally with Portsmouth, Southsea, and Isle of Wight Aviation Ltd until mid-1939. In April 1940, it was impressed into the RAF as AV968 before being relegated to an instructional airframe as 2758M.

The brand new D.H.84 Dragon 2 G-ADED being loaded and refuelled at the Barton pumps in June 1935. Completed at Hatfield and registered in May 1935, 'ED flew with Railway Air Services on the thrice-daily service from Barton to the Isle of Man via Blackpool, but survived less than a few weeks. On 1 July that year, the Dragon crashed while taking off from Ronaldsway, Isle of Man. Failing to lift off, the tail caught the boundary hedge and the Dragon burst into flames. Although the aircraft was completely burnt out, six passengers and pilot Capt. Robert Pierce miraculously survived.

D.H.86 G-ACVY photographed at the Barton fuel pumps on 12 June 1935. Completed at Hatfield in 1934, 'VZ was sold new to Railway Air Services and named *Mercury*. It was first used on the company's route between Croydon, Castle Bromwich, Barton, Belfast, and Renfrew. One of the early single-pilot variants, this D.H.86 soldiered on in airline service for fourteen years; it was scrapped finally at Langley in 1948.

Avro 643 Cadet G-ADEX at Barton on 12 June 1935. An improved version of the Avro 631 Cadet, the 643 featured a raised rear seat. Completed at Newton Heath, Manchester, in 1935, G-ADEX was delivered to Hon R. F. Watson and kept at Heston. In January 1937, it passed to L. C. Lewis at Hanworth before being sold abroad in September the same year.

The three-seat Percival Gull Four first flew in 1932 and proved to be a quantum leap in light aircraft design. In addition to being sold worldwide, pilots such as Jean Batten, Amy Mollison, and Edgar Percival himself all made notable flights in the Gull Four and the Gull Six. The latter featured a revised undercarriage and cabin top, and was powered by the de Havilland Gipsy Six engine. Percival Gull Four G-ACHM was completed in 1933, sold to I. C. MacGilchrist, and kept at Heston. When this photograph was taken at Barton on 6 July 1935, the aircraft had just passed to Brian Allen Aviation Ltd. It was subsequently sold to France in May the following year to Mlle Elisabeth Louse Spitzer, and based at Neuilly-sur-Seine as F-AQLZ.

D.H.84 Dragon 2 G-ADEE was registered in June 1935 to Railway Air Services Ltd, but its flying career was cut short five months later. On 26 October, while on the second stage of a journey to the Isle of Man in poor visibility, the pilot lost his way and the Dragon crashed into the slope of Fairsnape Fell, with fatal results for him and the sole passenger. The ill-fated Dragon is seen being refuelled at the Barton pumps on 6 July 1935.

The Short S.16 Scion was a useful twin-engine feeder liner first flown in August 1933. Capable of carrying five passengers, the Scion was usually powered by two Pobjoy engines varying in power from 75 to 90 hp. The Scion 2, with an additional passenger seat and general improvements, was introduced in 1935. Seen at Heston on 7 May 1935 is G-ACUZ, first flown in February from Rochester. It was owned by Airwork from May 1938, and was one of eleven Scions to be impressed into the RAF. As W7419, this Scion was taken off charge in April 1944.

An unusual sight at Heston and Hanworth from mid-1930 was the Breda 15 two-seater, built in Milan and powered by a 100-hp de Havilland Gipsy I engine. Six were allocated British registrations, but only two materialised. G-AAVL had several private owners before it passed to Pan Aero Pictures Ltd at Brooklands, which it is believed, used the aircraft for aerial photography; a number of postcards published at the time were credited to this company. 'VL is seen at Hanworth on 7 July 1935. It was dismantled in 1937.

At Croydon on 8 July 1935 is the prototype Avro 652 G-ACRM, the first of 11,000 Ansons produced from 1935-52. Named *Avalon* by Imperial Airways, 'RM and sister ship G-ACRN *Avatar* operated the airline's Croydon–Brindisi route until sold to Air Service Training (AST). After service with AST as a navigation trainer, G-ACRM was impressed into the RAF as DG655 in February 1940. After time at No. 3 Elementary Flying School and No. 11 Air Observers Navigational School, it then had a spell with No. 1 School of Photography, before passing to the Admiralty in July 1941 to serve with Nos 811 and 781 Squadrons at Lee-on-Solent.

Easily mistaken for a Percival Gull, the one-off, two-seat Hendy 302 G-AAVT was designed by Basil Henderson, and like the first batch of Percival Gull Fours, built at Yate by George Parnall & Company Ltd. Flown by Edgar Percival in the 1930 King's Cup air race, the aircraft was later rebuilt as the 302A, in which guise it featured a Cirrus Hermes IV engine and a modified cabin. G-AAVT is seen in this form at Hanworth on 13 July 1935. It was withdrawn from use at Gravesend in 1938.

Basil Henderson also designed the Hendy 3308, better known as the Heck. This two-seater was designed for Whitney Straight, built by Westland Aircraft Works in Yeovil, and first flown in July 1934. The Heck's speed range – 45 to 170 mph – was amazing, and exactly to Whitney Straight's demanding specification. Renamed Parnall Heck in May 1935, G-ACTC is seen at Hanworth on 13 July 1935, minus engine cowlings to reveal its 200-hp de Havilland Gipsy Six engine. Later that year, the Heck made an attempt on the Cape record, and although the journey out was fraught with many problems, the return to Lympne was made in the record time of 6 days, 8 hours, and 27 minutes. A further seven Hecks were built by Parnall Aircraft Ltd at Yate. The prototype was scrapped in 1937.

Better check the rigging! During 1932, a further batch of Bristol F.2b Fighters came on to the civil market, one of which was G-ABYT, formerly J8434 with the RAF. Registered in July 1933, the old Brisfit passed to J. P. W. Tophan in April 1934, and was based at Lympne, where it was photographed in a rather poor state on 17 July 1935. The following year, 'YT collided with a barbed wire fence; repairs were not carried out and the old fighter was scrapped shortly after.

In addition to BAC VII Drones constructed at Hanworth, manufacturing rights were sold to French company Société Aeronautique d'Aviation Nouvelle (SFAN) of Issy-les-Moulineaux, which produced two versions; the single-seat SFAN was powered by a 25-hp Ava engine, and the SFAN 4 side-by-side, two-seater fitted with a 35-hp Mengin. What appears to be a pristine SFAN 2 is pictured at Hanworth on 20 July 1935. What it was doing there is not clear. It was reported in *Flight* magazine that the French Air Ministry ordered forty Drones from the French company.

DETACHED   N⁰ 8857

JUBILEE

AIR DISPLAYS

VALID FOR ONE FLIGHT ONLY

MONGOOSE
___

3/6

PER PASSENGER.

Issued by Jubilee Air Displays Ltd.,
101, Leadenhall Street, London, E.C.3.
Subject to Conditions Printed Overleaf.
TO BE RETAINED BY PASSENGER.

Left: Jubilee Display ticket purchased by E. J. R. on 27 July 1935 for a flight in Leslie Anderson's Mongoose-powered Avro 504N G-ADBS.

Below: G-ACKZ D.H.83 Fox Moth, one of the last built, at Stretford on 27 July 1935, flying with Jubilee Air Displays Ltd. First registered in November 1933, this Fox Moth was sold to India, becoming VT-AJW in February 1938. It flew with Air Services of India until the registration was cancelled in October 1946.

Opposite above: Passengers climb aboard Avro 504N G-ADBS with Mongoose III engine running at Stretford, just south-west of Manchester, on 27 July 1935. The same day, E. J. R. had two short flights in 'BS. Owned by Leslie G. Anderson's company, Jubilee Air Displays Ltd, 'BS, its owner, and two passengers perished while joyriding at Bodmin on 15 August, just a couple of weeks after E. J. R.'s flights from Stretford. Built for the RAF as K1251 in 1930, this 504N was delivered to the Royal Air Force College. Demobbed in January 1935, it received its first Certificate of Airworthiness in April and was sold to Anderson.

Below: The prototype Short S. 16 Scion 1 G-ACJI, seen at Hooton Park on 30 July 1935, was first flown in February 1932. It was retained by the makers until sold to Yorkshire Airways Ltd in April 1937. In March 1940, the Scion was impressed into the RAF as X9375 and flew with No. 6 Anti-Aircraft Cooperation Unit from Ringway, Manchester, before detachment to No. 1 Ferry Pool at the Air Transport Auxiliary HQ, White Waltham. In September 1941, the Scion was relegated to instructional airframe status, and as 2725M, was delivered to No. 114 ATC Squadron, Ruislip (Middlesex Wing).

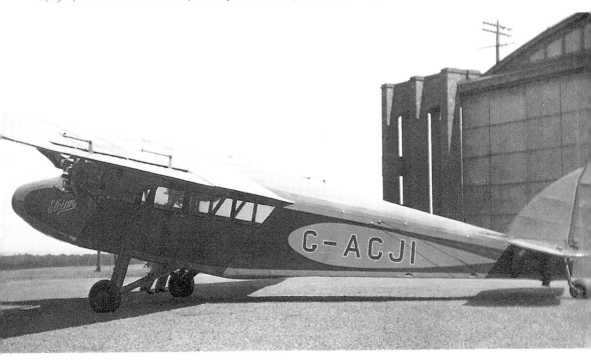

You have control. Armstrong Whitworth Atlas K2523 about to take off from RAF Sealand on 30 July 1935. One of fifty-three Atlas Trainers built at Whitley and delivered to the RAF between September 1931 and July 1932, K2523 flew with Nos 2 and 5 FTS before being relegated to instructional airframe 723M in October 1935. The Atlas was the RAF's standard army cooperation aircraft during the late 1920s and early 1930s. Powered by a 400-hp Jaguar IVC radial engine, this advanced dual control trainer differed from the standard Atlas in having an altered rear cockpit and omission of the Scarff gunring, message hook, and forward gun.

Westland IV feeder liner G-EBXK was first flown in February 1929. Powered by three 95-hp Cirrus III engines, it carried six people, including the pilot. Interestingly, the airliner was fitted with Wapiti rudders and had no brakes; instead, it relied on tailskids to reduce speed on the ground. After conversion to Wessex configuration, G-EBXK joined Cobham's National Aviation Day displays (NAD) based at Ford, touring Britain during the 1935 season. Here, it is seen when the NAD display team visited Redditch on 6 August 1935. That's not an airbrake sticking up vertically – the cockpit roof is open. The tri-motor was withdrawn from use in 1936.

D.H.80A Puss Moth G-AAXY, known locally as *Jacksie*, at Hooton Park on 8 August 1935. Originally delivered new to Shell Mex & BP Ltd in July 1930, the Puss Moth's last pre-war owner was Thomas Gracey, who kept the aircraft at Brooklands. Impressed into RAF service as DJ711 in February 1941, for a while the Puss was used as a taxi aircraft by the Air Transport Auxiliary from its White Waltham headquarters, but was reduced to spares at Witney, Oxfordshire, in August the following year.

D.H.83 Fox Moth G-ACEX was built in 1933 and delivered to Cobham's National Aviation Day displays at Ford until sold to Provincial Airways Ltd, Croydon, in whose colours it is seen during a visit to Crownhill, Plymouth, on 7 August 1935. In April 1936, it flew with Pines Airways, Porthcawl, until impressment caught up with it in December 1939. As X2866, it was badly damaged while landing at Wroughton and never flew again.

Seen at Crownhill, Plymouth, on 7 August 1935 is smart D.H.89A Dragon Rapide G-ADFY, doped in an attractive light green and brown colour scheme. First registered to W. H. R. Moorhouse in June 1935 and based at Heston, the Rapide was sold abroad in August 1936.

Hawker Osprey III K3634 on the slipway at Mount Batten on 9 August 1935. Delivered to No. 2 ASU in May 1934, and in common with most Osprey floatplanes, it was supplied to a catapult flight and had a built-in dinghy located in the starboard upper wing. During 1935, K3634 was delivered to 444 Flight, but had become instructional airframe 1000M by October 1937.

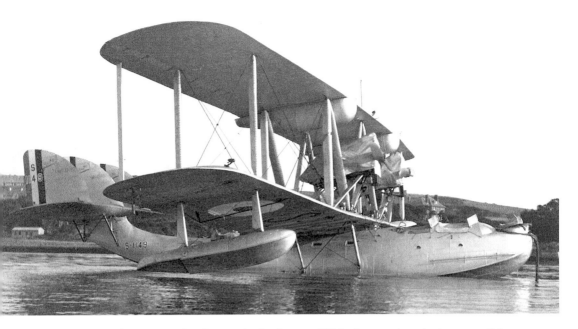

During 1927-28, the RAF, using four Supermarine Southampton II flying boats, undertook a long-range flight to open up Empire routes to the Far East and Australia. The quartet covered 27,000 miles, including flying round Australia, at a fairly leisurely pace of 80 mph. One of the aircraft was S1149, seen at Mount Batten on 9 August 1935. The Southampton II was powered by two 500-hp Napier Lion VA engines and carried a crew of four.

It is not generally remembered that the Junkers Ju 52 was powered originally by a single engine. Primarily a cargo aircraft, it made its first flight in 1930, and five examples were built. In 1932, a three-engine version was flown and designated Ju 52/3m. The multi-purpose aircraft was designed to carry fifteen to seventeen passengers and could also be flown as a bomber, freighter, troop carrier, or glider tug; all were roles in which it excelled. Standard Ju 52/3ms were powered by three 525/600-hp BMW Hornet engines. The largest civil operator of the type was Deutsche Lufthansa, with more than 230 in operation during the 1930s. Seen at Croydon on 16 August 1935, is DLH Junkers Ju 52/3mge D-AXOS *Oswald Boelcke*. So far as is known, this aircraft ended up with the Luftwaffe.

The Airspeed A.S. 6 Envoy was a twin-engine development of the single-engine A. S. 5 Courier, and was designed by Hessell Tiltman and N. S. Norway (the novelist Nevil Shute) in 1933, flying early in 1934. The six-eight-seat feeder liner had a retractable undercarriage and was powered by a pair of Wolsley A.R. 9 radial engines. A.S. 6A Envoy G-ADBA was registered in April 1935 to Cobham Air Routes, but operated by Olley Air Services, in whose livery it is pictured at Croydon on 8 August 1935. Following a period with North Eastern Airways, 'BA entered RAF service as P5778. It was used first by the Electrical Wireless School, then by No. 9 FTS, and finally ended up with No. 2 Electrical Wireless School before being relegated to instructional use.

The Czechoslovakian-designed Praga E.114 first flew in 1934. It was an all-wood, very light (584 lb empty), side-by-side two-seater powered by a 36-hp Praga B engine. OK-PGB, the second prototype, visited England on a sales tour and is seen at Croydon on 16 August 1935. The Praga had attracted the interest of F. Hills and Sons Ltd, and between 1936-38, the woodworking company produced a batch of thirty-five Hillson Pragas powered by the Praga B engine, built under licence by Jowett Cars Ltd. Ten Hillson Pragas were operated by the Northern Aviation School and Club Ltd based at Barton, Manchester. Both E. J. R. and J. G. E. undertook flying lessons in these aircraft under the Civil Air Guard system (see Chapter Eight). The method of entry into the Praga was novel, as seen in this photograph; a section of the wing's leading edge behind the cockpit, incorporating the cabin top, lifted backwards.

Eleven Fokker F. XIIs were built, and prototype PH-AFL flew in 1931. Powered by three 425-hp Pratt & Whitney Wasp C radial engines, the F. XII carried sixteen passengers and two crew. At Croydon on 16 August 1935 is PH-AFV, delivered to KLM in 1931 and named *Valk* (Falcon). In March 1936, this F. XII was acquired by Crilly Airways, later absorbed by Croydon-based British Airways Ltd, and registered G-ADZH. In August 1936, along with several other British registered Fokker F. XIIs, it was sold to Spain.

Produced in large numbers by SABCA during 1928-32, the Fokker F.VIIb-3ms was powered by at least a dozen varieties of engine in the 200-300-hp range, which obviously helped sales. Seen at Croydon on 8 August 1935, is the arrival of OO-AIJ, registered to Sabena in January 1931. The long exposure necessary to capture the shot has virtually doubled the number of people on the tarmac. The Certificate of Registration for the aircraft was cancelled in August 1938.

Cierva C.30 G-ACVX was built by A. V. Roe and Company Ltd at Newton Heath, Manchester, in 1934 and registered to the Hon. Mrs Victor Bruce before passing to the Redhill Flying Cub in September 1936. In October 1937, it was sold to Holland and became PH-ASA, but was damaged beyond repair at Oostwold in May 1938. It is seen at Croydon on 16 August 1935 while registered to its first owner.

A line-up of aircraft at Yeadon, Leeds, on 25 August 1935 featuring D.H.80A Puss Moth G-ABKG, nearest the camera. First registered in May 1931, this widely travelled Puss Moth had a number of owners, including Jim Mollison, who kept it at Stag Lane. At the declaration of war, 'KG was owned by Airwork Ltd, and on impressment by the RAF as W6416 in January 1940, was sent to No. 6 School of Technical Training, soon becoming instructional airframe 2068M.

Avro 631 Cadet G-ABYC at Woodford on 18 September 1935. Built in 1932, it was registered to Yardley and Company Ltd in July and then acquired by the Lancashire Aero Club at Barton, Manchester, in November 1934. The Cadet was scrapped at Barton in 1951.

The purposeful Avro 636 A14 for the Irish Army Air Corps (IAAC), pictured at Woodford on 18 September 1935. This handsome two-seat fighter looked more like a product from the other side of the Atlantic, whereas it was the ultimate development of Roy Chadwick's Avro 621. Four were built, all for the IAAC. Powered by a 460-hp Armstrong Siddeley Jaguar VIC engine, the Avro 636 had a top speed of 175 mph. The IAAC aircraft were delivered to Baldonnel in August 1935 and remained in service for several years.

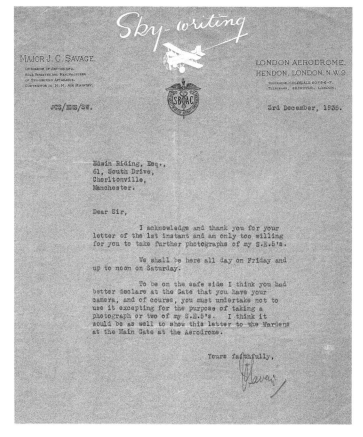

Above: The pilot of Avro 640 Cadet G-ACFT has just swung the prop and is running to board the aircraft at Woodford on 19 September 1935. Built there in 1933, this three-seater was sold first to the Scottish Motor Traction Company Ltd at Renfrew and spent time joyriding with two of its brethren. In July 1935, 'FT passed to Aircraft Facilities Ltd. On 7 August 1940, the Cadet was a victim of a hangar fire at Hooton Park that destroyed several other aircraft.

Left: In November 1935, E. J. R. wrote to the Savage Skywriting at Hendon asking permission to photograph the company's skywriting S.E.5as. Major Savage replied personally on 3 December giving the OK for E. J. R. and J. G. E. to do so on the condition that they were for personal use only. The striking notepaper is reproduced here – note the address is London Aerodrome, Hendon.

Around fifty First World War S.E.5a fighters appeared on the British civil register during 1920-28. The greater proportion were converted for aerial skywriting and owned by Major Jack Savage's company, Savage Skywriting Co. Ltd at Hendon. After initial experiments with S.E.5a G-EATE, with which black smoke issued from an extended exhaust pipe beneath the fuselage, the main S.E.5a fleet was modified to take two fuselage-length exhaust pipes, joined at a Y-junction at the tail, to emit white smoke. Business was brisk, and at least thirty modified S.E.5as were registered to Savage during the boom years of skywriting. This all came to an end in 1929 and the fleet was dispersed, many of the aircraft being scrapped. One survivor was G-EBIC, photographed at Hendon on 6 December 1936, devoid of its long exhaust pipes and being worked upon. The aircraft was stored for many years at Brooklands by Richard Nash before passing to RAF Colerne, where it was restored and given the spurious serial B4563, later changed to F938. Following five years in storage at RAF Henlow, the S.E.5a returned to Hendon, where it became one of the first exhibits of the new RAF Museum in 1972.

CHAPTER SEVEN

Around London (1936)

We were once threatened with being marched off Castle Bromwich by the CO (Squabbling Bleeder Bains) for attempting to photograph a service Avro 504N. (sufferin' cats!)

Letter from E. J. Riding to A. J. Jackson in 1943

Since August 1935, E. J. R. had been apprenticed to A. V. Roe & Company Ltd at Newton Heath, Manchester. By January 1936, he was working at the company's Failsworth factory, inspecting Hawker Audaxes (Hundreds of Army cooperation Audaxes were sub-contracted to A. V. Roe, and Avro 621 mainplanes, tailplanes, and rudders etc. He was also engaged on the inspection of subsidiary Audax aerofoils prior to covering, Audax ribs, and Avro 621 mainplanes returned from service for modification.)

British Airways began operating on a temporary basis from Heston Airport on 1 January, before moving its operational base to Gatwick on 17 May. On 20 January, the country and commonwealth mourned HM King George V's death at Sandringham, after a reign of twenty-five years.

E. J. R. had a 5-minute flight in Avro 504K G-EASF from Hooton Park with pilot W. Hobbs on 2 February. The 504 belonged to the North British Aviation Company and had been converted to dual control.

During 6 to 9 February, Flt Lt Tommy Rose flew from Lympne to Cape Town (7,300 miles) in 3 days, 17 hours, and 37 minutes, in Miles M.3B Falcon Six G-ADLC, the aircraft in which he won the previous year's King's Cup air race, beating Amy Mollison's 1932 record by 13 hours and 17 minutes. The return journey was made during 3 to 9 March in 6 days and 7 hours.

6 March 1936 will forever remain an important and momentous day in British aviation history. It was the day when, with Capt. J. 'Mutt' Summers at the controls, the prototype Supermarine F.37/34 K5054 made its first flight from Eastleigh's grass aerodrome. The sleek fighter was not to receive the name Spitfire until May; and perish the thought, one of the names considered for this most aggressive of fighters was Shrew! Shortly after, on 10 March, Fairey chief test pilot Chris Staniland took the less impressive Battle prototype K4303 on its first airing, some months *after* the type was put into quantity production.

During 4 to 12 May, Amy Mollison flew from Gravesend to Cape Town, approximately 6,700 miles, in Percival Gull Six G-ADZO, in 3 days, 6 hours, and 26 minutes, beating Tommy Rose's February flight by 11 hours and 19 minutes. On the return, she bettered his flight from Cape Town to Croydon by 1 day, 14 hours, and 40 minutes.

The unmarked prototype Miles M.11 Whitney Straight (Special) G-AECT was first flown on 3 May from Woodley. Wealthy American Whitney Willard Straight had 'sold' his idea of an efficient, general-purpose, light aeroplane to designer Fred Miles, hence the aircraft's name.

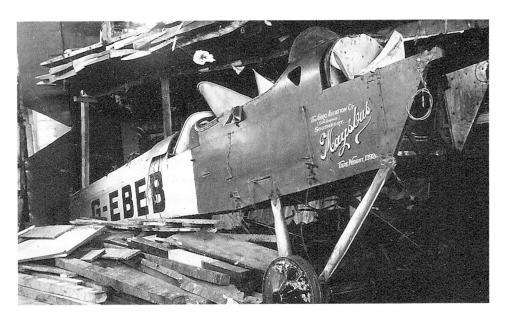

The red and silver fuselage of Airco D.H.6 G-EBEB, minus its 80-hp Renault engine, shoved in a corner of a hangar at Hesketh Park, Southport, on 26 January 1936. Named *Maybus*, this 'new' D.H.6 was assembled at Hesketh Park in 1925. In company with G-EBWG *Silver Wings,* also doped silver and red, it flew with the Giro Aviation Company Ltd from Southport sands. After giving many thousands of trippers their first taste of flying, the aircraft were withdrawn in 1930 and 1931 respectively. Both languished in a dismantled state at Hesketh Park well into the 1930s. More than fifty D.H.6 trainers of the 2,000 built for the RFC took up British registry; indeed, the very first aeroplane to receive civil registration letters in the UK, as distinct from the K numbering system, was D.H.6. G-EAAA.

D.H.60G Moth G-AAYY, doped silver and red, outside the main hangar at Stanley Park on 1 January 1936. Note the blind flying hood behind the rear cockpit and Spartan Cruiser II G-ACZM at the hangar entrance. The first C of A for 'YY was issued in June 1930 and registered to J. W. Chalmers of Hampstead Square, London, until 1936. In June that year, the Moth was acquired by British Airways before being sold in December to Ceylon as VP-CAC. Following a period with the Aero Club of Ceylon, the Moth was impressed there as MA939 in July 1942.

Westland Wallace K5072 of No. 503 Squadron at a snowbound Castle Bromwich on 23 February 1936. Built originally as Westland Wapiti K2319, it was converted to a Wallace in 1935, and transferred to the Air Training Corps at RAF Aldergrove later that year before being damaged beyond repair following a crash landing there in September 1937.

Aircraft with folding wings were all the rage before the war. Two such are seen at Castle Bromwich on 23 February 1936. Nearest the camera is D.H.60X Cirrus Moth G-EBTH, an early production model first registered in September 1927 to David Kittel and named *Silvry 3*. In 1940, the Moth was presented to an ATC squadron at Sheldon, Birmingham, which burnt it in 1951. Behind the Moth, also with wings folded, is GAL ST.4 Monospar 2 G-ACHU, withdrawn from use in May 1939.

During May, E. J. R. journeyed south, and on 19 May, had a 5s, 15-minute flight from Croydon in Surrey Flying Services' D.H.80 Puss Moth G-ABLB, flown by J. Woodman. A few days later, on 23 May, he enjoyed three short flights in three different types: an Empire Air Day 4s circuit round Hooton Park in light and dark blue Avro 548 G-EBIU with G. W. Haigh; another 4s circuit in Avro 504K G-ABAA with L. A. Lewis; and finally, a 20-minute trip with J. S. Taylor in Avro Avian G-AAYV from Hooton Park to Woodford.

Gatwick Airport was opened officially on 6 June. The month was to prove auspicious for the first flights of other aircraft that were to play an important part, in the early years especially, of the Second World War. On 15 June – coincidentally – prototypes of the Vickers Wellington K4049 and Westland Lysander K6127 got airborne for the first time. The Lysander's maiden flight was from Boscombe Down, with test pilot Harald Penrose flying it back to its birthplace Yeovil. On 21 June, at Radlett, the Handley Page Hampden K4240 prototype also flew for the first time, followed soon after by the Bristol Blenheim I prototype K7033 on 25 June.

The official opening of Weston-Super-Mare Aerodrome took place on 25 June, and two days later, the seventeenth annual RAF Display was staged at Hendon. The New Types Park included Spitfire, Hurricane, and Battle prototypes for the first time. A new and popular feature was a flying exhibition of 'old crocks', although many of the ancients could only taxi. Two days later, the SBAC's sixth annual display and exhibition was held at a new venue, Hatfield. There was an opportunity to examine a predominance of civil aeroplanes, and the show was declared, 'Bigger and better than ever...'

At Rochester, the Short Empire boat prototype G-ADHL *Canopus* made its first flight on 4 July, followed soon after, on 10 to 11 July, by the fifteenth King's Cup air race at Hatfield. It took the form of an elimination contest over a course of 1,224 miles, and a final course of 300 miles. The race was won by Charles Gardner in Percival Vega Gull G-AEKE, at an average speed of 164.5 mph.

Before the Second World War, four examples of the Beech 17 were imported into the UK from the USA. The first was G-ADDH, seen here in the snow at Castle Bromwich on 23 February 1936. Powered by a 225-hp Jacobs engine, the four-seater cruised at 200 mph and was a truly remarkable performer for its day. Registered in the UK in June 1935 to Amy Mollison, and kept at Croydon, 'DH was damaged beyond repair in October 1936 when Amy forgot to lower the undercarriage on landing near Orpington, Kent. The aircraft was damaged beyond repair and its remains were sold as spares to France.

The design of the Spartan Cruiser Tri-motor originated with Edgar Percival's Saro-Percival Mailplane G-ABLI, built in 1931. After Percival sold his interest to Saunders-Roe Ltd, which eventually tied up with Spartan, the concept was developed further under the Spartan name into the Spartan Cruiser I, powered by three 120-hp de Havilland engines and carrying six passengers and two crew within a metal fuselage. Next came the Spartan Cruiser II, of which twelve were built, and finally the Cruiser III, powered by 130-hp de Havilland Gipsy Major engines, of which three were constructed. The last of them was G-ADEM, seen at Stanley Park on 8 March 1936. Sold originally to Spartan Air Lines, 'EM passed to British Airways the month this photograph was taken, and in August 1936, ended up with Northern and Scottish Airways Ltd. Its career came to an untimely end on 20 November 1936 when it crashed spectacularly while taking off in fog at Blackpool; the aircraft hit a hangar and caught fire. The pilot and the only passenger lost their lives and four aircraft in the hangar were destroyed.

On 28 September, Sqn Ldr F. R. D. Swain, flying the Bristol 138, literally rose to new heights when he set the world altitude record at 49,967 feet.

During 5 to 15 October, Jean Batten set off on her travels again, and flew the 14,000 miles from Lympne to Auckland, New Zealand, in Percival Gull G-ADPR, in 11 days, 1 hour, and 25 minutes, entering the record book as the first woman to fly solo from Australia to New Zealand.

During 29 September to 1 October, the most gruelling of races was staged. The Schlessinger Race, starting at Portsmouth and ending at Johannesburg, was won by C. W. A. Scott and Giles Guthrie, flying Percival Vega Gull G-AEKE, the only aircraft from nine starters not to crash; it covered the 6,150 miles in just less than 53 hours, at an average speed of 156 mph.

The year ended in controversy with the abdication of King Edward VIII on 10 December. Brave King George VI succeeded as monarch; his brother chose to forsake the British throne in order to marry American divorcee Mrs Wallis Simpson.

By the end the end of 1936, there were around seventy-five light aeroplane clubs in the UK, of which forty-eight participated in the Air Ministry scheme for providing financial assistance to approved clubs. Total membership was 11,087, and at the end of December, 3,287 members held pilots' 'A' licences. The previous year's figures were 9,112 and 2,489 respectively.

When the de Havilland Aircraft Company began thinking about a successor to the D.H.60 Gipsy Moth, it came up with a two-seat cabin biplane with a family resemblance to the D.H.85 Leopard Moth. The D.H.87A Hornet Moth featured side-by-side seating, and the prototype G-ACTA was first flown in May 1934 from newly-opened Hatfield. Production began immediately, and early Hornet Moths featured pointed wings, which soon proved a problem, particularly for inexperienced pilots. In order to reduce the stalling speed, square-tipped mainplanes were introduced. The revised model was designated D.H.87B. In addition, some Hornet Moths built with pointed wings were retro-fitted with square-tipped mainplanes. Seen at Castle Bromwich on 8 March 1936 is G-ADKD, registered in October 1935 and impressed into the RAF in February 1940 as X9321. It flew with No. 6 Coastal Patrol Flight, ending its wartime use as a hack aircraft for Rolls-Royce. 'KD was restored to the register after the war, but withdrawn from use in October 1947.

The number of Royal Aero Club aviators' certificates issued during 1936 was 1,144, compared to 955 in 1935, while 'A', 'B', and 'C' gliding certificates totalled 280.

At the end of 1936, a total of sixty accidents involving British registered aircraft were recorded, although many minor accidents were not included. The greater percentage of fatal accidents involved private and subsidised club flying; 50 per cent were the result of errors of judgement or faulty airmanship. As usual, stupidity on the part of pilots accounted for a number of fatalities, as the following examples illustrate: 'A series of manoeuvres, which amounted to reckless flying and complete disregard of regulations on the part of the pilot, a nosedive to earth following a stall from a height of about 200 feet. Both occupants of the aeroplane were killed.'

Another report referred to one of a spate of accidents with H.M. 14 Pou de Ciels: 'The accident involved an ultralight aeroplane of foreign design and amateur construction. Very shortly after the start of the flight, the machine was seen gradually to develop a nose-down attitude and dive at high speed into the ground. The pilot was instantly killed.'

Built at Hagerstown, Maryland, USA Fairchild 24 C.8C G-AECO, formerly NC15664, was imported brand new into the UK in spring 1936. Doped red and blue with silver trim, it is seen at Castle Bromwich on 8 March that year. The aircraft's first owner, W. MacLeod, kept 'CO at High Post, Wiltshire. In December 1940, the four-seater was impressed into the RAF as BK869, attached to No. 3 Ferry Pilots Pool and later 60 Group Conversion Flight, before ending its days with No. 1347 ATC squadron at Elmdon, Birmingham.

Designed originally for the 1924 Lympne trials, the pretty Westland Widgeon had been produced in four versions, culminating with the IIIA in 1929-30. The prototype, weighing only 815 lb fully loaded and powered by a mere 35-hp, was first flown in September 1924, but badly damaged during the qualifying trials at Lympne. It was rebuilt as the Widgeon II with almost double the engine power. The Mk III became the standard production version, having a plywood fuselage and an all-up weight of 1,400 lb. Thirty or so Widgeons were built, including red and silver G-EBRO, seen at Walsall on 8 March 1936. First owned by the makers, 'RO passed through the hands of several owners, including I. P. Tidman, who kept the aircraft at Walsall. Following a period based at Portsmouth, the Widgeon was scrapped during the Second World War.

The Vickers Viastra was an immensely strong and rugged ten-passenger workhorse first flown in October 1930. The prototype was powered by three 230-hp Armstrong Siddeley Lynx V radials, but the four subsequent Viastras dispensed with the engine in the nose and were fitted with a variety of powerplants of 490-650 hp. The Viastra X G-ACCC was the final aircraft and fitted out as a seven-seat VIP transport for the Prince of Wales (later King Edward VIII and latterly Duke of Windsor). First flown in April 1933, 'CC was used rarely by the Prince, although thousands saw him arrive in it at the 1934 RAF Display at Hendon in June. By the time this photograph was taken at Croydon on 14 April 1936, 'CC had forsaken its Brigade of Guards red and blue colour scheme for one of overall silver, having been acquired by the Air Ministry in May 1935 as a radio test aircraft for Imperial Airways, based at Croydon, where it was scrapped in 1937.

Westland Wessex G-ACHI at Croydon on 17 April 1936. Note how the cockpit roof hinged forward to allow access. Built in 1933 and delivered to Imperial Airways, the tri-motor later became part of the Air Pilots Training fleet at Hamble until withdrawn from use there in May 1940. 'HI was powered by three 140-hp Armstrong Siddeley Genet Major 1A engines, giving the 57-foot, 6-inch-span aircraft a cruising speed of 100 mph.

In 1936, the British Aircraft Company (1935) Ltd was renamed Kronfeld Ltd, and the Kronfeld Super Drone was introduced. The new model featured a 23-hp Douglas Sprite, which on paper, gave the Drone a top speed of 70 mph. Seen at its Hanworth birthplace on 18 April 1936, with port wing folded, Super Drone G-AEAN is being prepared for flight while an ugly little boy stares at E. J. R. This Drone, in company with G-AEEO (see page 109), toured Britain with C. W. A. Scott's Air Display during the 1936 season until destroyed in a crash at Southend in July.

The metal-fuselage Blackburn B-2 was first built in 1932, and was a well thought out training aeroplane. Rugged in construction to withstand mishandling by trainee pilots, it incorporated sensible side-by-side seating and was characterised by having no wing stagger, giving it a somewhat upright appearance. Around forty were registered in Britain, many operating with Flying Training Ltd at Hanworth, one of which was G-ADLG, seen there on 18 April 1936. In October 1939, 'LG moved north to No. 4 EFTS at Brough, only to return south in February, ending up with the ATC at Welling, Kent, and acquiring the serial 2888M.

The pretty little Robinson Redwing was a practical side-by-side training type that handled well in the air, and which also had folding wings. First flown in October 1930, the prototype was powered by a 75-hp ABC Hornet. The Redwing II, of which ten were built, featured the 80-hp Armstrong Siddeley Genet IIA radial. G-ABMF was first registered to comedian Will Hay (who once owned S.E.5a G-EBTO), and then passed to the Wiltshire School of flying at High Post in August 1934. It was still owned by the school when this photograph was taken at Hanworth on 18 April 1936, where judging by its immaculate appearance, it had just emerged after a C of A renewal. The Redwing's last known whereabouts appear to have been somewhere in the Midlands during the Second World War.

Around forty Comper CLA.7 Swifts were produced during 1929-34, first at Hooton Park and latterly at Heston. Production Swifts were initially powered by the British Salmson A.D. 9 radial engine, but the majority sported the 75-hp Pobjoy R. Swift G-AAZC, built in 1930, exchanged its original Salmson engine for the Pobjoy and passed through several private owners before it was acquired by Airwork Ltd at Heston in May 1938. The Swift is seen outside the Olley Air Services hangar at Croydon on 19 April 1936 with someone wondering where the oil is coming from. 'ZC was withdrawn from use in April 1943.

Above: On 19 April 1936, E. J. R. arrived at Croydon and paid 5 bob (25p) for a flight in Surrey Flying Services D.H.80A Puss Moth G-ABLB, *Wild Oats*. The pilot was J. Woodman and the flight lasted 15 minutes. 'LB remained with Surrey Flying Services right up to the war and was impressed into the RAF as X9400 in April 1940, eventually becoming instructional airframe 2306M.

Left: This near-vertical aerial photograph of Tattenham Corner, Surrey, was taken at 1,500 feet from D.H.80A Puss Moth G-ABLB on 19 April 1936 during E. J. R.'s 5-bob flip in the aircraft. The absence of road traffic is especially noticeable.

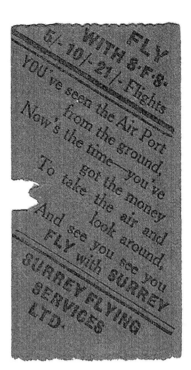

Right: Both sides of an entry ticket to Croydon Airport with a plug for Surrey Flying Services Ltd on the reverse. 'You've seen the Airport from the ground, now's the time – you've got the money to take the air and look around and see you see you see FLY with SURREY.'

Below: D.H.53 Humming Bird G-EBXN received its C of A in May 1928 when its first civilian owner was the RAE Aero Club at Farnborough. Part of a batch of six D.H.53s, J7271 was delivered to the RAF in 1924 and flown at RAF Netheravon before taking up civil registry. Seen at Squire's Gate, Blackpool, on 26 April 1936, 'XN was then owned by J. Gillett and later sold and based at Speke, Liverpool. On the outbreak of war, 'XN was stored at Hooton Park, where it was destroyed in the fire of 8 July 1940.

Spartan Cruiser II G-ACZM, in the livery of British Airways, seen outside the main hangar at Stanley Park, Blackpool, on 24 April 1936, was owned originally by Spartan Airlines, which operated several Cruisers from Croydon to the Isle of Wight. When Spartan Airlines was absorbed by British Airways in 1936, 'ZM spent a brief period at Stanley Park before being sold to Northern and Scottish Airways Ltd and finally Scottish Airways Ltd at Refrew. After being withdrawn from use in January 1940, the Cruiser was scrapped at Refrew in April 1942. Carrying six passengers and a crew of two, most Cruisers, including 'ZM, were powered by three de Havilland Gipsy Major engines, giving a cruising speed of 115 mph.

Armstrong Whitworth Argosy II G-AACJ was completed in 1929 and sold to Imperial Airways operating from Croydon. Named *City of Manchester,* the twenty-passenger airliner was purchased by United Airways Ltd and transferred to Stanley Park in 1936, from where it completed one season of pleasure flying before being sold to British Airways and withdrawn from use shortly after. The Argosy II was fitted with more powerful 420-hp Armstrong Siddeley Jaguar IVA radial engines and had a cruising speed of 80 mph. 'CJ is seen at Stanley Park on 26 April 1936 with its Jaguar IVAs covered. Note the rudder-like vertical servo flaps on the lower wing.

The one-off Vickers Type 212 Vellox G-ABKY, a heavy freighter seen at Croydon on 9 May 1936, was powered by two 580-hp Bristol Pegasus radial engines, flying first in January 1934. In May 1936, the Vellox was sold to Imperial Airways, and doped silver overall with black lettering, used briefly on night freight work. On 10 August 1936, 'KY was destroyed during a night take-off from Croydon, crashing into the garden of a house in Wallington and catching fire. All four crew perished in the blaze. The probable cause was a failure of the starboard engine, the Vellox having just been re-engined with 600-hp Bristol Pegasus IIIs.

The Short S.16 Scion 2 was introduced in 1935 and featured raised engine nacelles and revised cabin glazing. Around fifteen were built at Rochester, mostly powered by two 90-hp Pobjoy Niagara III radial engines. Seen in the Redwing hangar at Croydon on 9 May 1936 is G-ADDO, first flown in July 1935, delivered to the Earl of Amhurst and kept at Heston. Olley Air Services Ltd acquired the Scion in July 1936, although this photograph would suggest an earlier date. In August 1939, 'DO went to Great Western & Southern Air Lines Ltd at Shoreham, and in August 1940, was impressed into RAF service as AX864. Based at Elmdon, Birmingham, it was used as a company hack by Austin Motors and finally taken off RAF charge in April 1944.

Two examples of the dumpy Boulton and Paul P.71A were built and delivered to Imperial Airways at Croydon in early 1935. Whereas the earlier P.64 had been designed as a mail plane, both P.71As could be modified quickly to take seven VIP passengers in addition to freight. Seen at Croydon on 9 May 1936 is G-ACOX, named *Boadicea*. Powered by a pair of 490-hp Armstrong Siddeley Jaguar VIA radial engines, 'OX came down in the English Channel on 25 September that year while on a mail flight. Although the body of the captain was recovered, 'OX was lost and thus the cause of the accident never determined.

During the 'Flea Craze' of 1935-36, a number of aircraft companies embarked upon producing small batches of HM.14 Mignet Pou du Ciels. One of the first constructors to show interest was E. G. Perman and Co. Ltd. Located in a mews off Gray's Inn Road, London, the company built nine, the second of which was G-ADPV registered in January 1936, sold to E. W. Cavendish and kept at Heston. Powered by a 25-hp Scott Squirrel, 'PV is seen at Croydon on 9 May 1936. Although the H.M.14 was not officially banned following a number of fatal accidents due to faulty design, many projects were abandoned, and many completed aircraft pushed into corners and forgotten. By the end of 1939, 'PV had been withdrawn from use.

Although only eight were built, the Handley Page H.P. 42 was a commonplace sight at Croydon throughout the 1930s. G-AAXC *Hercules* is seen sailing over the hangars only seconds from touchdown on Croydon's grass aerodrome in May 1936. An HP.42W, 'XC entered service with Imperial Airways during the summer of 1931, soldiering on with the company until wrecked by a gale at Bristol Whitchurch on 19 March 1940.

Pictured in a hangar at Barton on 23 May 1936, a few days before it was registered, is Mignet H.M.14 G-AEII. Powered by a 35-hp ABC Scorpion, this 'Flea' was doped blue and built by Henry D. Killick at Bowdon, Cheshire. The owner had plans to fly the 'Flea' across the Irish Sea, but after a number of incidents at Barton, probably as a result of the unreliable engine, the registration was cancelled and the aircraft given away.

D.H.60X Moth G-AAMP outside the Brian Lewis hangar, Hooton Park, on 26 May 1936. Built in 1930, this Moth was first delivered to National Flying Services Ltd at Hanworth and doped in the club's distinctive black and orange colour scheme. The Moth's last pre-war owner was William Moss, who kept the aircraft at Chorley, Lancashire, and stored it there during the early part of the war. 'MP was later donated to an Air Training Corps Squadron squadron at Brough.

An interesting resident at Barton during 1936 was Avro 641 Commodore VT-AFN. Powered by a 215-hp Armstrong Siddeley Lynx IVC radial, the 641 five-seat tourer was a direct descendant of the open cockpit Avro Tutor. Only six were built, the sole British-registered example being G-ACNT, constructed in 1934 and broken up at Woodford in 1939. VT-AFN, doped blue and silver, was the last built, and although sold to the Maharajah of Vizianagram in October 1934, it soon returned to the UK because its structure was deemed unsuitable for Indian conditions.

Avro 621 Tutors K3387 and K3435 at Hooton Park on 26 May 1936. These two trainers were part of a batch of 288 delivered to the RAF between March 1933 and December 1935. K3387's ten-year RAF career included spells with No. 6 FTS and No. 610 Squadron, in whose markings it is seen. In 1941, the Tutor was part of the ATA Training Unit, and after many other postings, was finally struck off RAF charge in March 1944. The aircraft behind K3387, also in 610 Squadron markings, had a similar career, but ended up with the Signals Flight at Old Sarum, Wiltshire, and was taken off charge in June 1944.

Pictured in a field at Timperley, Cheshire, on 27 June 1936 is C. W. A. Scott's Flying Displays' Avro-built Cierva C.30A G-ACUT. First registered to Airwork Ltd in September 1934, the Autogiro flew the 1936 season with Scott, and was sold the following March. The registration was cancelled in December 1937.

Cierva C.30 Autogiro G-ACUT in flight at Timperley on 27 June 1936.

Avro 504N G-ACRE spent the 1936 season with C. W. A. Scott's Flying Displays and is seen at Timperley on 27 June 1936. Formerly E9408 with the RAF, 'RE was registered in May 1934 and owned by Capt. Percival Phillips, who had formed the Cornwall Aviation Company in 1924. Phillips joined forces with Scott for the 1936 season, and was later to meet his death in 'RE in spectacular style. On 13 February 1938, he was flying cross country in very close formation – just feet from – Winifred Crossley, who happened to be driving a car! His passage necessitated much hedge and tree-hopping, and arriving near Gamlingay, Cambridgeshire, he misjudged one particular line of trees and crashed. He was pulled clear of the burning aircraft, but nonetheless died of his injuries.

Airspeed Ferry G-ACFB was built in 1933 for Midland & Scottish Air Ferries Ltd, and during 1936, was acquired by C. W. A. Scott's Flying Displays. Sporting an all-red colour scheme, the ten-seat Ferry flew pleasure trips during the 1936 season. At the end of that year, the Ferry passed to Air Publicity and was later impressed into the RAF in February 1941 as DJ715.

The pretty Miles M.2 Hawk was the brainchild of talented designer Fred G. Miles, and first appeared in 1933, heralding a whole family of Hawk types. Because Miles had managed to acquire a haul of cheap Cirrus engines from Canada, the M.2 was offered at an attractively low price. It was considered to be viceless, and had the added attraction of folding wings. Seen at Woodley, Reading, in June 1936, G-ACOP was registered in mid-1934 and bore the initials of its builder Charles Owen Powis. Note the Philips & Powis logo on the rudder. The Hawk spent its short life with P & P School of Flying at Woodley, but crashed there on 4 August 1936 after the front control column became detached during a loop.

Avro 548A G-EBIU was first registered in May 1924 to North Sea Aerial and General Transport Company Ltd and became a reserve school trainer. In October 1934, 'IU was acquired by Williams & Company, Blackpool, and is seen resting between pleasure flights on the sands at Rhyl, North Wales, on 22 July 1936. Note the coat hanging from the four-bladed propeller. On 17 May 1937, the ancient biplane was damaged beyond repair when pleasure flying from Rhyl beach.

A very unusual sight at Heston during 1936 was the appearance of Romanian-registered ICAR Universal YR-CGS, belonging to Prince Constantin Soutzo, seen there on 1 August. Designed in 1934 and developed from the licence-built Messerschmitt M.23b, the Universal was a two-seat trainer powered by a 150-hp Siemens-Halske Sh 14 radial engine. The front seat has been removed, and in its place, a long-range tank installed, giving the aircraft a 6-hour endurance. YR-CGS was registered in Romania in January 1936, and is reported as having crashed on 31 December 1938.

Around 130 D.H.9s were allocated for British registry, many of them going to The Aircraft Disposal Co. Ltd at Croydon where most were converted for civil use. Many were given temporary markings for ferrying to the Belgian Air Force and elsewhere, but several dozen served useful lives as joyriders in the UK. Others were used for experimental work, and G-AACP and G-AACR were employed in this role by Alan Cobham for flight refuelling trials from Ford during 1932. 'CP was registered in February 1929, and saw service with Surrey Flying Services at Croydon before joining 'CR at Ford. A couple of years later, it passed to Brian Field and then to Aerial Sites Ltd at Hanworth, where tasks included banner towing. Note the banner rig beneath the cockpit and what appears to be a banner lying across the rear fuselage coaming. Not long after this photograph was taken at Hanworth on 1 August 1936, G-AACP was dismantled.

Looking similar in appearance to the D.H.85 Puss Moth, the French Caudron Phalene (Moth) was first flown in March 1932, and around 240 of all versions were built. F-AMKL, seen at Croydon on 2 August 1936, was one of five C.286/6 Super Phalene's and powered by a D.H. Gipsy Major engine. Registered in April 1933 and owned by Jacques de Peyerlmnof of Paris in 1936, it was sold in 1937 to Club des Martinets.

The single-seat Tipsy S.2 OO-TIP was built by Avions Fairey S.A. at Gosselies, Belgium, in 1935, and powered by a 28-hp Douglas Sprite two-cylinder engine. Flown to England in May that year, it was demonstrated extensively wherever light aviation flourished, often in the expert hands of Fairey test pilot Chris S. Staniland. Here, it is pictured at West Malling on 4 August 1936, minus the Sprite engine. The Tipsy was scrapped there in 1938.

Pictured at the pumps at West Malling on 4 August 1936 is D.H.80A Puss Moth G-ABWA, first registered in April 1932. While based at West Malling, it was owned by Flg Off J. K. Lawrence. In December 1936, it crashed at Seine Le Havre, France, and was destroyed.

Cream and brown D.H.60G Moth G-AACZ, owned by Malling Aviation Ltd, seen in front of the company's hangar on April Fool's Day 1936. First registered in December 1928, the Moth was broken up three months after this photograph was taken.

The Short S.22 Scion Senior powered by four 90-hp Pobjoy Niagara III radial engines was produced during 1935-36. Five seaplane versions were built, of which three were destined for the Irrawaddy Flotilla Co. Ltd., Rangoon. One of these, VT-AHI, is pictured at Rochester on 4 August 1936, a week before its first flight and subsequent delivery to Burma. It later flew with Palestine Airways as VQ-PAD before being impressed into RAF service in August 1940 as Z7187 and used by the Communications Fight at Lydda until February 1942. Subsequently, it went to No. 55 Repair and Salvage Unit and was taken off RAF charge in September that year.

Almost hidden from view, and with its three 540-hp Bristol Jupiter XIF engines covered, Short S. 8/8 Rangoon G-AEIM at Rochester on 4 August 1936. A military adaptation of the Short S.8 Calcutta, the Rangoon featured an enclosed cockpit and nose, and midships gun positions. First flown as the prototype Rangoon S1433 in September 1930, 'IM was later stripped of all armament and converted for use as a civil conversion trainer, receiving its first C of A in September 1936, shortly after this photograph was taken. After a couple of years based at Hamble with Air Pilots Training Ltd, the Rangoon was scrapped there in 1938.

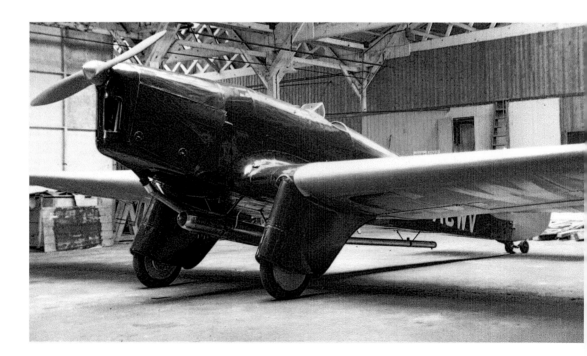

Only two genuine First World War Sopwith Triplanes survive, one of which is N5912, seen at Hendon on 7 August 1936. Built in 1919, it served with No. 2 School of Aerial Fighting, and by 1924, was part of the Imperial War Museum collection, stored at the Science Museum, South Kensington. Moved to Cardington in the early 1930s, the Triplane nearly perished after it was dumped there *c.* 1936. Luckily it was rescued, and removed to Hendon where it was restored, flying in that year's RAF Pageant bearing the number 5. After a repeat performance at the 1937 pageant, the Triplane was once again stored post-war at RAF Kemble in company with other First World War survivors. Its first reappearance was at Farnborough in July 1950; countless other static displays followed. The aircraft arrived at the RAF Museum, Hendon, in 1972, where it is currently on display, having been moved to the re-sited Grahame-White factory building adjacent to the main museum in 2003.

Opposite below: When one recalls Major Savage's Hendon-based skywriters, automatically his large S.E.5a fleet comes to mind. But during 1935, a couple of Miles M. 2F Hawk Majors were also equipped with Savage smoke- producing gear. G-ACWV and G-ADGA were kitted-out by the Savage-owned British Instrument Co. Ltd at Hendon, where the all-red 'WV was photographed on 7 August 1936. This was probably scrapped during the Second World War, while 'GA was shipped to India where it carried on skywriting, based at Juhu, Bombay, during 1938.

The L.V.G C.VI, designed in 1918 as a two-seat reconnaissance and artillery observation biplane, was powered by a 250-hp Benz Bz IVa engine. An example was acquired by the RAF after the First World War, and following tests at Martlesham Heath, passed into the care of the Imperial War Museum. Shortage of space necessitated moving the L.V.G to the Science Museum, where it remained until it was returned to the RAF and sent to Cardington in 1932. In 1936, it was 'rediscovered' and sent to Hendon to join Sopwith Triplane N5912. It is seen here on 7 August 1936, shortly after its arrival. After restoration to airworthy condition, the L.V.G made a surprise appearance at the 1937 RAF Pageant at Hendon, after which it was returned to Cardington. In 1945, it passed to No. 5 M.U at RAF Kemble, and like Triplane N5912, made an appearance at Farnborough in 1950. In 1959, the Shuttleworth Trust acquired the L.V.G on loan, but a second restoration to airworthiness did not begin until 1965. The first post-restoration flight took place at Old Warden on 28 September 1972; the L.V.G was displayed regularly in mock dogfights with the collection's Bristol Fighter until it was returned to the RAF Museum in 2003, destined for conservation at Cosford.

Opposite above: Former S.E.5a G-EBIB, first registered in 1924 to Major Jack Savage, was also at Hendon on 7 August 1936, but looking somewhat different. Gone were the long skywriting exhaust pipes and the civil scheme which had given way to First World War colours. It was in this form that the S.E.5a was flown at the following year's RAF display at Hendon and in 1939 Major Jack Savage gave the aircraft, now bearing the RAF serial number F937, to the Science Museum, South Kensington. In 1972 the fighter returned to Hendon and has been exhibited at the RAF Museum ever since.

Below: Production of the Lynx-powered Avro 504N began in March 1927, and it was supplied to the RAF in large numbers as an *ab initio* trainer until replaced largely by the Avro Tutor in the mid-1930s. Dozens of former RAF 504Ns were sold on the civil market, since they were ideal joyriders or banner-towing aircraft. G-ADBM started life as K1055 in 1929, and for a while was on the strength of the Central Flying School. It was sold in April 1934 and acquired by Air Travel Ltd in March 1935. From September that year, in company with several of its brethren, it was employed by Heston-based Air Publicity Ltd for banner towing, in which guise it is seen at Haldon (Tynmouth) having its pots inspected on 9 August 1936. In June 1940, it was back into RAF uniform, and as AX871, was used by the Special Duty Flight at Christchurch. Several Avro 504Ns were used to tow gliders from a strip at Worth Matravers, near Swanage, Dorset. The gliders were released out to sea and tests conducted to determine if approaching wooden aircraft could be detected by radar. AX871 spent only a few weeks on this work before it was lost in a crash at RAF Hawkinge on 1 August 1940.

BAC Drone G-AEJP, completed at Hanworth in August 1936, is seen there on 10 August, looking pristine in clear varnish with black lettering, shortly before delivery to the Aberdeen Flying Club at Dyce. The Drone continued flying until its C of A lapsed shortly before the war.

On 11 August, J. G. E. visited the Imperial War Museum (IWM), Lambeth, which had reopened on 7 July 1936, having moved from its previous location at the Imperial Institute, South Kensington. On display was R.E.8 F3556, built by Daimler and delivered to the RAF in October 1918. Its arrival in France coincided with the signing of the Armistice on 11 November, and it is probable that F3556 remained crated. In 1920, the R.E.8 was exhibited at Crystal Palace, and remained there until moved to the IWM's present location. The original plan was to restore the R.E.8 to flying condition, but owing to a change in policy, restoration to static only status was completed in 1980. The aircraft is presently on display at the IWM Duxford. More than 4,000 R.E.8 two-seat corps reconnaissance and artillery spotters were built, but only F3566 and an example in Brussels survive.

Opposite above: Pictured at the IWM, Lambeth, on 11 August 1936 is Sopwith Camel 2. F1 N6812, in which Sub.-Lt S. D. Culley shot down Zeppelin L.53 on 11 August 1918 after being launched from a lighter towed into wind by HMS *Redoubt*. It was the last Zeppelin of the war to be brought down. Afterwards, Culley landed on the water near the lighter, and both he and the Camel were retrieved none the worse for wear. Built by William & Beardmore, N6812 was exhibited at the IWM's first home at Crystal Palace, right from the opening in June 1920. In 1936, it moved to the new Lambeth home of the IWM building. In 1988, Skysport Engineering Ltd restored the Camel to the markings in which it was flown by Sub.-Lt Culley.

Built in 1916 by Lincolnshire firm Ruston, Proctor, & Co. Ltd., B.E.2c 2699 served with No. 50 Home Defence squadron, based at Dover, and flew anti-Zeppelin patrols. It was probably painted black, and was withdrawn from use in May 1918. Presumably, the aircraft was acquired by the IWM *c.* 1920, exhibited at Crystal Palace, and then moved to Lambeth in 1936, where this photograph was taken on 11 August 1936. This B.E.2c was beautifully restored by Skysport Engineering and is currently displayed at Duxford.

Chocks away! D.H.60X Moth G-ABUB about to depart Crownhill (Roborough), Plymouth, on 8 August 1936; the engineer is waiting for the pilot to signal 'chocks away'. This particular Moth was well-travelled, starting life as G-AUFT, later VH-UFT, and used by Jim Mollison for his record flight from Wyndham, Australia, to the beach at Pevensey Bay in 8 days, 9 hours, and 23 minutes during 25 July to 7 August 1931. In April 1932, the Moth was registered G-ABUB to Sir Alan Cobham, and when this photograph was taken, had passed to acclaimed racing car driver Dick Seaman. The Norfolk & Norwich Aero Club owned 'UB when war broke out. It was impressed into the RAF as X5029, and following a spell in storage, the much-travelled Moth ended life ignominiously as a decoy.

Short S.16 Scion 2 G-ADDX was first registered to champion racing driver Dick Seaman and kept at Ramsgate. When this photograph was taken at Crownhill (Roborough), Plymouth, on 12 August 1936, the Scion was owned by Plymouth Airport Ltd. In April 1939, it was acquired by Southern Airways Ltd, but remained based at Plymouth. In April 1940, it was impressed into the RAF as X9430 and delivered to No. 6 Anti-Aircraft Co-operation Unit, ending its wartime service with Air Service Training in August 1941 until struck off charge in April 1942.

Why the chap is busting a gut swinging the props of D.H.90 Dragonfly G-AEDH at Croydon on 12 August 1936 will never be known. The sleek, five-seat Dragonfly luxury tourer has been described as a scaled down Dragon Rapide, and certainly there were similarities. Proportionally, the wings, cabin, and engines seemed to have been pushed forward; the short nose perhaps accentuated this impression. The monococque construction was a departure from the company's usual method of a spruce-and-plywood box structure, as with the Hornet Moth. With two 130-hp de Havilland Gipsy Major engines and nice lines, the Dragonfly cruised at 125 mph and made an excellent de luxe tourer. Unfortunately, it had a tendency to ground loop unless it was 'wheeled-on' during landing. Consequently, many were lost in landing accidents. 'DH was registered in July 1936, and at the outbreak of war was with Western Airways, based at Weston-Super-Mare. It was impressed as AV987 in May 1940 and used by the Station Flight at Ringway, Manchester, until taken off charge in January 1941.

This typical everyday view from Croydon's control tower was taken on 15 August 1936. In the foreground are D.H.83 Fox Moths G-ACFF and G-ACFC. Dominating the photograph is British Airways D.H.86 G-ADEA, in front of which are D.H.60G III Moth G-ACHH and D.H.60G Moth G-ABTP. Behind the tail of 'EA are D.H.80A Puss Moth G-ABTD, another Fox Moth, and D.H.60X Moth G-ADIL. In the background, at right, in front of Rollason's hangar, is Airspeed A.S. 6A Envoy G-ADBA.

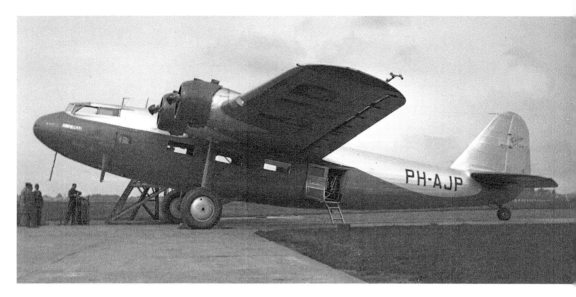

The handsome Fokker F. XXII transport first appeared in 1935. Powered by four 500-hp Pratt and Whitney Wasp radials, the F. XXII carried twenty-two passengers in four separate cabins; cargo and baggage were stored in the wings. Seen at Croydon on 12 August 1936 is PH-AJP, the prototype, named *Papegaai* (Parrot), and delivered to KLM in March 1935. After service with the Dutch national carrier, it was sold to Scottish Aviation, registered G-AFZP and used as a navigation trainer. In October 1939, it was impressed into RAF service as HM160, surviving the war. Overhauled by Scottish Aviation, it then flew with Scottish Airlines on Prestwick–Belfast services under charter to British European Airways until August 1947. In July 1952, its mortal remains were burnt at Prestwick.

German wing walker and aerial trapeze artist Oskar Dimphe, also a bit of a comedian, stands obligingly in front of his unidentified homebuilt biplane D-EJEF at Croydon on 15 August 1936.

Bellanca Pacemaker G-ABNW at Croydon on 15 August 1936. Built by the Bellanca Aircraft Corporation at New Castle, Delaware, in 1931, this six-seater came to Britain in 1932, via Italy, where it had been registered I-AAPI. Later owners included the Hon. F. E. Guest and C. S. J. Collier, the latter basing the aircraft at Doncaster. When this photograph was taken, the Bellanca was in the hands of Airwork Ltd and doped silver overall with brown trim and lettering. On 26 June 1934, E. J. R. flew as a passenger with J. G. E. in 'NW from Barton to the Woodford Pageant and back, with A. Weedon as pilot. On the onset of war, the Bellanca was impressed into service as a naval communications aircraft and took up the military serial DZ209. Powered by a 300-hp Wright R-975 Whirlwind radial engine, the 46-foot, 4-inch-span monoplane had a maximum speed of 150 mph.

On 27 June 1936, the assortment of aircraft that comprised C. W. A. Scott's Flying Displays Ltd alighted in a field at Timperley, Cheshire, to entertain the locals. Seen here is D.H.82A Tiger Moth G-ADWG in striking chequerboard scheme, in which Miss Winifred Crossley flew aerobatic displays. When Scott's outfit went bust, 'WG was sold to the Cinque Ports Flying Club based at Lympne, Kent. It ended its days as VT-AMA thousands of miles away in India, to where it was dispatched in January 1940.

The prototype Airspeed Ferry was first flown in 1934, delivered to Sir Alan Cobham, and used extensively by his National Aviation Day display, giving thousands their first experience of flying. Ferry G-ABSI passed to C. W. A. Scott's similar organisation for the 1936 season, and is seen at Reddish, Manchester, on 23 August 1936. After a period with Air Publicity Ltd at Heston, the Ferry passed to Portsmouth, Southsea, and Isle of Wight Aviation for a few months in 1939 before being impressed in to the RAF as AV968.

Seen at Barton, Manchester, on 6 September 1936 is the much-travelled prototype Miles M.3 Falcon G-ACTM. First flown as U3 in September 1934,'TM took part in the MacRobertson Mildenhall–Melbourne air race the following month, flown by Harold Brook. He arrived at Melbourne after taking nearly 27 days, but the return flight was made in a record time of 7 days, 19 hours, and 50 minutes. Brook attempted another record flight to Cape Town in July 1937, but crash-landed in the dark in Egypt. The Falcon was repaired and kept at Barton for a while in 1936, but its subsequent fate is unknown.

Brand new D.H.82A Tiger Moth G-AELD of the Liverpool & District Aero Club by the pumps and clubhouse at Hooton Park on 12 September 1936. 'LD was lost in a crash while pleasure flying from the beach at Prestatyn, North Wales, on 11 April 1937. Note the blind flying hood behind the rear cockpit.

The prototype Hawker Hurricane K5083 at Brooklands on 23 October 1936; the cowlings are removed to reveal the fuel tank in front of the cockpit and the Rolls-Royce Merlin C engine. The first flight had taken place on 6 November 1935 in the hands of Hawker test pilot P. W. S. 'George' Bulman. After various handing and performance trials, K5083 became a maintenance airframe and was assigned the serial number 1211M in January 1939.

On the day of E. J. R.'s visit to Brooklands on 23 October 1936, a fire broke out under the engine shop of the Brooklands Aero Club, causing considerable damage to the first and second hangars. Members and staff managed to save all but six of the aircraft.

POPULAR FLYING LTD.
THE NATIONAL AVIATION PAPER

Telephone :
TEMPLE BAR
3323

DIRECTORS
H. C. TINGAY
THEO. A. STEPHENS
W. E. JOHNS

34/35 SOUTHAMPTON ST.
STRAND
LONDON :: W.C.2

November 13th, 1936.

Mr. Edwin Riding,
61 South Drive,
Chorltonville,
MANCHESTER.

Dear Mr. Riding,

　　　　　　Thanks very much for sending me the exceptionally good snapshots.   I do not know if I shall be able to use them because the story is now rather cold, but I am glad to have them for reference.

Yours sincerely,

(W. E. Johns,)
Editor.

Monospar ST-25 Universal G-AEDY was built as an ST-25 Jubilee in early 1936, and is seen at Hooton Park on 27 December. For a short period during 1936, this aeroplane flew with a single, enlarged fin, and was renamed the De Luxe; the sole example. It subsequently reverted to its original, twin-fin configuration, and following a period with Aircraft Facilities at Hooton, joined the fleet of Hooton-based Utility Airways Ltd bearing the name *Alcaeus*. 'DY was lost in a crash near Hanworth on 10 January 1940 while in the care of Rollasons.

Opposite below: Three photographs of the Brooklands hangar fire were sent to W. E. Johns, Editor of *Popular Flying*, for possible publication in the December 1936 issue. This letter of thanks to E. J. R. from Johns, dated 13 November 1936, must have been a little disappointing, particularly as a paragraph about the incident appeared in the December issue, but with no pictures.

CHAPTER EIGHT

Touring with Busby (1937)

In later years, we acquired a very ancient and dilapidated Austin Seven for the magnificent sum of £4, which considerably widened our scope. In 1937, we did a tour, covering 1,300 miles in our ten days' holiday, and managed to get to more than twenty 'new' aerodromes.

Letter from E. J. Riding to A. J. Jackson in 1943

The first photographic visit of the year was to Castle Bromwich on 17 January. Earlier, on 13 January, Fairey's chief test pilot Chris Staniland had flown K5099, one of the prototype Fulmars, on its first flight at the company's Great West Aerodrome. The Air Registration Board was formed on 1 March; among its duties was the survey of aircraft in relation to the issuing of Certificates of Airworthiness.

E. J. R.'s next opportunity for photography occurred on 14 March when he travelled to Norman Giroux's place at Hesketh Park, Southport, and came across veterans D.H.6 G-EBWG, Avro 548As G-ABMB and G-ABSV, and Avro Avian IV G-EBZM. It was so dark in the hangar that exposures in excess of 3 minutes were necessary.

The prototype Miles Magister U2/G-AETJ was first flown on 20 March; the RAF's first monoplane trainer. Curiously, when Magister deliveries to the RAF ceased in January 1941, the service continued accepting the Tiger Moth biplane until the end of the war.

The world's newspapers on 7 May were filled with horrific images of the German airship *Hindenburg* enveloped in flames as it fell onto escaping passengers after exploding while landing at Lakehurst, New Jersey, the day before.

Two days later, E. J. R. had a 6-minute flight in Surrey Flying Services' D.H.84 Dragon G-ACIU from Croydon, piloted by S. F. Woods.

There was countrywide jubilation on 12 May when the coronation of HM George VI and HM Queen Elizabeth took place at Westminster Abbey, London. On 28 May, Neville Chamberlain succeeded Stanley Baldwin as Prime Minister.

Meanwhile, on 20 May, the prototype D.H.91 Albatross E.2 G-AEVV made its maiden flight at Hatfield. On 31 May, air operations at Squires Gate, Blackpool, were transferred to Stanley Park Aerodrome, and on the same day, Exeter Airport was officially opened.

The prototype Airspeed Oxford L4534 was first flown on 19 June, and 11 days later, the world altitude record was raised to 53,937 feet by Flt Lt M. J. Adam in the Bristol Type 138A high-altitude monoplane.

The eighteenth and final RAF Display, held at Hendon on 26 June, was adjudged the most successful ever, with a record attendance of 200,000 paid admissions. In addition to the New Types Park, there was a display of First World War aircraft; Bristol Fighter S.E.5a, Sopwith Triplane, and German LVG were popular attractions. A couple of days later, the seventh annual two-day SBAC show was held up the road at Hatfield, where 5,000 guests inspected products from twenty different firms. Geoffrey Tyson delighted onlookers by looping an Avro Anson.

Smart little Southern Martlet G-AAVD was built to the order of Southern Aircraft director Lionel Bellairs, and first flown in March 1930 by F. G. Miles. Powered by an 80-hp Armstrong Siddeley Genet II engine, the 25-foot-span biplane cruised at 95 mph and had a range of 200 miles. 'VD passed through several ownerships before ending up in derelict condition at RAF Turnhouse towards the end of the war. The aircraft is seen at Castle Bromwich on 17 January 1937 when owned by RAF officer Lionel Saben.

The sleek, ten-passenger, all-metal Lockheed Electra 10A was powered by two 450-hp Wasp Junior radials and had a cruising speed of 185 mph. In 1936, when British Airways Ltd was looking for a faster replacement for D.H.86A four-engine biplanes used on Scandinavian routes, it ordered four, the second of which was G-AEPP, seen at Croydon on 8 May 1937 shortly after entering service. Also carrying ten passengers, the Lockheed was 50-mph faster in the cruise than the D.H.86. 'PP's career was cut short on 13 December 1937 when it crashed at Croydon, hitting petrol pumps while landing at night in a blizzard. No-one was hurt, but the aircraft was written off.

From of a number of Lockheed 12As imported into Britain before the war, the first was G-AEMZ, pictured in front of Gatwick's 'beehive' airport building on 8 May 1937. Registered a month earlier, it was used by the Secretary of State for Air and based at RAE Farnborough from August 1938. Once impressed into RAF service as R8987 on declaration of war, it remained at Farnborough, where it was damaged in April 1942 after swinging off the runway. It was taken off RAF charge the following month. The all-metal Lockheed 12A was powered by two 450-hp Pratt and Whitney Wasp Juniors and carried a crew of two and six passengers.

A rare sight in the UK before the war was any product of the Wichita, USA-based Cessna Aircraft Corporation. It would be another twenty years or more before Cessna types would become an everyday sight at airfields in the UK. Back in 1936, the first of two Cessna C-34 Airmasters imported is seen at Croydon on 8 May 1937, G-AEAI having been acquired by Surrey Flying Services Ltd. Powered by a 145-hp Warner Super Scarab 40, the four-seater had a respectable 145 mph cruising speed, and unusually for the period, the C-34's cantilever (internally braced) wing did away with drag-inducing lift struts. 'AI remained at Croydon until the war, and in October 1941, was impressed into RAF service as HM502. In October 1942, the Airmaster was sold to Dowty Equipment Ltd, which used parts of 'AI to keep airworthy its own Airmaster G-AFBY. 'AI was restored to the register in June 1946, but damaged beyond repair after catching fire while being refuelled at Squires Gate, Blackpool, in September 1950.

The prototype Savoia Marchetti S.73 first flew in June 1934 and went into production early the following year. Of mixed metal and wooden construction, the S.73 normally carried five crew and fourteen passengers, and was powered by three 600-hp Gnome Mistral 9Kfr radial engines, giving a cruising speed of 165 mph. OO-AGP, seen at Croydon on 8 May 1937, was delivered to Sabena, and flew on the Ostend–London route until captured by the Germans at Haren in May 1940.

During the 1930s there was a steady trickle of Stinson high-wing monoplanes imported into the UK from the maker's plant at Wayne, Michigan, USA. These large, Lycoming-powered four/five-seaters were generally the property of the well-heeled and aristocracy. Seen at Croydon on 8 May 1937 is five-seat Stinson SR-9 Reliant G-AEVY, registered the same month to J. R. Bryans. It was impressed into the RAF as W7984 in February 1940, and was on the strength of No. 24 Communications Squadron at Hendon until transferred to No. 510 Squadron in October 1942. It was later assigned to the Station Flight at RAF Andover and taken off RAF charge in September 1948.

E. J. R. was back in Southport on 17 July, where he took the opportunity to take a 10-minute, 7s flight with S. N. Giroux, from Southport Sands, in all-white D.H.83 Fox Moth G-ACCB. Southport and Hesketh Park were old haunts, and in a letter to A. J. Jackson, E. J. R. recalled:

What a glorious haven of rest for aged aeroplanes Hesketh Park at Southport used to be. I knew Giroux well, and he used to let us play to our hearts content. He used to like to keep all his junk around him. About half of his hangar space was sheer, unadulterated junk. It went back in layers according to the years, and if you dug far enough, you came to aged D.H.6s of a bygone age. I don't mean G-EBEB and G-EBWG – they were comparatively to the fore. Round about the fifth row of the stalls – there were wings stacked in twenties, some still in RFC colours. G-EARD, 'RL, and others I remember. Then, in a place of sanctity (among the rudder, elevator, and bucket seat department), were the mangled remains of poor old G-EAFH. How near I came to missing her can only be realised when you know that my pictures were taken at the end of April 1935 [the aircraft was written off 31 May 1935].

Now alas, Southport is no longer the place we knew. Martin Hearn Ltd took old Giro's over and I believe all the relics were destroyed. What madness – this mass execution makes one wild. The Hooton and Maylands fires were perfect examples of needless vandalism.

I remember the time when Giroux decided to change over to Avros (c. 1931). Having a stock of Renault engines to hand, he plumped for 548s instead of 504Ks and acquired that already ancient relic G-EAFH, which we used to go and watch being reconditioned by Berkshire Aviation Tours at Barton. We were thrilled to bits one morning when a dirty big crate came up in a lorry containing a four-bladed prop, the first we'd ever seen. Not long afterwards, the firm built two more 548s from 504K bits and went to Southport from Barton as G-ABMB and G-ABSV. I don't think they ever did another cross-country flight again! The last time I saw 'MB flying was in August 1934, and after that she was always there in the hangar fully rigged right up to the time I left work down here. 'SV was dismantled and lay in the 'orchestra stalls' for a long time with her 'bag' half stripped off.

He also had G-EBXX's fuselage suspended in the cross-trusses of the hangar together with stacks and stacks of brand new Avro spares.

After Southport, the following day, E. J. R. was in Rhyl, where he had another 5s flight from the foreshore in Avro 504K G-ABAA, with Les Lewis. E. J. R. was to become intimately acquainted with this aircraft during the coming year.

On Saturday 31 July, E. J. R. and J. G. E. embarked upon a tour of Southern England in *Busby*, the former's Austin Seven, to photograph as many aeroplanes as they could find. They set off from South Drive, Chorlton-cum-Hardy, with the car loaded up with suitcases, a couple of tents, and cooking utensils. They headed south, travelling via Newcastle-under-Lyme and Banbury to their first port of call – Witney Aerodrome, near Oxford. Originally a First World War Royal Flying Corps training school with Avro 504Ks, de Havilland D.H.5s, and Bristol F.2Bs, Witney had remained inactive from 1919 until December 1932, when it was reopened by Universal Aircraft Services Ltd (UAS). In 1934, UAS formed the Witney & Oxford Flying Club. Also based at Witney was the Witney Aeronautical College, a residential flying school offering practical training in flying, navigation, wireless and/or engineering 'for an assured career in commercial flying or engineering'. Solo flying was charged at £1 per hour; board residence was an additional £1 10s per week.

On arriving, the two lads parked on the hardstanding in front of the UAS hangar and were confronted with a pair of red and silver D.H.60 Moths, G-AAKO and G-EBZI, of the Witney & Oxford Flying Club. Out came E. J. R.'s Goertz folding 620 camera, and the first of more

Sabena's black and silver Fokker F.VIIb/3m OO-AIH at Croydon on 8 May 1937. First registered in December 1929, this SABCA-built F.VIIb was powered by three 365-hp Gnome Rhone Titan radials, giving a cruising speed of 123 mph. OO-AIH and several other Sabena F.VIIb tri-motors were seized by the Germans at Haren in May 1940; their ultimate fates are unknown.

From 1937 until the beginning of the war, Barton airfield resounded to the sound of Praga B engines as Hillson Pragas of the Northern Aviation School & Club carried out circuits and bumps, flown often by Civil Air Guard students. Old Trafford firm F. Hills and Son Ltd (hence the prefix Hillson), had acquired a licence to build the Czechoslovakian Praga E.144, and around thirty were produced. Ten went to the Barton school, including G-AEPJ, pictured by Barton's 1933 control tower on 16 May 1937. Note how the leading edge of the Praga's wing centre section is folded back to allow access to the side-by-side cockpit seating. 'PJ was first registered in February 1937 and scrapped during the war.

A line-up of No. 610 Squadron Hawker Harts at Hooton Park, seen through the wing struts of a Tiger Moth on 27 May 1937. In the foreground is K3881, built by Armstrong Whitworth in 1934 and delivered to the squadron in January 1937. The badge on the fin is a garb (a bundle or sheaf). Behind is Hart Trainer K5895, built by Vickers in early 1936 and delivered to the unit in April 1937. No. 610 (County of Chester) Squadron of the Royal Auxiliary Air Force was formed at Hooton Park in February 1936 and remained there until moving to RAF Wittering in October 1939.

B.A. Swallow II G-AEMS at Hooton Park on 27 May 1937. Powered by a 90-hp Pobjoy Cataract III radial engine, 'MS was registered in September 1936 to Merseyside Aero & Sports Ltd and later flew with the Liverpool Aeroplane Club until crashing at Bromsborough, Cheshire, in January 1938.

than 200 or so photographs taken during the tour was exposed. Inside the hangar, they came across something much more exotic – a civil-registered Bristol F.2b Fighter. The silver and black First World War veteran had been converted and registered G-ACCG to UAS in March 1933, and then sold to T. Mavrogordato. Fitted with a Rolls-Royce Falcon III of some 275 hp, the old fighter looked immaculate. By the side of 'CG stood an anonymous F.2b, minus engine and fabric covering. Tripods were set up, and after exposing film for approximately a fortnight at f8, it was time to leave Witney and head for Blackheath, London, where they had arranged to spend the night with E. J. R.'s aunt.

The next day, Sunday, they arrived at Maylands Aerodrome near Romford, Essex. Opened in 1928, Maylands came to prominence when coach entrepreneur Edward Hillman formed Hillman's Airways in 1931. By the time E. J. R. and J. G. E. visited the little field, Hillman's had moved away to nearby Stapleford Tawney, and Maylands had become home to Romford Flying Club. On arrival, one of the club's D.H.60 Moths, G-EBTG, was flying circuits and bumps, but it was the sight of a relic from the 1925 Lympne Trials that caused the greatest excitement. There was much activity centred on Parnall Pixie G-EBKM, which had arrived the previous year. Built in 1924, the then unregistered third Pixie had turned up unannounced at the 1925 Lympne Trials, causing quite a stir. Following evaluation at the Aeroplane & Armament Experimental Establishment (A&AEE) at Martlesham Heath as J7324, this Pixie was returned to the makers at Yate and registered G-EBKM. Flown sporadically until the following year, it was put into storage and remained forgotten until sold to private owner F. J. Cleare at Maylands in April 1936. The ageing ultralight was issued with a Permit to Fly in August 1937, a week after the accompanying photograph was taken, and eventually passed to Ray Bullock in 1939.

E. J. R. in his 1928 Austin Seven BU 5575, *Busby.*

E. J. R.'s Austin Seven *Busby* outside United Aircraft Services' First World War hangar at Witney Aerodrome, near Oxford, on 31 July 1937.

E. J. R. standing by the Witney and Oxford Aero Club's silver and red D.H.60X Moth G-EBZI. Built in 1928, 'ZI was withdrawn from the register on C of A expiry in April 1938.

Opposite: M. N. Mavrogordato's smart Bristol F.2b Fighter G-ACCG doped silver overall with black nose and lettering. Formerly J6790 with the RAF and converted for civil use in 1933, it was first registered to United Aircraft Services, Witney, in March 1933. The registration was cancelled in July 1939.

A few years later, E. J. R. wrote to A. J. Jackson:

Talking about G-EBKM, we bowed in reverence over its mortal little frame down at a place called Blue Anchor in Cornwall just before the war started. Her owner Ray Bullock, whom everybody for at least 25-miles around knew by sight [he apparently flew quite low], was hobbling about on crutches and with both arms in slings, supervising preliminary repairs. How far the job proceeded I don't know, but he was extraordinarily keen for one who'd all but killed himself a few months previously. I fancy he was Cornwall's only aviation supporter, and it seems a pity there aren't a few more of his stamp in the country.

The next port of call was Croydon, then London's Airport, but it was to be a brief stopover because the pair wanted to visit Gatwick and Redhill before the end of the day. It was August Bank Holiday weekend (celebrated at the beginning rather than end of the month until 1965), and the aerodrome was exceptionally busy. It was later reported that 7,000 passengers passed through the London terminal that day, nearly a third of the month's total. In one hangar, Comper Swift G-ABWH was spotted, dwarfed by a couple of dark blue Curtiss Condors. Looking rather like a biplane version of the Douglas DC-2, the Condor was a fifteen-seat airliner built by the Curtiss-Wright Corporation at St Louis, Missouri. Powered by two 700-hp Wright Cyclone radial engines, it had a retractable undercarriage and a cruising speed of 150 mph. Four new Condors were shipped to Britain during 1933 and assembled at Southampton for operation by Croydon-based Eastern Air Transport. In 1937, the Condors were sold to International Air Freight Ltd and converted to freighters. During the following year, they operated a successful twice-daily service from Croydon to Brussels and Amsterdam. Because of the worsening international situation, the company went under in September 1938, and the freighters were purchased by the Air Ministry, earmarked for use as flying classrooms. They remained in storage until they were moved to No. 30 M.U. at RAF Sealand and presumably scrapped.

An unidentified Bristol F.2b in the United Aircraft Services hangar at Witney, minus its Rolls-Royce Falcon III engine and revealing its wooden structure.

The prototype Heston Phoenix, of which only six examples were built, was first flown in August 1935. Powered by a 200-hp de Havilland Gipsy VI engine, the smooth lines and retractable undercarriage all contributed to a respectable cruising speed of 135 mph. The all-yellow, five-seat Heston Phoenix II G-AESV, owned by Standard Telephones and Cables Ltd, is pictured at Redhill in the late afternoon of 1 August 1937. It was the only Phoenix to survive the war, but its flying career ended when it crashed on top of a French Alp in April 1952. Owner 'Tiny' Pilgrim escaped unhurt and legend records that he managed to salvage the Gipsy engine, although how he achieved this remains a mystery.

Surrey Flying Services' D.H.80A Puss Moth G-ABHB, in which E. J. R. and J. G. E. had a quick circuit at Croydon on 1 August 1937. First registered in December 1930, the aircraft ended its days during impressment with the RAF as X9405. On 3 November 1940, while serving with the Air Transport Auxiliary, it hit a hedge while taking off from a field near Ashby-de-la-Zouch and was written-off.

In 1932, three Gipsy-engined Comper CLA.7 Swifts, G-ABWH, G-ABWW, and G-ACBY, were built specifically for racing. 'WW was raced in the 1932 King's Cup on behalf of the Prince of Wales and came second. In May the following year, the same Swift was prepared for the prestigious Coupe Deutsch de la Meurth Race held at Etampes, France, and although it averaged a respectable 149 mph in the hands of its designer, it was completely outpaced by French competitors. Of the Gipsy Swift trio, the most travelled was 'WH. In 1934, it was shipped to the USA to compete in the Cleveland races, for which it was registered N27K. Returning to the UK in 1935, it was kept at Croydon, where this photograph was taken on 1 August 1937. Minus its Gipsy engine, the Swift still bears its American marks; note the non-standard sliding hood. In July 1939, the Swift was shipped to Australia to become VH-ACG. Over the ensuing years, it was modified extensively and was still airworthy at the time of writing.

As it was a nice, bright, sunny day with good visibility, E. J. R. and J. G. E. each decided to take a joyride in one of Surrey Flying Services' aircraft. After parting with 5 bob, E. J. R. climbed into the back seat of D.H.80A Puss Moth G-ABHB behind pilot P. Q. Reiss for a 10-minute flight around the local area. J. G. E. had a similar flight soon after. During that Bank Holiday weekend, Surrey Flying Services carried more than 700 passengers on similar flights.

With the noise of the Puss Moth's Gipsy engine still ringing in their ears, the two were soon on their way in *Busby*, hood down, to Redhill – their next port of call. British Air Transport (BAT) purchased the Redhill Aerodrome site in May 1934 after being forced out of Croydon in 1932 when all instructional flying there was prohibited. Incidentally, the first hangar at Redhill was erected by Boulton & Paul – and centrally heated! The first aircraft to attract our travellers was Heston Phoenix G-AESV. One of six built, this unsuccessful but practical contender for the touring aircraft market featured a retractable undercarriage, as well as other advanced features. Registered a few months earlier and owned by Standard and Telephone Cables Ltd, the all-yellow 'SV was based at Hatfield, and was a special flying laboratory, stuffed with radio installations for airborne demonstrations. The sole Phoenix to survive the war, its flying career ended when it came to grief on top of a French Alp in April 1952.

Also photographed in the evening light at Redhill was the all-silver D.H.60 Moth K1884. Delivered to RAF Kenley in February 1931, this Moth arrived at Redhill in July to fly with No. 15 Elementary & Reserve Flying Training School (ERFTS), operated by BAT. After leaving Redhill, E. J. R. and J. G. E. dropped into Gatwick, but took no photographs, returning to E. J. R.'s aunt for the night.

The next day, Monday 2 August, they drove to Hanworth, where they came across Aeronca C-3 G-AELY. C-3s were built in Cincinnati, Ohio, by the Aeronautical Corporation of America Inc. Following shipment to the UK, 'LY was registered in December 1936 and delivered to Hanworth to join an ever-growing fleet of bright yellow C-3s operated by London Air Park Flying Club.

The Parnall Pixie was designed for the 1923 Lympne Trials for ultralight aeroplanes. The following year, the Air Ministry ordered two slightly modified Pixies for trials, one of which was J7324. This aircraft was registered to the makers as G-EBKM in December 1924 and took part in the following year's Lympne Races. In April 1936, the Pixie passed to F. J. Cleare and was kept at Maylands, Romford, where this photograph was taken on 1 August 1937. After being sold to Ray Bullock in January 1939, the Pixie was badly damaged when it crashed near Colan, Cornwall, in April 1939.

D.H.60M Moth K1884, pictured at Redhill on 1 August 1937, was delivered to the RAF in February 1931, and eventually found its way to Base Training Flight at Gosport. When this photograph was taken, it had just been delivered to No. 15 ERFTS. In January 1939, it became 1240M.

One of several all-yellow, American-built Aeronca C-3s operated by the London Air Park Flying Club during the late 1930s, G-AELY was photographed at its Hanworth base on 2 August 1937. Powered by the licence-built version of the twin-cylinder Aeronca E.113C engine, the dual ignition Aeronca JAP J-99, C-3s cruised at around 80 mph and sounded like a derated V1 pulse jet. 'LY was one of sixteen C-3s erected at Hanworth, first registered in July 1936 and scrapped during the Second World War. The Peterborough-based Aeronautical Corporation of Great Britain Ltd produced a licence-built version of the C-3 from 1936-38 called the Aeronca 100, fitted with the JAP J-99 engine. Sales were poor and production was discontinued after six months.

D.H.60G Moth G-AAET was completed at Stag Lane in 1929 and owned first by speedster Malcolm Campbell. It is seen at Hanworth on 2 August 1937 when owned by the London Air Park Flying Club. Its last peacetime operator was the Christchurch-based Bournemouth Flying Club. In June 1940, the Moth was impressed into RAF service as AW126, but scrapped at RAF St Athan in 1941.

These American-built aircraft were powered by a 26-hp Aeronca E.107A twin-cylinder, air-cooled engine, and were a very cheap form of flying. London Air Park offered dual instruction at £1 18s per hour, or £1 for solo flying, and claimed prospective pilots could gain an 'A' licence for approximately £15. On the other side of the field sat a group of Hawker Hart trainers, operated by No. 5 ERFTS. The lads then went on to visit Heston Aerodrome, purchased by the Government that year, but no photographs were taken.

The next day, the pair left London for Gravesend Aerodrome, near the village of Chalk, Kent. Opened officially on 12 October 1932, Gravesend was operated by Gravesend Aviation Ltd, which also ran the Gravesend School of Flying. When customs facilities were granted in December 1933, Gravesend was used regularly as a diversionary airport when nearby Croydon was fogbound. During 1934-36, the Percival Aircraft Company had a factory on the aerodrome, and Essex Aero Ltd moved in shortly after. A few weeks following E. J. R.'s visit, the Air Ministry established No. 20 ERFTS at Gravesend. Today, like so many former airfields, Gravesend is covered by a housing estate. But on that sunny Tuesday morning, at least one *rara avis* awaited our intrepid snappers; in the main hangar, they came across the one and only C.L.W. Curlew. This low-wing, all-metal monoplane had been built at Bexley Heath, Kent, the previous year. Assembled and test-flown at Gravesend in September 1936, it was immediately acquired by Essex Aero Ltd. Powered by a 90-hp Pobjoy Niagara III, the 26-foot, 6-inch-span trainer was scrapped in 1948. Other subjects for E. J. R.'s camera at Gravesend were Avro Avian IVs G-AADL and G-AAHN, and elderly Westland Widgeon G-EBRO.

Before heading for Bekesbourne, near Canterbury, there was time to call into Short Brothers' at Rochester. There, they came across the lower half of the Mayo Composite S.21 G-ADHK, named *Maia*, which had made its first flight only days before on 27 July. The first composite flight, with the S.20 G-ADHJ Mercury attached to the top of 'HK, was made on 21 January 1938;

Fairchild 24-H HB-EIL at Hanworth on 2 August 1937, owned by Werkzeugmaschinenfabrik Oerlikon and based at Dubendorf, Zurich. In the 1930s, this Fairchild was sold in Germany as D-ECAF and was still flying in the 1970s. The three-seat Deluxe Model H was introduced in 1937 and was powered by a 150-hp Ranger in-line engine, giving a cruising speed of 120 mph. The Model H was also available with Edo floats.

During the latter half of the 1930s, No. 5 ERFTS operated Hawker Hart Trainers. Seen at Hanworth on 2 August 1937 is K6529, delivered in February that year. This Hart survived a nocturnal coming together with Hawker Audax K7403 at RAF Ansty in January 1939, ending its days as a wartime instructional airframe.

the first airborne separation took place on 6 February. After photographing *Maia*, E. J. R. and J. G. E. headed for Canterbury and their first night under canvas.

On the morning of 4 August, E. J. R. and J. G. E. chucked their camping paraphernalia into the back of *Busby* and headed for Bekesbourne Aerodrome. Situated 4 miles south-east of Canterbury, near the village of Bekesbourne, this former Royal Flying Corps emergency landing ground was active from 1916 and first occupied by F.K.8s and B.E.12s of No. 50 Squadron. In June 1917, S.E.5as of No. 56 Squadron were based there temporarily to combat daytime raids on London by German Gotha bombers. The little sloping field was upgraded in 1918 with the addition of two large hangars, but in 1920, Bekesbourne was de-requisitioned, becoming the home of the Kent Flying Club until the Second World War, when the aerodrome was closed. In May 1940, Bekesbourne was again re-opened, this time as a base for No. 2 Squadron's Westland Lysanders engaged on armed reconnaissance raids on targets in France. After Dunkirk, the airfield was abandoned and obstacles placed strategically to prevent further use.

Parking *Busby* in front of the main Kent Flying Club hangar, the place was pretty quiet that Wednesday morning. Photographs were taken of D.H.60G Moth G-ABJZ, registered in 1931 and destined to crash in 1939. In the hangar was orange and black Miles M.2 Hawk G-ADGI, registered in May 1935 to the Kent Flying Club. The Hawk then passed to Airsales & Service Ltd, also based at Bekesbourne, and was impressed into the RAF as AW150 in June 1940, but taken off RAF charge in August 1941.

Busby's next stop was Lympne Aerodrome, 2.5 miles west of Hythe. Lympne originated in 1916 as an RFC Emergency Landing Ground, before becoming the home of the School of Aerial Gunnery. After the war, its role changed to that of an important civil customs airfield and a favoured departure point for international transport flights and record attempts because of its proximity to the continent. During the 1920s, it also became the venue for light aeroplane competitions, known as the Lympne Trials, and in the 1930s, for many international flying rallies. In 1936, Lympne once again housed the military, temporarily becoming an RAF bomber station; Hawker Hinds of Nos 21 and 34 Squadrons mingled with the civil population. By the outbreak of the Second World War, Lympne had full-time military status once more, re-commissioned as Daedalus II, an outstation of RNAS Lee-on-Solent.

One of the first sights to greet them on arrival at Lympne was G-EBTD, one of the more notable D.H.60 Moths, outside one of the hangars. Built as a 60X in 1927, this Moth was upgraded to a 60G in 1928. Its bog-standard Gipsy I engine was sealed, and between December 1928 and September 1929, 'TD flew on an engine reliability test, running 600 trouble-free hours and covering the equivalent of 51,000 miles.

Inside another of the hangars, the sight of the one-off Hendy Hobo G-AAIG caused sighs of delight. Designed by Basil Henderson and built at Shoreham in 1929 by the Hendy Aircraft Company, the Hobo was powered originally by a 35-hp A.B.C. Scorpion II engine. It was first flown in October 1929 by Edgar Percival, and later purchased by wealthy Lord Patrick Crichton-Stuart, who modified the aircraft for racing, replacing the Scorpion with a 90-hp Pobjoy Cataract. In this guise, the owner flew the Hobo into first place in the 1934 Hatfield–Cardiff Race at an average speed of 125 mph. On 30 August 1940, the Hobo was a victim of a German air raid on Lympne.

Other photographs taken there included shots of the Cirrus-engined B.A. Swallow G-AEYW and the Cinque Ports Flying Club's D.H.82A Tiger Moth G-ADWG, first registered in April 1936 and destined to go to India in January 1940 as VT-AMA.

Opposite above: K1195 was the trainer version of the standard army co-operation Armstrong Whitworth Atlas. It was delivered to No. 5 ERFTS at Hanworth in 1931, before being transferred to No. 2 Aircrew Selection Unit. It was struck off RAF charge in March 1935, but returned to Hanworth where it was photographed on 2 August 1937, minus its 400-hp Jaguar IVC engine.

Messrs Cole, Levell, and Welman formed the CLW Company at Bexley Heath in 1935 to embark on the Curlew, an ambitious, all-metal, two-seat trainer. Powered by a 90-hp Pobjoy Niagara III radial engine, the monoplane featured a lightweight cantilever wing, which helped keep the empty weight down to just less than 1,000 lb. First flown at Gravesend in September 1936, the Curlew was sold to Jack Cross' Essex Aero Ltd, also based at Gravesend, and is seen there on 3 August 1937. Though the Curlew survived the war in storage, it was scrapped in 1948.

This smart, Genet II-powered Avro 594 Avian IV G-AADL was first registered on 3 January 1929 and based at Maylands by Premier Aircraft Construction until November 1937. Pictured at Gravesend on 3 August that year, 'DL was withdrawn from use following C of A expiry in August 1938.

Lacking its empennage, at first glance G-AAHN resembles a D.H.60 Moth, but is actually an Avro 594 Avian IV, on overhaul at Gravesend on 3 August. This Avian's penultimate pre-war owner was locally-based Horton Kirby Flying Club. In February 1940, the Avian became instructional airframe 2079M until scrapped at Squires Gate, Blackpool, in 1945.

From Lympne, *Busby* headed to RAF Hawkinge, 2 miles north of Folkestone, where No. 2 Squadron's Hawker Audaxes were based, and where it was not possible to take photographs.

The next day, 5 August, *Busby* pushed on to Shoreham Airport, 1 mile north-west of Shoreham-by-Sea. This famous aerodrome had been established on waterlogged ground in February 1911. By 1937, it had become an established airport and featured an impressive terminal building, opened on 13 June the previous year. Used predominantly by civil aircraft up to this time, Shoreham had just become the home of No. 16 E&RFTS; the Martin School of Air Navigation gained an RAF volunteer training contract just a few days before E. J. R. arrived with his camera.

The top of the new terminal provided a good vantage point from which to photograph D.H.84 Dragon II G-ADCR, which had just disgorged passengers. This Dragon II, with individually framed windows and faired-in undercarriage struts, was registered in April 1935 to Blackpool & West Coast Air Services Ltd and based at Squire's Gate. It was later operated by Isle of Man Air Services until lost in a crash at Squires Gate on 25 June 1938.

In one of the Shoreham hangars, E. J. R. and J. G. E. came across orange and black Monocoupe 70 G-AADG. Built by Mono Aircraft Inc. of Illinois, this tandem two-seater was built in 1928, coming on to the British register in December. In 1931, it was fitted with an 80-hp Armstrong Siddeley Genet II radial engine, and was flown throughout the 1930s. Although it survived the war in storage, sadly it was broken up at Gatwick in 1947.

In the same hangar were newly-arrived Tiger Moths, Hawker Harts, and Hinds of No. 16 E&RFTS, including Tiger Moth K4256. Delivered to Kenley in January 1935, K4256 passed to No. 16 ERFTS in June 1937. Following a chequered career involving several accidents, this Tiger was finally struck off RAF charge in June 1950.

A bit of a scoop for E. J. R. and J. G. E. at Rochester on 3 August 1937 was Short S.21 G-ADHK *Maia*, better known as the lower component of the Short-Mayo S.20/S.21 Composite. Built in 1937 and first flown in July, the flying boat was used as a navigational trainer. For piggyback flights, a pylon structure was erected on top of the fuselage, onto which S.20 G-ADHJ *Mercury* lowered by a 50-ton crane. The first combined flight was made on 21 January 1938 and the first airborne separation flown successfully on 6 February. 'HK was destroyed by a Heinkel He 111 of the German 8th Staffel during a night raid on Poole Harbour on 11-12 May 1941.

Lympne on 4 August 1937 with D.H.82A Tiger Moth G-ADWG, now devoid of its chequered paint scheme, and D.H.60G Gipsy Moth G-ABOG in the background. 'WG appears elsewhere in this book and was sold to India as VT-AMA in January 1940. 'OG was impressed into the RAF as AW149 the same year.

E. J. R. and J. G. E. packing up camp at Lympne, Kent, on 4 August 1937 during the *Busby* tour of southern England. The next stops were Shoreham and Ford.

Opposite: Plugs again! J. G. E. under the bonnet of *Busby* on the Kington–Rhayader road in mid-Wales.

The next stop was Ford Aerodrome, nearly 3 miles to the west of Littlehampton, not far from Arundel. Sometimes known alternatively as Yapton, Ford was built by German prisoners of war and completed in 1918. Occupied at first by RFC and units of the American Expeditionary Force, all aerial activity at Ford ceased from January 1920 until the Ford Motor Company leased the airfield as a maintenance base in 1931. Three years later, Ford moved out and Sir Alan Cobham moved in. There, he established Flight Refuelling Ltd, experimenting with Armstrong Whitworth A.W. 23 K3585 and a couple of Handley Page Harrows. The A.W. 23 was designed as a replacement bomber/transport for the Vickers Valencia and powered by two 810-hp A.S. Tiger VIs. When the Bombay was chosen for the role, the sole A.W. 23 was loaned to Flight Refuelling in February 1937 for flight refuelling trials with Short Empire flying boats. In April 1939, it took up civil registration G-AFRX and was stored at Ford until destroyed during a German air raid on 18 August 1940.

In one of the hangars, E. J. R. and J. G. E. came across Vickers Virginia X K2668, powered by two 570-hp Napier Lions. Delivered originally to RAF Hawkinge in September 1932, this Virginia flew with Manston-based No. 500 (County of Kent) Squadron, coded K and named *Richborough Castle*. In 1936, Virginias J7771 and K2668 were sold by the Air Ministry to Sir Alan Cobham's Flight Refuelling for flight refuelling trials, and were kitted out for this work at Ford.

Outside, parked on the grass at Ford, was General Aircraft Monospar ST.4 G-ABVS. During its six-year flying life, this Monospar had a string of owners, including Flying Hire Ltd and Geoffrey Alington. For a short period during 1933, 'VS was registered EI-AAU to Western Air Transport at Oranmore, Ireland. It ended its days with a private owner at Lympne; the registration was cancelled in July 1939.

Photographs were also taken of the Yapton Aero Club's D.H.60 Moths G-EBZL and G-EBZC, on which Lettice Curtis, of wartime Air Transport Auxiliary fame, had learnt to fly; she gained her pilot's licence at Ford in July 1937. The airfield closed to flying in 1980.

The next day, Friday 6 August, E. J. R. and J. G. E. popped back to Ford before heading for Portsmouth Aerodrome via RAF Tangmere, where it was not possible to take photographs. Opened officially on 2 July 1932, close to the city centre, Portsmouth will be remembered as the home of Airspeed Ltd and the Portsmouth, Southsea, and Isle of Wight Aviation Company Ltd. After moving there from York into a brand new purpose-built factory in March 1933, Airspeed put Couriers, Envoys, and Ferries into production. At the time of E. J. R.'s visit, the first production batch of fifty Oxfords for the RAF was under way. Portsmouth Airport closed to flying in December 1973.

On Saturday 7 August, *Busby* headed for Southampton and Eastleigh Airport, often referred to as Atlantic Park Aerodrome, harking back to its pre-1930s title. Situated on the northern side of Southampton, the airport's origins extended back to 1918, when it was commissioned as an American Naval Air Station and used to assemble D.H.9As for dispatch to France for units of the US 10th Bombing Group. In 1926, Eastleigh became the home of the Hampshire Aeroplane Club, and was developed into a municipal airport in 1932, by which time Supermarine Aviation had moved in to carry out flight-testing. In March 1936, K5054, prototype of the immortal Spitfire, made its first flight from Eastleigh. At the time of E. J. R.'s visit, No. 22 Squadron's Vickers Vildebeests were in temporary residence, but more interestingly, Saro A.19 Cloud G-ABHG, Kay 33/1 Gyroplane G-ACVA, and Ford 5-AT-E Tri-motor G-ACAE were discovered and photographed in one of the hangars.

Blackpool & West Coast Air Services purchased D.H.84 Dragon 2s G-ADCP and G-ADCR in February 1935 for use on the Blackpool–Isle of Man route. Later, both aircraft passed to newly-formed (September 1937) Isle of Man Air Services. 'CR is seen on the apron shortly after arrival at Shoreham on 5 August 1937. Note the Isle of Man Air Services logo on the aircraft's rudder. On 25 June 1938, 'CR crash landed at St Just, Land's End Airport, in very poor weather. Capt. Dustin was killed, but his six passengers survived in what was the airport's first fatal accident.

In December 1928, a snub-nosed, side-by-side seat cabin monoplane was shipped to the UK from Moline, Illinois. Monocoupe 70 G-AADG's original 55-hp Velie radial engine was soon replaced with a more powerful 80-hp Armstrong Siddeley Genet II. After several owners, 'DG ended up at Maylands Aerodrome, Essex, spending the war in storage before being broken up at Gatwick. The Monocoupe is seen hangared at Shoreham on 5 August 1937.

The Vickers Virginia heavy bomber, descended from the Vimy of the immediate postwar period, first entered service with the RAF in 1924, lingering on until 1937. The bomber was of all-metal construction with fabric covering, and featured nose and tail gunner's positions; later models had their tail skids replaced with tail wheels. Nearly half of the 125 or so Virginias produced for the RAF were Mk Xs, powered by two 570-hp Napier Lion Vs, and able to carry a 3,000-lb bomb load. Vickers Virginia X K2668 'K', photographed at Ford on 5 August 1937, was delivered to the RAF in 1932 and served with No. 500 Squadron, bearing the name *Richborough Castle*. Together with Virginia 'M', it was put at the disposal of Sir Alan Cobham's Flight Refuelling Company, and flown from RAF Hawkinge to Ford, where it was modified for tanker refuelling trials. The rear end of K2668 is fitted with a refuelling hose, which was wound out to "M" in flight; a fairly hazardous business. Once Cobham had finished with K2668, it was sold in January 1938.

Above and below: A close-up of Vickers Virginia X K2668 at Ford. The bomber normally carried a crew of four, and was armed with a Lewis gun in the nose and twin Lewis guns in the tail. For Cobham's flight refuelling tests, the guns were removed and the nose and tail positions modified.

Armstrong Whitworth 23 K3585 at Ford on 5 August 1937. Designed unsuccessfully as a replacement for the Vickers Valentia transport biplane, it nonetheless served a useful life during development of the Whitley. In 1939, it passed to Flight Refuelling Ltd, was registered G-AFRX and based at Ford, from where it carried out many flight refuelling sorties with Short Empire flying boats. During 1940, night refuelling flights were flown from Boscombe Down. K3585 was destroyed during a German air raid on Ford in June that year.

Saro Cloud 'HG was built for the Hon. A. E. Guinness and completed in 1930. At the time of its first flight, by Sqn Ldr L. S. Ash in December, the Cloud was powered by three 215-hp Armstrong Siddeley Lynx IVC radial engines. However during the following year, these engines were exchanged for two 425-hp Pratt & Whitney Wasp C radials. The handling of the Cloud was further enhanced with the fitting of an auxiliary aerofoil, located above the engines, and the addition of twin fins and rudders. The Cloud was based at Eastleigh throughout the 1930s, and sold to Imperial Airways for crew training duties in January 1940. Following an accident in June 1941, the fuselage ended its days in 1952 as a caravan.

Ford 5-AT-E Tri-motor G-ACAE, also owned by Guinness, was imported from the USA in 1933, where it was initially registered as NC440H. Based in Dublin and Heston, this tri-motor was impressed into the RAF as X5000 in April 1940, though its service life was cut short after a forced landing on the shore of Belfast Lough, County Down, in September that year. Like the owner's Saro A.19 Cloud, the tri-motor was powered by Pratt & Whitney Wasp C radial engines.

The one-off Kay 33/1 Gyroplane G-ACVA was designed by David Kay, built by Oddie, Bradbury, and Cull Ltd at Eastleigh in 1934, and first flown on 18 February 1935. Powered by a 75-hp Pobjoy R radial engine, 'VA remained airworthy until 1947, and is currently on loan to the Museum of Flight, East Fortune.

The next stop was RAF Worthy Down, 3 miles north of Winchester. Opened in August 1918 as an RAF & Army Co-operation School, by the mid-1930s, Worthy Down had become home to Handley Page Heyfords of Nos 7 and 102 Squadrons. At the time of E. J. R.'s visit, a few of No. 35 Squadron's Fairey Gordons were still around, although most of the aircraft seen from the hedge were Hawker Hinds of No. 49 Squadron, shortly to be replaced by Vickers Wellesleys. Worthy Down remained active until October 1946, reopening as HMS Ariel II in 1952; it was home to the Air Electrical School until 1960.

The Saro A.19 Cloud G-ABHG was first flown in December 1930 and powered by three 215-hp Armstrong Siddeley Lynx IVC radial engines. By the time it had been delivered to the Hon. A. E. Guinness, 'HG had been re-engined with two 425-hp Pratt and Whitney Wasp C radials. In order to improve directional control, twin fins replaced the original single fin, and to lower the landing speed, an auxiliary aerofoil wing was mounted above the engines. The Cloud was named *Amo* and based at Eastleigh, Southampton, where this photograph was taken on 7 August 1937. In January 1940, 'HG was sold to Imperial Airways and used for crew training until damaged badly at Ibsley in June 1941.

Kay Gyroplanes Ltd was formed by Scotsman David Kay in 1933 to explore further his idea of producing an autogiro, which had collective pitch control combined with a rotor hub that could be tilted for lateral control. This system had earlier been rejected by Cierva on the grounds that it was too complicated, although the system was later incorporated in his autogiros. Following production of the unregistered Type 32/1 in 1932, Kay's Gyroplane Type 33/1 was built by Oddie, Bradbury, & Cull Ltd of Eastleigh and registered G-ACVA. Powered by a 75-hp Pobjoy R engine, 'VA was first flown in February 1935 and was still at Eastleigh when photographed on 7 August 1937. Note the four-bladed propeller. The Gyroplane survived the war and was withdrawn from use in 1947 following a final flight at Perth. Acquired by the Museum of Transport, Glasgow, in 1969, the Gyroplane can now be seen at the National Museum of Scotland, Edinburgh.

D.H.60G Moth G-AACY was first registered in November 1928, and following a period with Airwork Ltd, joined the Hampshire Aero Club fleet at Eastleigh where it was photographed on 7 August 1937. By 1939, the Moth was owned by a Frank Wallis and based at Broxbourne. In May 1940, 'CY was impressed into RAF service as AV991, and following a period with No. 7 Air Gunners School at RAF Stormy Down, taken off charge in May 1943 and scrapped.

The Blackburn Bluebird first appeared in 1924, and the intention was that the prototype should take part in that year's Air Ministry trials for low-powered, two-seat aircraft. Unfortunately, it was not ready in time, but entered instead in a similar competition sponsored by the aviation-minded *Daily Mail* newspaper. It caused plenty of interest, probably because of its practical and social side-by-side seating. In 1927, it became the first British side-by-side two-seater to be put into production. Several marks of Bluebird were produced, culminating with the completely redesigned Mk IV, first produced in 1928. Registered in March 1930, G-AAUG spent a while on floats, operating on the River Humber with the Reserve School at Brough. By July 1934, 'UG had moved south to High Post, Wiltshire, where it was photographed on 7 August 1937. Owned by Robert Giddings, 'UG was lost in a crash at High Post in March 1938 and its remains were sold for scrap.

On Sunday 8 August, E. J. R. and J. G. E. arrived at High Post, Wiltshire, via Old Sarum. Situated remotely, just north of Salisbury, High Post Aerodrome was opened in 1931. It became the residence of the Wiltshire Light Aeroplane & Country Club, and later the Wiltshire Flying Club. In September 1939, all civil flying ceased, and during the war, High Post was used extensively by Supermarine to test fly Spitfires (mostly Mk Vs, VIIs, and XIIs) built locally at Salisbury. The company retained a presence at High Post for a while after the war. The prototype Attacker TS409 was not only assembled there, but also made several trial flights from the grass field. By the time Supermarine had transferred operations to nearby Chilbolton, the Wiltshire School of Flying had returned, but only for a short period before moving on to Thruxton. High Post was closed to flying in June 1947.

At High Post, E. J. R. and J. G. E. took photographs of D.H.60G Moths G-AAAL, G-AABJ, and G-AABH. More interesting was the Blackburn Bluebird IV G-AAUG, owned by Robert Giddings. After a brief period with Auto Auctions Ltd at Heston, this Bluebird returned to Blackburn at Brough for use as a trainer with the Reserve School there. During June 1930, it is recorded that 'UG was flown with floats. In July 1934, the Bluebird passed to Giddings and was based at High Post, where it remained until crashing there on 20 March 1938.

Come 9 August, E. J. R. and J. G. E. were peering through hedges bordering RAF Boscombe Down. Although unable to enter the security-conscious aerodrome, they were able to snap Vickers Virginia III J7132, as obligingly it took to the air right in front of them. Delivered to No. 7 Squadron in July 1924, J7132 was rebuilt to become the prototype Mk IX in 1927, and up-rated to Mk X standard in 1929. The old bomber passed to No. 215 Squadron in April 1936, and when photographed, had just arrived at the A&AEE, where it carried on flying until 1940. What a shame that it was not preserved.

Also at High Post, Wiltshire, on 7 August was D.H.60G Moth G-AAAL. First registered to Winifred Spooner in 1928, it was acquired by Malcolm Campbell Ltd and based at Heston until joining the Wiltshire School of Flying. The last pre-war owner was the Isle of Wight Flying Club at Lea, later known as Sandown, where 'AL was lost in a take-off crash in August 1939.

Blackburn Bluebird IV G-AACC seen at High Post on 7 August 1937. First registered in June 1939, it spent most of its life in the north of England, notably with North Sea Aerial & General Transport Ltd at Brough. When Messrs Kent and Forth purchased the Bluebird in July 1937, it was based at Hooton Park, and it remained there until destroyed in the disastrous hangar fire of 8 July 1940.

Plugs! With not another vehicle in sight, E. J. R.'s Austin Seven BU5575 *Busby* receives attention on the Stockbridge Road near Worthy Down on 7 August 1937. On that day, E. J. R. and J. G. E. visited the aerodromes at Eastleigh, RAF Worthy Down, Old Sarum, and High Post.

The airport buildings at Bristol Whitchurch on 9 August 1937 with a B. A. Swallow standing in front of the Norman Edgar premises. The airport was opened formally on 31 May 1930 and managed by the Bristol & Wessex Aeroplane Club until taken over by Bristol Corporation in 1935.

The Bristol & Wessex Aeroplane Club's immaculate Avro 643 Cadet G-ADFD seen outside the main hangar at Bristol Whitchurch on 9 August 1937. The Cadet survived the war, was given to the Air Training Corps at Wimborne, Dorset, in 1951, and scrapped ten years later. Introduced in September 1934, the Cadet was powered by a 135-hp Armstrong Siddeley Genet Major radial engine and featured a raised rear seat for the instructor. Very few examples were built, but the type's successor, the 643 Cadet Mk ll with a 150-hp Armstrong Siddeley Genet Major 1A, fitted with an inverted fuel system, was built in large numbers for the Royal Australian Air Force and Hamble-based Air Service Training.

Journeying ever westwards, stops were made at RAF Netheravon and RAF Upavon, but no photographs were taken until reaching Yatesbury Aerodrome, east of Calne. First opened in 1916 as a training station, Yatesbury closed in 1919, but gained a new lease of life in 1935 when the Bristol Aeroplane Company set up an RAF Reserve Training School there. Flying began in earnest in February 1936 with Tiger Moths, some of which were snapped on that Monday. In 1938, the school became No. 10 E&RFTS, and Hawker Harts were added to the fleet. Yatesbury closed in April 1969.

Leaving Wiltshire, *Busby* and its occupants headed for Somerset, to Bristol's Whitchurch Airport, located 2 miles south of the city. Opened officially on 31 May 1930 and run by the Bristol & Wessex Aeroplane Club, it was taken over by Bristol City Council in 1935. In 1938, No. 33 E&RFTS was formed at Whitchurch, and shortly before the war, the airport was requisitioned by the Air Ministry. During the early part of the war, the first Air Transport Auxiliary pilots were trained there before a move to ATA headquarters at White Waltham. After the war, the Bristol & Wessex Aeroplane Club resumed flying from Whitchurch until its closure in 1957.

After calling in at nearby Filton and Yate, where again no photographs were taken, E. J. R. and J. G. E. toured Wales before returning to Manchester.

In ten days, they covered 1,300 miles, repaired 16 punctures, and between them, took a couple hundred photographs.

Holiday over, on 1 September, E. J. R. started work with Northern Aircraft Products, Manchester. This involved inspection of Fairey Battle bomb doors, dash boards, and flooring, as well as Armstrong Whitworth Whitley engine rings and other detailed work, after which he moved on in October to AID duties at the Blackburn Aeroplane & Motor Company at Brough.

Vickers Virginia X J7132 seen shortly after take-off from Boscombe Down on 9 August 1937. Delivered to No. 7 Squadron in 1924 as a Mk III, J7132 was upgraded to Mk VII, then Mk IX, and finally a Mk X, powered by two 570-hp Napier Lion V engines. When this photograph was taken, the Virginia was serving with No. 58 Squadron at Boscombe Down. Note the slight sweep-back of the outer mainplanes introduced with the Mk VII.

In 1936, part of the former First World War airfield at Yatesbury, Wiltshire, was developed as the base for the Bristol School of Flying, purchased and operated by the Bristol Aeroplane Company. The School's Tiger Moths began moving in from Filton during February, including G-ADNY, seen at Yatesbury with several of its brethren on 9 August 1937. The Bristol School of Flying became No. 10 E&RFTS in February 1938, and the sight of a mixture of civil-registered Tiger Moths and RAF Hawker Hart trainers on circuits and bumps became the norm. 'NY was shipped to the warmer climes of India during the early part of the war.

During September and October, E. J. R. pushed the boat out by beginning flying lessons (eight in all) with the Northern School of Aviation. Instruction was on Hillson Pragas G-AEUN, 'UM, 'UK, and 'PJ, with tutors R. F. Graesser and T. N. Winning. After completing about 3 hours of instruction, he discontinued lessons. A succession of letters from the school demanding payment probably tells all! Later, in 1939, J. G. E. also started lessons, beginning in February and continuing spasmodically until he stopped on 1 August, almost at the point of going solo.

The sixteenth annual King's Cup air race was held during 10 to 11 September. It took the form of eliminating heats on the first day, over a course starting at Hatfield and calling at airports all round the country, totalling 786 miles. The second day's course covered 656 miles. The race was won for the second successive year by Charles Gardner, flying Percival Mew Gull G-AEKL at an average speed of 234 mph.

On 19 September, E. J. R. had a 5-minute, 3s 6d flight with Lancelot 'Pop' Rimmer in North British Aviation's silver and grey-lettered Avro 504N G-AEGW from Orford, Lancashire.

It was 11 October when E. J. R. joined Blackburn Aircraft, Brough, in the AID department. His work there involved inspection of Shark and Skua components, floats, and Skua wing sub-assemblies. He left Blackburn on 14 February the following year for Martin Hearn Ltd at Hooton Park, Cheshire.

Meanwhile on 16 October, the Short S. 25 Sunderland prototype K4774 made its first flight in the hands of John Parker from Rochester.

On 30 October, E. J. R. was at Hedon Aerodrome, Hull, and had a 35-minute flight in BA Swallow G-AEVZ with Dick Caws. He was there again on 27 November for another 45 minutes in the Swallow, again with Dick Caws. His next visit was on 19 December, when

On 19 December 1937, E. J. R. flew with R. A. Caws in the Hull Aero Club's D.H.60X Moth G-AAMS from Hedon Aerodrome, Hull. The half-hour flight took in Spurn Head, and much of it was flown at 2,000 feet above fog. 'MS was first owned By National Flying Services Ltd at Hanworth and was once the property of the Master of Semphill. Immediately prior to the war, it was on the strength of the Airwork Flying Club at Heston. The Moth was impressed into RAF service in January 1940 as X5018 and scrapped in 1943.

E. J. R. in the front seat of D.H.60X Moth G-AAMS taxiing out from Hedon with Dick Caws on 19 December 1937. Note the blind flying hood folded behind the rear cockpit. E. J. R. flew again with Caws in 'MS on 2 January 1938, via Cottingham and Ferrybridge, returning to Hedon in pouring rain.

Pilot Dick Caws photographed by E. J. R. flying B.A. Swallow II G-AEVZ on 22 November 1937. Many years later, on 1 September 1985, the author was given a flight in 'VZ by Ron Souch from Hamble, and took a similar photograph during a pre-breakfast flight over the Solent.

Dick Caws took him on a 30-minute flight in D.H.60 Moth G-AAMS around Spurn Head and the local area. That month, the first Hawker Hurricane fighters entered service with No. 111 Squadron based at RAF Northolt.

At the end of 1937, there were approximately seventy-eight light aeroplane clubs in Great Britain, and of these, fifty-three were included in the Air Ministry scheme for affording financial assistance to approved clubs.

The number of Royal Aero Club aviators' certificates issued during the year totalled 981, compared with 1,144 in 1936. The decrease was judged to be due to the number of potential candidates joining RAF Volunteer Reserve Schools.

At the end of the year, a total of ninety-eight licensed and permanent aerodromes existed, an increase of two on the previous year. There were thirty-five licensed municipal aerodromes, and an additional eighteen sites had been purchased.

During 1937, 2,458 pilots' 'A' licences were issued, compared with 2,447 the previous year, bringing the total of current 'A' licences to 4,694, an increase of 337 over the previous year. This figure included 200 'A' licences held by women.

The total number of registered aircraft over the same period was 1,660, compared with 1,682 the previous year; 274 had been registered for the first time.

During the year, there were thirty-seven accidents in which serious injury or death occurred. About 60 per cent were attributed to faulty judgement or poor airmanship. In two accidents, passengers were thrown from the aircraft in mid-air: one during aerobatics; the other after the aircraft hit turbulence.

Designed as a torpedo bomber for the Fleet Air Arm, some Blackburn T.2 Dart seaplanes were civilianised and attached to the RAF Reserve civil training school at Brough, run by the North Sea Aerial & General Transport Co. Ltd, a subsidiary of the Blackburn Aeroplane and Motor Company. Fitted with floats initially, G-EBKH continued as a seaplane trainer, but eventually put on wheels to soldier on until May 1933. The unsuitably named Dart was then taken by road to Reg Fowler's garage in Hatfield, Yorkshire, where this close-up photograph was taken on 24 December 1937. Left to rot, its skeletal remains were still there nearly twenty years later.

CHAPTER NINE

Ever Increasing Roundels and Lots of Flying (1938)

Hooton was always my favourite aerodrome, and I think one-fifth of my pre-war photographs were taken there.

Letter from E. J. Riding to A. J. Jackson in 1943

The year started with the usual round of visits to local aerodromes in the North West and West Midlands: Hooton Park, Blackpool, Walsall, Castle Bromwich, RAF Sealand, Ringway, and Speke. It was also the first year that E. J. R. began building up serious flying hours in full-size aeroplanes. On New Year's Day, he visited Hedon Aerodrome, Hull, to fly once again with Dick Caws in his B.A. Swallow II G-AEVZ, making a 15-minute flight in formation with D.H. 60X Moth G-AAMS. The following day, E. J. R. had another flight with Caws in the Swallow in poor visibility, flying into cloud at 2,000 feet. Less than an hour after landing, the pair flew to Brough and back in the Moth. Nearly fifty years later, in September 1985, the author flew with Ron Souch in the same Swallow from Hamble, out over the Solent and back before breakfast.

E. J. R. was working at Brough when, on 13 January, Avro 652a K6301 messed up a landing and ended up sliding along on its belly. Fortunately, there were no human causalities, although the Anson was a write-off.

The Air Ministry announced on 20 January that the annual RAF Display at Hendon was to be discontinued because of its unsuitability to host modern aircraft, and that, 'It was not in the public interest to show the latest types of military aircraft and engines, and that the immense amount of work devolving upon the British aircraft industry at the present time makes undesirable the diversion of time and energy to organisation of a display.'

At Hamble on 24 January, the prototype Armstrong Whitworth A.W.27 Ensign G-ADSR made its first flight in the hands of Charles Turner-Hughes, before being flown to Baginton, Coventry, for further testing. At the time, the Ensign was the largest airliner to be built in Britain; only fourteen were produced.

During February, Sqn Ldr J. W. Gillan hit the headlines when he flew a Hawker Hurricane from Edinburgh to RAF Northolt in 48 minutes, averaging 409 mph for the journey. Even more spectacular, the piggy-back Short S.20 Mercury seaplane G-ADHJ and Short S.21 flying boat G-ADHK combination made their first in-flight separation over Rochester on 6 February. Two weeks later, on 21 February, the Miles M.17 Monarch prototype G-AFCR made its first flight at Woodley, Reading.

By this time, having left Blackburn in February, E. J. R. was working for Martin Hearn at Hooton Park, and this happy, eight-month interlude is the subject of the next chapter. While engaged in full time work, visits to other aerodromes were necessarily limited mostly to weekends.

Right: From October 1937 until February 1938, E. J. R. worked in the AID Department at Blackburn Aircraft Ltd Brough. Here he is, aged twenty-one, examining Blackburn Shark fittings in works inspection in Blackburn's viewing room.

Below: Oh, calamity! This was the scene at the end of the runway at Brough on 13 January 1938 after Avro Anson I K6301, inbound from RAF Leconfield, overshot on landing. Built in 1937, the Anson was delivered to No. 75 Squadron at RAF Driffield in March 1937, but transferred later to Ferry Flight, Cardington.

J. G. E. and E. J. R., looking like CID officers, pictured with the mortal remains of Avro 504K G-EASF at Hooton on 20 February 1938. Formerly D5858 with the RFC/RAF, this venerable 504K flew with Cobham and Holmes Aviation before passing to distinguished Imperial Airways pilot Capt. O. P. Jones. After a stint with Northern Air Lines at Barton, the tired biplane was owned finally by Lancelot 'Pop' Rimmer and dismantled at Hooton in 1937. Another photograph of this forward fuselage section appears on page 211.

On 8 May, the great and the good of the aeronautical world attended the Royal Aeronautical Society's garden party, held at Fairey's Great West Aerodrome. While the Spitfire and Hurricane were absent, there was great interest in the collection of 'old crocks' supplied by Richard Nash and Richard Shuttleworth, some of which can still be seen at Old Warden in the care of the Shuttleworth Collection. The Empire Air Day celebrations on 28 May were more popular than ever, when despite appalling weather, eighty-eight aerodromes were opened to the general public.

The official opening of Ringway Airport, Manchester, took place on 25 June, attended by E. J. R., who arrived in style from Hooton in Avro 640 G-ACFT, piloted by a Miss Spiller. A dozen or so photographs were exposed, and the return flight made so late in the evening that they landed in darkness. Meanwhile down south, to make up for the absence of the RAF display, the *Daily Express* sponsored a great air display at Gatwick. Attended by thousands, it was billed by the newspaper as the 'display of the century', although *The Aeroplane* took issue with this claim, suggesting that it was only 'reasonably good'. The display included a Hendon-like set piece – an oil refinery 'bombed' by Fairey Battles. On the same day, Wolverhampton's municipal airport was opened officially by Flg Off Arthur Clouston, although it had been in use by Boulton and Paul for about a year.

First registered in July 1930, Avro 616 Avian IVM G-ABCD had passed through several private ownerships by the time it was acquired by N. S. Jones in August 1935 and kept at Walsall where this photograph was taken on 8 March 1938. In August that year, the Avian passed to the South Staffordshire Aero Club Ltd and remained at Walsall until December, when it was destroyed.

In yellow and aluminium training colour scheme, Hawker Hind trainer L7227 had just been delivered to No. 610 Squadron when photographed at Hooton Park on 13 March 1938. Built at Hawker's Kingston factory in 1938, it was part of a batch of twenty Hind trainers produced between February and June 1938, remaining with the squadron until taken off RAF charge in October 1943.

Hawker Hart K4441 was built by Armstrong Whitworth at Whitley Abbey during the winter of 1934-35. Among others, it served with No. 610 Squadron at Hooton Park, where this photograph was taken on 13 January 1938. After flying with a couple of FTS units, the Hart was struck off RAF charge in July 1940.

On 2 July, Alex Henshaw won the seventeenth King's Cup air race in Percival Mew Gull G-AEXF at an average speed of 236 mph for the 1,012-mile course, which consisted of twenty laps of a triangular circuit of 50.6 miles, starting and finishing at Hatfield. Luton Airport was opened officially by Sir Kingsley Wood, Secretary of State for Aviation, on 16 July.

Towards the end of July, E. J. R. took a busman's holiday, travelling south to visit Hanworth, Broxbourne, and Croydon. At the latter, he photographed a variety of aircraft, including a Lufthansa Ju 52, Curtiss Condor, and the inevitable H.P.42.

On 1 September, the Civil Air Guard (CAG) scheme came into being, having been announced officially the previous July. Via light aeroplane clubs, the idea was to make flying training available to a much wider audience at lower than flying club charges. Membership was open to men and women between eighteen and fifty who were British subjects and resident in this country. The public response was immediate, and by the end of the year, no fewer than 30,200 applications had been received, including nearly 6,500 from women. Members of H.M. Forces and persons with reserved occupations were not eligible. CAG members were trained to Class 'A' pilot licence standard and then required to undertake 10-hours flying practice each year. Flying rates varied between 2s 6d and 10s per hour, but were more expensive at weekends. By the end of the year, 300 CAG members had achieved licences.

Immediately on leaving the employment of Martin Hearn in September, E. J. R. worked for a few weeks as an engineer for Lancelot J. 'Pop' Rimmer's Hooton-based North British Aviation Company up until the end of the joyriding season. It involved plenty of flying for him, and is covered in the next chapter.

The country sighed with relief when Prime Minister Neville Chamberlain returned to Heston Aerodrome from Munich on 30 September, famously waving his 'Peace for our Time' piece of paper.

On 30 October, E. J. R. had a 35-minute flight in D.H.87B Hornet Moth G-ADMJ from Woodford with C. Doodson.

Elementary trainer Avro 621 Tutor K3311 was delivered to the RAF in 1933, and after a time with No. 5 FTS, passed to No. 610 Squadron at Hooton Park, where it was photographed on 13 March 1938. On 8 April 1939, the Tutor's Armstrong Siddeley Lynx IVC engine cut out, causing the aircraft to stall during a night landing at Hooton Park; the aircraft was badly damaged.

The three-seat Fairey Battle light bomber entered RAF service in March 1937, and with the outbreak of war in September 1939, the type was the first to be sent to France. But the days of the Battle as an operational bomber were short and it was soon relegated to training duties. Battle I K7698, built at Stockport, was delivered to the No. 142 Squadron a few days before this photograph was taken at Hooton Park on 29 April 1938. K7698 was still with the squadron when it went missing near Laon during a raid on 19 May 1940.

The Gloster Gladiator, the RAF's last biplane fighter, entered service in January 1937. Like the Fairey Battle, by the time went to France at the outbreak of war, it was already outdated. Gladiator K7925 was delivered to No. 50 Squadron in May 1937, and is seen at Hooton Park on 20 April 1938, its 640-hp Bristol Mercury VIS engine ticking over while the pilot prepares to settle into his seat. After a couple of accidents, K7925 ended up in the Middle East, first with No. 1411 Flight and then with No. 267 Squadron. It was struck off charge following a landing accident at RAF Heliopolis on 30 June 1942.

Opposite below: Netherthorpe Airfield, not far from Worksop, Yorkshire, was opened in August 1935 and became the headquarters of the Sheffield Aero Club. In 1938, the club possessed three D.H.60 Moths, including silver and blue D.H.60M G-AAVE, seen at Netherthorpe on 1 May 1938. First registered in June 1930, 'VE had a string of owners before settling at Netherthorpe. In January 1941 the Moth was sold in India'.

Above: The Avro 652A Anson I reconnaissance aircraft, developed from the six-passenger Avro 652, began its long RAF career in March 1936. Built at Woodford, Anson I K6234 is seen at Hooton Park on 20 May 1938. After delivery to the School of Navigation, this aircraft spent time with No. 6 FTS and then No. 48 Squadron, with which it was flying when ditched at night on 2 October 1939 off East Stoke, Hayling Island, after an engine problem.

Below: The Avro Prefect was the RAF's version of the civil Avro 626, seven of which were supplied to the Service in mid-1935, although many others were delivered to foreign air forces. The first aircraft, K5063, undertook trials at the Aeroplane & Armament Experimental Establishment before delivery to No. 2 Aircrew Selection Unit, and is seen at Woodford on 22 May 1938. In June, the Prefect was relegated to a maintenance airframe, becoming 1594M.

The prototype Fairey Albacore L7074 first flew on 11 December. From early 1941, E. J. R. was to get to know the Albacore intimately while working in the AID department of Fairey Aviation at Hayes. Engaged on their inspection, he flew as an 'observer' on fifty test flights in this Swordfish replacement, mostly with test pilot F. C. Dixon, from Fairey's nearby Great West Aerodrome. On 17 April 1949, Dixon was to lose his life while flying the Fairey Gyrodyne G-AIKF.

On 28 December, the D.H.95 Flamingo prototype G-AFUE got airborne for the first time at Hatfield, piloted by Geoffrey de Havilland, Jnr.

By the end of the year, around seventy-four light aeroplane clubs existed in the UK. The flying members of approved clubs totalled 9,100, of whom 3,960 held pilots' 'A' licences. The figures for the previous, pre-Civil Air Guard year were 7,187 and 3,418 respectively. During the year, 2,659 private pilots' 'A' licences (including 300 CAG members) were issued, compared with 2,458 the previous year. The number of 'A' licences current at the end of the year was 5,352, (including 210 held by women), an increase of 658 over the previous year.

The number of Royal Aero Club Aviators' certificates issued during 1938 totalled 1,172, compared with 981 the previous year. A sharp increase in the last quarter was attributed to the institution of the Civil Air Guard.

At the end of 1938, there were 108 permanent licensed aerodromes, compared to 98 the previous year.

A familiar sight on Southport sands during the 1930s was a pair of white D.H. 83 Fox Moths taking off and landing every 10 or so minutes, giving four trippers at a time their first taste of flying. Norman Giroux, trading as Giro Aviation, had started flying from the beach in the 1920s with D.H.6s, basing his aircraft at nearby Hesketh Park, on the beach with two maintenance hangars set back on land. The two Giro Fox Moths are seen together on Birkdale Sands on 11 June 1938. About to take off is Norman Giroux himself in G-ACEJ, with G-ACCB in the background. 'EJ was completed in 1933 and sold to Scottish Motor Traction Co Ltd, based at Renfrew, until acquired by Norman Giroux in July 1936. 'CB was sold to Midland & Scottish Air Ferries Ltd in 1933 and also based at Renfrew until bought by Giroux in January 1936. Both Fox Moths were stored during the war, somehow escaping impressment. They resumed joyriding with Giroux after the war. 'CB received a dunking when ditched off Southport on 25 September 1956. All was not lost however, because it was restored to life in 1988. 'EJ carried on at Southport until sold to Norman Jones of the Redhill-based Tiger Club in 1966. On 17 July 1982, it crashed at Old Warden and was burnt, but its few mortal remains were the basis for a 'restoration' and the old Fox was rebuilt in 1986. It has since revisited the sands at Southport and featured in the BBC's *Coast* series.

Norman Giroux heads off with another load of holidaymakers from Birkdale Sands in D.H.83 Fox Moth G-ACEJ on 11 June 1938.

Gloster Gladiator K6136 being escorted across Ringway on 25 June 1938. Delivered to No. 72 Squadron in February 1937, K6136 was shipped out to the Middle East in May 1939 and flew with No. 112 Squadron. While carrying out a slow roll at Erkowit in the Sudan on 18 June 1940, the Gladiator crashed. The pilot was killed and the aircraft damaged beyond repair.

So impressed was Anthony Fokker with the Douglas DC-2 that he obtained the rights to assemble and distribute the airliner in Europe. The eighteen-passenger DC-2-115 was powered by two 720-hp Wright Cyclone SGR-1820-Ft radial engines, giving a highly creditable cruising speed of 200 mph. Seen here at Ringway on 25 June 1938 is Douglas-Fokker DC-2 PH-AKP *Perkoestoet*. Together with several others, it was destroyed at Schiphol on 10 May 1940.

Also at Ringway on 25 June was Railway Air Services' D.H.86B G-AEWR *Venus*. Although almost a contemporary of the Douglas DC-2, the two designs appear to be generations apart; one a sleek, all-metal, twin-engined, high-performance monoplane, the other a biplane made of fabric-covered wood and propelled by four engines. Of the sixty or so D.H.86s built, two-thirds flew with UK airlines, including Imperial Airways, Jersey Airlines, Railway Air Services, and British Airways. 'WR, one of the last examples, was lost during the evacuation of France in June 1940.

The Westland Lysander two-seat army co-operation aircraft entered RAF service in 1938 and was to carry out a variety of roles, including air-sea rescue and spy-dropping. As a target tower, it was shot at by friendly fire! The first squadron to receive Lysanders was No. 16, based at RAF Old Sarum, one of whose aircraft, L4678, is seen at Ringway on 25 June 1938. After service with No. 16 Squadron, L 4678 was sold to Finland in February 1940. Note the line of Gloster Gladiators behind.

The Airspeed Oxford advanced trainer was a military development of the Airspeed Envoy and first entered RAF service in 1937. Early Oxfords were fitted with dorsal turrets for gunnery training, but these were deleted with the Oxford II, which was used generally for pilot training. Built at Portsmouth, Oxford L4566 was delivered to No. 5 FTS at RAF Sealand, where it is seen on 28 June 1938 and was the subject of much interest. Subsequently, it flew with No. 14 FTS and No. 28 FTS, but was taken off RAF charge in September 1943 and allocated the maintenance serial 3851M.

The Vickers Wellesley general purpose bomber was first flown in June 1935, entering RAF service in April 1937. Famously constructed to the Barnes Wallis' geodetic method of construction, the Wellesley was powered by a single 925-hp Bristol Pegasus XX radial engine. By the outbreak of war, the type was outmoded and therefore sent to East Africa. The Wellesley is probably best known as a pre-war long-distance record breaker. In November 1938, two flew non-stop from Ismailia to Darwin, a distance of 7,162 miles, fitted with long-range tanks. Wellesley K7757 is at RAF Sealand on 28 June 1938. Delivered to No. 207 Squadron in August 1937, it spent time at Aboukir aircraft depot. During a ferry flight to Aden, the aircraft caught fire, and after making a forced landing at Dar Majahar on 15 August 1940, was abandoned.

No, this is not the high speed version of the D.H.9, but the wingless mortal remains of G-AACP (see page 121), lying abandoned at Hanworth Park on 23 July 1938. Last owned by Aerial Sites Ltd and used for banner-towing, this old D.H.9 had led a varied life that included use by Sir Alan Cobham for early flight refuelling experiments at Ford. As can be seen from this photograph, the two rear cockpits have hinged decking to allow more working space for flight refuelling work. Sadly, 'CP was dismantled shortly after this picture was taken.

The British Aircraft Manufacturing Co. Ltd at Hanworth, formerly The British Klemm Aeroplane Co. Ltd, had already produced the highly successful and viceless B.A. Swallow and the B.A. Eagle, when in 1936, the company embarked upon a twin-engine, six-seat monoplane featuring a retractable undercarriage and a pair of de Havilland Gipsy Major engines. Only three Double Eagles were built, the prototype first taking to the air in July 1936. The second aircraft, G-AEIN, is pictured at Hanworth on 23 July 1938 with its 200-hp Gipsy VIs ticking over. 'IN was sold to Lord Willoughby de Broke, and the aircraft came to public notice when it flew into third place in the 1936 King's Cup air race. Shortly before the war, the Double Eagle was acquired by North Western Air Transport Ltd at Speke, Liverpool, but with the onset, was impressed into the RAF, given the RAF serial number ES950, and used as an instructional airframe. As interesting as this innovative aircraft was, the Double Eagle was competing for a market already filled adequately by more traditional types, such as the D.H.90 Dragonfly.

Broxbourne Aerodrome was opened officially on 14 June 1931 and was home to the Herts & Essex Flying Club; the boundary between the two counties ran across the airfield. It was run by the Frogley brothers of speedway fame. Seen here is the London Transport (Central Buses) Sports Association Flying Club's D.H.60G-III Moth G-ACGX on July 24 1938. This Moth had previously been owned by Hillman's Airways Ltd and Croydon Airways Ltd. 'GX was impressed into the RAF as X5131 and used as an airfield decoy. Half parked in the hangar with wings folded is the LT Club's D.H.60M Moth G-AASL.

Although it is generally known that Junkers Ju 52s were in service with British European Airways immediately after the Second World War, the fact that the type was flying with a British airline beforehand may raise a few eyebrows. This classic, three-engined workhorse was flying with many European airlines in the 1930s, and during 1937-38, British Airways acquired three from Sweden for use as freighters, basing them at Gatwick. One of the trio was G-AERU, named *Juno*, seen picketed at Croydon on 25 July 1938 with G-AERX just visible behind. By this time, the fleet had been re-engined with Pratt and Whitney Wasp engines. In November, by which time *Juno* had been absorbed into British Airways, the Ju 52s were shipped to Lagos and used on the trans-African route between Takoradi and Khartoum. Shortly after arrival, *Juno* was cannibalised to keep the two remaining aircraft airworthy.

There must have been thousands of photographs taken of Handley Page H.P.42s landing at Croydon during the 1930s. This one shows G-AAUD's stately arrival on 25 July 1938. Although not a particularly brilliant picture, it does show off the word *Imperial* beneath the fuselage. 'UD was an H.P.42W (Western), registered to the airline in January 1930, and named *Hanno*. Having served ten years with Imperial, *Hanno* succumbed to gales at Bristol Whitchurch airfield on 19 March 1940 and was destroyed.

Curtiss T.32 Condor G-AEWE at Croydon on 25 July 1938. Looking like a biplane version of the Douglas DC-2, this somewhat curious design was powered by two 700-hp Wright Cyclone radial engines, featured a retractable undercarriage, and cruised at 150 mph. Accommodation was for fifteen passengers and two crew. Earlier that year, 'WE and three other Condors had been acquired from Eastern Air Transport in the US by Croydon-based International Air Freight Ltd. With seats removed, they were used as freighters, capable of carrying a useful 5,565 lb on twice-daily services to Brussels and Amsterdam. The Condors were not in service for long; in October, the Air Ministry acquired all four, earmarking them for conversion to flying classrooms for the RAF. Nothing came of the plan and the Condors remained hangared at Croydon until September 1939 when they were taken by road to RAF Sealand and scrapped.

Looking like a cut-price Monospar ST-25, the one-off Hordern-Richmond Autoplane was a very light, low-powered, three-seater designed by E. G. Hordern and the Duke of Richmond and Gordon. The aircraft was built by Heston Aircraft Co. Ltd at Heston in 1936, registered G-AEOG, and given an Authorisation to Fly in October that year. Powered by two 40-hp Continental A40 engines, the Autoplane cruised at 85 mph and had an all-up weight of 1,750 lb. 'OG was first registered to the Duke, ownership later being transferred to Hordern-Richmond Aircraft Ltd at Denham. This interesting twin was scrapped during the war.

One of the more unusual looking aeroplanes of the late 1930s was the twin boom, pusher-engined, one-off Arpin A-1 G-AFGB, seen at Hanworth on 25 July 1938. This two-seat cabin monoplane was designed by M. B. Arpin, built at West Drayton and test flown at Hanworth on 7 May 1938. Featuring a MacLaren crosswind tricycle undercarriage, the A-1 was powered originally by a 68-hp British Salmson A.D.9R radial engine and caused a great deal of interest when shown at that year's RAeS garden party. But the A-1 was underpowered, so in 1939, a 90-hp Blackburn Cirrus Minor was fitted, upgrading the pusher to A-1 Mk II. After evaluation by the British Army at Old Sarum, the A-1 survived the war in storage, but was scrapped in December 1945.

No, this Piper J-3 Cub has not hit something and lost half its propeller! It has been fitted with a single-blade Everel airscrew, with a metal button covering where the second blade would normally be. Surprisingly, the single blade improved take-off performance on the Cub and described a larger arc when turning – 6 feet, 4 inches as against 5 feet 9 inches with a 'normal' propeller. The Everel was also lighter and cheaper to buy. Piper Cub G-AFIO was imported from the USA and registered in July 1938 by Piper agent A. J. Walter, who also introduced the Everel propeller to the UK. The Cub was flown at Hanworth, where this photograph was taken on 25 July 1938. 'IO was scrapped during the war and the Everel propeller never caught on.

The Miles M.14 Magister is remembered as the RAF's first monoplane trainer and began equipping flying training schools in 1936. It was powered by a 130-hp de Havilland Gipsy Major I engine, as was its biplane rival, the D.H.82A Tiger Moth. Magister L6900 was built at Woodley in 1937 and delivered to No. 3 FTS at Hamble. Later, it flew with No. 16 EFTS at Burnaston, and later still with the Air Transport Auxiliary, presumably as an elementary trainer. In February 1946, it was packed off to Argentina. It is seen at Speke Airport, Liverpool, on 26 August 1938 wearing wheel spats that were normally discarded because they clogged up constantly, especially when operating from water-sodden airfields.

A line-up of Hawker Nimrods pictured at Hooton Park on 2 September 1938, with K2834 in the foreground. Delivered in 1933, this Nimrod had already served with No. 802 Squadron in Malta before joining No. 800 Squadron at Gosport when photographed at Hooton. Three days later, it was damaged following a poor landing at RAF Worthy Down and struck off charge the following month.

D.H. Moths G-EBTZ and G-ABES of the Worcestershire Flying Club (WFC) at their home aerodrome, Tilesford/Pershore, on 2 September 1938. 'TZ was first delivered to Air Taxis Ltd in 1927 and then flew with the WFC until impressed into RAF service as AW146 in June 1940, ending up with No. 1092 ATC Squadron Bridgend with maintenance serial 2833M. 'ES, behind, was registered in 1930 to the Hon. H. C. H. Bathurst and was still owned by WFC when impressed into the RAF as AX792. Its only excitement came on 24 June 1941 when it had engine failure near Stirling. Unfortunately, the field chosen for an emergency landing was occupied by cattle and the Moth ended up in a hedge.

First flown from Witney in April 1937, the diminutive and beautifully-formed Chilton DW1 prototype G-AESZ, designed by A. R. 'Reggie' Ward and the Hon. Andrew Dalrymple. It is seen at Hooton on 7 September 1938, probably when owned by J. A. Talbot of Plymouth. The Chilton survived the war, but crashed at Felixstowe, Suffolk, on 24 May 1953 and looked like a write-off. Enter Roy 'Mr Chilton' Nerou, who restored the Chilton to the register in June 1984. After a thorough restoration, 'SZ flew again on 1 September 2001 and continued to remain airworthy at the time of writing.

Opposite: The beautifully proportioned Hawker Nimrod single-seat, carrier-borne fighter replaced the FAA's Fairey Flycatcher, entering service in 1932. Powered by the Rolls-Royce Kestrel and carrying two fixed, synchronised Vickers guns, the Nimrod remained in service until 1939, its role having been taken over by the Gloster Gladiator and the Blackburn Skua. Hawker Nimrod II K5057 is seen at Hooton Park on 4 September 1938. Delivered in November 1935, it spent time at 'C' Flight Gosport, where it lost an undercarriage leg on landing in February 1937. After repairs, K5057 flew with No. 800 Squadron, coded '105', as seen here, and then with No. 803 based at Worthy Down, before going to the Admiralty in May 1939.

Above and below: Imagine turning up for work one day when in flies the legendry Amy Mollison (née Johnson). This happened at Hooton Park on 9 September 1938 when she arrived in Tipsy B G-AFCM for reasons unknown. Within minutes of the engine stopping she was surrounded by the lads from Martin Hearn, who no doubt remembered the incident for the rest of their lives. 'CM was originally the Belgian-built OO-DOS and given British registration in May 1938 by aircraft agent Brian Allen Aviation Ltd at Hanworth. Although it survived the Second World War, the Tipsy was burnt at nearby Slough in 1952.

Above and below: Two views of Gloster Gladiator I K8004 taken at Hooton Park on 9 September 1938. Delivered to No. 72 Squadron in August 1937, and thereafter serving with many other units, K8004 had a penchant for hitting balloon cables. The first occasion was on 20 April 1942 when it flew into a balloon cable at Plymouth, but landed safely. On the second occasion, it hit a cable while carrying out a forced landing in fog at Oswestry in November 1943, ending its flying career.

This page and oppsite above: D.H.83 Fox Moth G-ACEY was first registered in March 1933, spending the season with Cobham's National Aviation Day displays. The following year, it passed to Provincial Airways Ltd, and in 1935, flew with Crilly Airways Ltd based at Braunstone. The final owner was Hooton-based Utility Airways Ltd and it was during this ownership that disaster occurred. Now named *Athene*, 'EY was due to joyride at the opening of Walsall airfield on 24 September 1938. The pilot Flt Lt W. Hill attempted to take off uphill on a windless day with the Fox Moth overloaded, the result of which is seen in this sequence of photographs, referred to as the 'Fall of *Athene*' in E. J. R.'s photograph album. The pilot was later sacked, but the Fox Moth lived to fly again, only to fall victim to the infamous Hooton Park hangar fire of 8 July 1940.

NORTHERN AVIATION SCHOOL & CLUB LTD.

BARTON AIRPORT, MANCHESTER.

Regd. Office :
Trafford Park.
Manchester, 17.

Telephone: Trafford Park 2661 (6 lines)..

Directors:
A. G. Murrell (Chairman)
W. J. Asley
W. R. Chown
J. F. Morland
E. J. Murrell
G. C. Scholfield
F. B. Osborne

Secretary: E. B. Goldson

Telephone: ECCles 3582

Please reply to: Barton Airport.

7th. October, 1938.

E.J.Riding Esq.,
61,South Drive,
Chorltonville,
MANCHESTER.

Dear Sir,

     May we remind you that the enclosed account
is owing to us, and we should be glad to have a remittance
at your earliest convenience.

     It is extremely helpful to us when members
respond to an informal reminder, such as this letter is
intended to be, and your attention therefore will be
much appreciated.

     Yours faithfully,

     For and on behalf of,
The NORTHERN AVIATION SCHOOL & CLUB LTD.,

. . . .
Commercial Manager.

A letter from the Northern Aviation School & Club Ltd, dated 7 October, asking E. J. R. to settle his account for fees owing for flying instruction on the school's Pragas.

CONTRACTORS TO H.M. & FOREIGN GOVERNMENTS

TELEPHONE : COLLYHURST 2731(4 LINES)
TELEGRAMS: "TRIPLANE, MANCHESTER."

CABLE CODES: BENTLEYS AND BENTLEYS SECOND

A. V. Roe & Co. Limited

Newton Heath,

Manchester, 10

DESIGNERS AND CONSTRUCTORS OF AEROPLANES AND SEAPLANES

LONDON OFFICE : 166, PICCADILLY, W. 1.
TELEPHONE : REGENT 3551-2.

Ref. RHD/ACJ.

3rd November, 1938

TO WHOM IT MAY CONCERN.

Mr. E. J. Riding was employed by this Company from September 1935 to September 1937, and during this time was engaged in the various sections of the Inspection Department, such as, Goods Received, Finished Wings, and other covered components, Dope Room Inspection, etc. etc.

At the end of this period he left this firm of his own accord in order to take up another position.

A. V. ROE & COMPANY, Limited.

CHIEF INSPECTOR.

Above: Easily mistaken for a D.H.53 Humming Bird, Martin Monoplane G-AEYY did in fact incorporate a number of D.H.53 components that had been used in the construction of Clarke Cheetah Monoplane G-AAJK. The Cheetah had begun life in 1929 as a biplane, using the lower wings of Halton Mayfly G-EBOO, and in 1930, was converted into a monoplane. Designed and built by C. H. Latimer-Needham and Harold Best-Deveraux at Denham in 1937, G-AEYY was first flown in October 1937. It crashed during the next flight and was rebuilt with a plywood fuselage. A subsequent owner used the aircraft to commute from Denham to Ringway and popped into Barton where this photograph was taken on October 23 1938. Shortly after, 'YY was damaged in a forced landing near Meir and stored for many years until the late Mike Russell acquired it in the 1970s with the intention of using parts of it to restore his D.H.53.

A.R.B. Form No. 26

AIR REGISTRATION BOARD.

TELEPHONE No. : TEMPLE BAR 9787-8.
TELEGRAMS : BORDAIR, RAND, LONDON.
ALL COMMUNICATIONS TO BE
ADDRESSED TO THE SECRETARY.

BRETTENHAM HOUSE,
LANCASTER PLACE,
STRAND, LONDON, W.C.2.

3rd November, 1938.

GROUND ENGINEERS' EXAMINATION

DEAR SIR,

With reference to your application dated 19th October, 1938.
to be examined for the grant of a Ground Engineer's Licence, I am to
notify you that you are required to present yourself for examination at

Air Registration Board, Liverpool Airport, Speke, LIVERPOOL 19.

on Friday, 11th November, 1938 at 10.0 a.m.

It will be necessary for you to present to the Board of Examiners for
perusal copies of testimonials from the referees you have nominated against
Clause 13 of your application on the C.A. Form 2B.

I am to request you to complete, detach and return the acknowledgment
slip at the foot hereof to me by return post.

Should you, owing to illness or other unavoidable circumstances, be
unable to keep this appointment, the earliest possible notice of such inability to
attend must be given to the Board. Unless such notice is given, it will not be
possible to remit the fee payable in respect of the first appointment and a further
fee (to be paid in advance) will be chargeable for any subsequent appointment
made.

Yours faithfully,

E.J. Riding, Esq.,
61 South Drive,
Chorltonville,
MANCHESTER 21.

Secretary.

Opposite below: To Whom it May Concern. A letter of reference from A. V. Roe and Co. Ltd, dated November 3 1938.

Mr. E. J. Riding was employed by this Company from September 1935 to September 1937, and during this time, was engaged in the various sections of the Inspection Department, such as, Goods Received, Finished Wings, and other covered components, Dope Room Inspection, etc. etc.

At the end of this period, he left this firm of his own accord in order to take up another position.

Top: Ground Engineers Examination Notice from the ARB dated 3 November 1938, requesting E. J. R.'s presence for an examination at the Air Registration Board, Liverpool Airport, Speke, on Friday 11 November 1938 at 10 a.m.

Bottom: An offer of a job with Brooklands Aviation Ltd, dated 7 December 1938.

TO ENSURE PROMPT ATTENTION PLEASE ADDRESS ALL CORRESPONDENCE TO THE COMPANY

BROOKLANDS AVIATION Lᵀᴰ

DIRECTORS:
F. SIGRIST, H.B.E., F.R.A.E.S. *Chairman.*
H. DUNCAN DAVIS, A.F.C. *Managing Director.*
J. W. MASSEY, *General Manager.*
A. P. BRADLEY, M.I.A.E., A.M.I.MECH.E.
SECRETARY:
K. M. DAVIS.

PHONE: MOULTON 325 & 326.
WIRES: AERO, NORTHAMPTON.
RLY. STATION: NORTHAMPTON.
SECRETARY:
SYWELL AERODROME.
M. KIRBY.

SYWELL AERODROME.
NORTHAMPTON.

7th December, 1938.

E.J. Riding, Esq.,
61 South Drive,
Chorlton Ville,
MANCHESTER.

Dear Sir,

In a recent conversation with Mr Hill he
mentioned to me that you were looking for a change. I
have at the moment a vacancy for a G.E. licenced on
Gipsy Major and Tiger Moth. If you are in any way
interested I would be obliged if you would communicate
with me and I will furnish you with the necessary details.

Yours faithfully,
p.p. BROOKLANDS AVIATION LIMITED,

Chief Engineer.

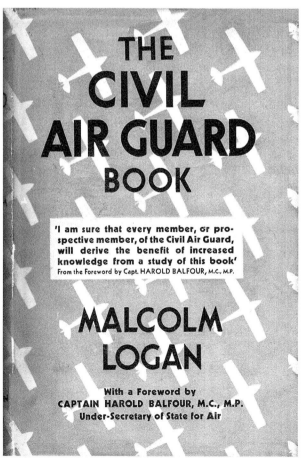

THE CIVIL AIR GUARD BOOK

'I am sure that every member, or prospective member, of the Civil Air Guard, will derive the benefit of increased knowledge from a study of this book'
From the Foreword by Capt. HAROLD BALFOUR, M.C., M.P.

MALCOLM LOGAN

With a Foreword by
CAPTAIN HAROLD BALFOUR, M.C., M.P.
Under-Secretary of State for Air

Above: From 1938, the RAF received around forty-fives Miles M.16 Mentors for use on communications work and radio instruction. Mentor L4396 was delivered to No. 24 Communications Squadron, Hendon, in October 1938, and is seen during a visit to Hooton Park on 12 December that year. On 8 October 1940, it was damaged beyond repair during an air raid on Hendon.

Left: Malcolm Logan's book *The Civil Air Guard* was first published in 1939 by Nicholson & Watson. The aim of the book was to, 'Present the workings of the Civil Air Guard together with a brief outline of the elements of flying and the essential reading matter required by a pupil in pursuit of his "A" licence.' E. J. R. and J. G. E. had started to learn to fly on Hillson Pragas with the Northern Aviation School and Club Ltd at Barton, but after several hours of instruction, lack of finance prevented them from completing the course.

CHAPTER TEN

Hooton Park Heaven (1938)

There was an air about Hooton that I've never met anywhere else. Everybody used to drift
down to the 'drome after tea in the summer evenings and work for the fun of it – a thing
that you won't find in these days of mass production.

                                        Letter from E. J. Riding to A. J. Jackson in 1943

On leaving Blackburn Aircraft Ltd in February 1938, E. J. R. metaphorically fell on his feet
when he joined Martin Hearn Ltd at Hooton Park Aerodrome. During the late 1920s and early
1930s, Martin Neito Hearn had made a name as a daredevil wing-walker before this reckless
form of entertainment was banned in 1933. Yes, it has been revived in recent years, but so-called
wingwalkers are secured to rigs and freedom of movement is restricted to the waving of arms. In
Hearn's day, exponents of that dangerous art either rode atop suitable biplanes, standing on the
centre-section while holding onto a rope or wire, clambering along the wings, or nonchalantly
sitting on the top planes completely unsecured.

Martin Hearn was born in the district of Bury in June 1906, and educated at Salesian School,
Farnborough. He began his working life as an engineer before learning to fly. Gaining Royal
Aero Club aviator's certificate No. 8488 in January 1929 with the Lancashire School of Aviation
Ltd, he joined the most famous of all barnstorming companies, Berkshire Aviation Tours, *flying*
Avro 504Ks rather than riding on top of them! After a period with this outfit, Hearn joined Sir
Alan Cobham's National Aviation Day display as part of the Northern Air Transport element
of the 'circus'. His party trick was to sit on an Avro 504K's forward central skid, unrestrained,
while the aircraft performed loops! Initially, he wanted to stand on the aircraft's centre section
holding onto a wire while the aircraft performed the same manoeuvre, but the boss said no.

In December 1937, Hearn forsook such dangerous pursuits and started his own aviation business
at Hooton Park Aerodrome, Cheshire. At the same time, he became involved with the running of
Utility Airways, first registered in December 1936, and began operating D.H.83 Fox Moth G-ACEY
Athene on taxi, charter flying, and local pleasure flying. Later, the company acquired Monospar
ST-25 Universal G-AEDY and operated a 5-minute, Hooton–Speke route across the River Mersey,
saving an hour's journey by road. This particular Monospar had been built as an ST-25 Jubilee with
a single fin, but in an effort to improve the aircraft's directional control in the event of losing an
engine, it was converted to a twin-fin configuration and thereafter known as an ST-25 Universal.

Martin Hearn Ltd really came into its own during the Second World War when the company
became a Civilian Repair Unit, receiving lucrative Air Ministry contracts to assemble and repair
military aircraft. It is recorded that a total of 9,000 aircraft from North America were assembled by
the unit, among them P-47 Thunderbolts, P-38 Lightnings, and Douglas Havocs. It also specialised
in the repair of Spitfires, Mosquitoes, Ansons, and gliders. After the war, the company built the
prototype Slingsby Type 24 Falcon 4 at Hooton Park, first flown in April 1946. It also produced
examples of the Slingsby Type 26 Kite 2, Type 8 Kirby Tutors, and Type 21B Sedbergh TX Mk 1.

Left: Martin Neito Hearn (1906-92) – pilot, engineer, entrepreneur, wing-walker, and aerial trapeze artist. E. J. R. was employed in his aviation repair business at Hooton Park during 1938.

Below: Martin Hearn employees at Hooton in August 1938 cleaning down Bill Williams' Avro 504K G-ABAA after three months out in the open at Yeadon Aerodrome. Powered by a 140-hp Le Clerget rotary engine, 'AA was registered in September 1930 to G & H Aviation Ltd at Stag Lane, passing to Luff's Aviation Tours Ltd before being acquired by Bill Williams & Company at Squires Gate, Blackpool. It was dismantled at Brooklands in 1939, and is currently preserved at the Manchester Air & Space Museum. These photographs helped in the restoration process.

The company was later renamed Aero-Engineering and Marine (Merseyside), and serviced RCAF jet fighters. But Martin Hearn became tired of the red tape that was stifling aviation and ultimately turned his hand to a non-aviation business. He died in June 1992.

E. J. R. had great regard for him, and in a letter written to A. J. Jackson years after, he wrote, 'I believe the authorities had a great respect for the "old man". Every "board" I've had while in the AID have seemed favourably impressed at the mention of his name. It was a hard school, but a life that takes a long time to forget.'

The other great influence on E. J. R. during his time at Hooton Park was Lancelot J. Rimmer. Five feet, 5 inches in height, with brown eyes, dark hair, but of fair complexion, Rimmer was known by

Above: Seasoned aviator and respected engineer Lancelot J. 'Pop' Rimmer with Avro 504K G-ABAA at Hooton Park on 12 April 1938.

Right: The cover of the A. V. Roe *Handbook of Instruction for the Avro Avian Two Seater Light Aeroplane.* Priced at 1s, this thirty-page publication was to, 'Ensure that the Avian owner shall be provided with all the information necessary to maintain his machine without skilled technical assistance.'

Next page: This diagram from the Avro Avian Handbook shows how the aircraft should be rigged.

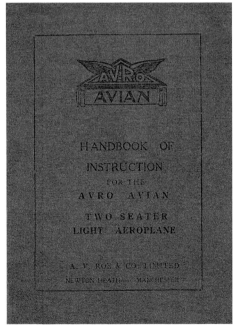

HANDBOOK OF
INSTRUCTION
FOR THE
AVRO AVIAN
TWO SEATER
LIGHT AEROPLANE

A. V. ROE & CO. LIMITED
NEWTON HEATH · MANCHESTER

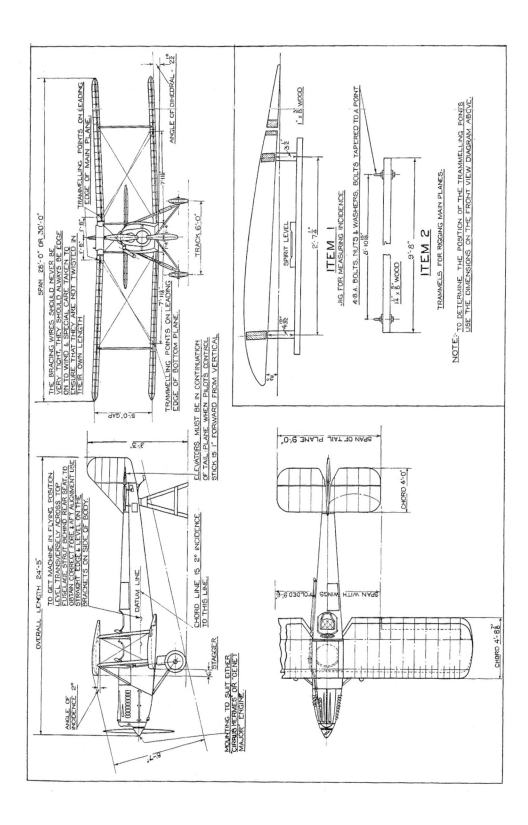

the aviation fraternity as 'Pop'. He was born on 19 February 1896 to Oswald and Mary Rimmer, and had five brothers and a sister. Before the First World War, the family upped sticks and settled in Medicine Hat, Canada, and in September 1914, Lancelot joined the Canadian Expeditionary Force (CEF) as a Corporal (20811), serving with the 10th Battalion. In March 1916, he was awarded the Military Medal, the equivalent of the Military Cross for commissioned officers. At about this time, he married Celia Gray, and they produced three sons and a daughter.

Later in the war, Rimmer transferred to the Royal Flying Corps. He was made acting sergeant in July 1917, and promoted to flying officer in February 1918. He probably flew as an instructor, for when in 1920 he joined the short-lived Hooton-based International Aviation Company (IAC), which operated from Douglas, Isle of Man, and elsewhere, its pilots were all former RFC/RAF instructors. They included G. S. Hughes, William Nichole, and Norman Giroux; the same Norman Giroux who later operated pleasure flights from the beach at Southport as Giro Aviation.

From 1919, IAC operated four D.H.6s; three had crashed or were damaged before the year was out. The fourth, G-EARC, was later sold to Norman Giroux and his Giro Aviation Company.

During the 1925 season, Rimmer was joyriding from the beach at New Brighton, flying the Liverpool Aviation Company's Avro 504K G-EAAY. The season was not without incident, for on two occasions, the 504 hit members of the public while taking off. The second occasion put the victim in hospital and the company was fined £100. It is not certain whether or not Rimmer was the pilot either time.

From 1926-28, Rimmer flew with the legendary Berkshire Aviation Tours Ltd, which operated around twenty-five Avro 504Ks at one time or another. He was also with short-lived South Wales Airways Ltd, set up by Robert Thomas, D. W. Griffiths, and himself in 1927, based at a strip at Coity Glamorgan. The company flew four Avro 504Ks for joyriding: G-EBNH, G-EBSG, G-ABLV, and G-ABLW.

In March 1929, Rimmer and E. E. Fresson started the North British Aviation Co. Ltd (NBAC) using three former Renfrew-based Beardmore Flying School Avro 504Ks: G-EBGZ, G-EBIS, and G-EBXA, all fitted with 110-hp Le Rhone engines. NBAC's joyriding territory from its Hooton Park base was the north of England. Year after year, its aircraft returned to lucrative sites in Lancashire, Cheshire, and the Lake District, flown by seasoned pilots including S. W. Sparks and 'Jock' MacKay, as well as Rimmer and Fresson. By 1931, the fleet had been joined by Avro 504Ks G-EBHE and G-EBSJ.

Fresson departed to form Highland Airways Ltd the following year. That in turn led to the creation of Scottish Airways Ltd in 1937.

In 1933, NBAC toured Britain with Sir Alan Cobham's National Aviation Day display 'circus', but as a separate unit. The pilots were Messrs Rimmer, MacKay, Sparks, and Idwal Jones. Later that year, the fleet was almost doubled with the acquisition of Northern Air Transport Avro 504Ks G-EASF, G-EAKX, G-EBKX, G-AAEZ, G-ABHJ, G-ABHK, and G-ABLL. Never had the firm had it so good! Having said that, by the beginning of the 1935 season, following a series of minor crashes, fortunately without injuries, the fleet had been reduced to just three aircraft.

The loss of Avro 504Ks G-EBKX and G-EBIS during the middle of the 1935 season reduced the 'fleet' to Avro 504K G-EASF and borrowed Short Scion G-ACJI. My father recalled that 'IS collided with a duck pond at Rainford on Easter Monday 1935, from which it failed to emerge.

The following year, Rimmer toured with C. W. A. Scott's Air Display, flying newly acquired Avro 504N G-ACOK, which he continued to fly until the Avro fell apart following a forced landing on the sands at Rhyl in July 1938, from where it had been joyriding. 'OK was replaced by Avro 504N G-AEGW, but by the time the company had closed down in October 1938, 'GW had seen little action.

While with Martin Hearn, E. J. R. was responsible for assisting in renewing the Certificate of Airworthiness of Avro 594 Avian III G-EBXY. The two photographs show work in progress at Hooton Park on 12 March 1938. First registered in May 1928, 'XY joined the fleet of the Liverpool and District Aero Club Ltd at Speke. It then passed to Blackpool & West Coast Air Services Ltd and was owned by the Blackpool & Fylde Aero Club Ltd when war stopped civil flying. 'XY was impressed into the RAF and given the maintenance serial 2078M.

Airspeed AS.5 Courier G-ACLF undergoing a C of A renewal at the hands of E. J. R. in March 1938. 'LF was completed at Airspeed's Portsmouth factory in 1933 and acquired by R. K. Dundas. It slipped out of the country during 1936, but was restored to the register the same year when bought by North Eastern Airways Ltd, based at Croydon, in whose colours it is seen. Finally, it joined Portsmouth, Southsea, and Isle of Wight Aviation Ltd in April 1939, before impressment into the RAF in March 1940 as X9342. The Courier's service role was as a taxi aircraft with the Air Transport Auxiliary until July 1942 when it moved to No. 25 OTU at RAF Finningley. By 1943, the Courier was at RAF Kemble in a dismantled state and was scrapped there soon after.

In December 1936, Utility Airways was registered, with W. Frank Davison and E. Joy Davison as directors. In May 1937, it inaugurated a shuttle service from Hooton to Speke, reducing an hour's car journey to just 5 minutes by air. Rimmer later became chief pilot of the company, whose fleet in 1938 consisted of Monospar ST.25 G-AEPA, D.H. 83 Fox Moth G-ACEY, two Avro Cadets, and an Avro 504N four-seater.

In 1942, he became a test pilot with Rootes Securities at Speke, flight testing Bristol Blenheims and Handley Page Halifaxes. He died on 5 January 1980, aged eighty-three.

Rimmer's second eldest son Reginald Frank Rimmer was obviously a chip off the old block, joining the RAF on a short service commission in March 1937. Following a period with No. 10 FTS at RAF Tern Hill, he joined No. 66 Squadron at Duxford. After damaging a Heinkel He.111 over Dunkirk in June 1940, Rimmer Jnr was posted to No. 229 Squadron, and later destroyed a Dornier Do. 117. On 15 September 1940, he shared in the destruction of another Heinkel He.111, but on the afternoon of 27 Septemeber, the twenty-one-year-old, flying Hawker Hurricane I V6782 'T', was shot down by Bf 109s over Franchise Manor Farm, Burwash. His final resting place is at Hoylake Grange, Cheshire.

This page and opposite above: On 3 July 1938, Miss N. Garsed and her female passenger took off from Stanley Park, Blackpool, in D.H.60G-III Moth Major G-ADHE for a short flight to Manchester. Somehow, they managed to run out of fuel, making a spectacular arrival in a field at Penkridge, a few miles south of Stafford, as the accompanying photographs illustrate. Amazingly, both women escaped unhurt. Looking at the close-up of the cockpit in particular, it is apparent that they were lucky to escape with their lives. The wrecked Moth was collected and repaired by Martin Hearn and was soon back in the air. 'HE was first registered to H. E. Evans, whose initials the Moth bore. It not only survived the war, but remained airworthy until crashing at Rickmansworth, not far from its Denham base, on 22 March 1958.

Below: Built at the London Air Park, Feltham, in 1936, BAC Drone G-AEEO joined the fleet of C. W. A. Scott's Air Display Ltd just in time for that year's season. In October, it passed to Lancelot Rimmer at Hooton Park before being purchased the following month by J. Boumphrey. On 8 July 1940, the Drone and several other aircraft were destroyed in the infamous Hooton Park fire. Here it is at Hooton Park on 5 May 1938 after renewal of its C of A by Martin Hearn.

Disaster! Bill Williams, owner of Avro 504K G-ABAA, and G. 'Les' Lewis, pilot, discussing damage to the starboard wing tip, axle, and tail end sustained on the first flight of the season at Holmes Chapel on 15 April 1938. The Avro was dismantled and transported by road to Hooton Park for repair. Lewis was fired!

WORKING WITH MARTIN HEARN

E. J. R. worked for Martin Hearn Ltd at Hooton Park Aerodrome between March and September 1938. According to his notes, he carried out the following:

- Assisting with the Certificate of Airworthiness renewal for Avro 504K G-ABAA for Williams & Company, which included re-rigging and re-doping etc.
- Assisting with C of A renewal on Avro 504N G-ACOK for Lancelot Rimmer.
- Assisting with C of A renewal for D.H.84 Dragon G-ADCP, including dismantling, cleaning, repairs to numerous ribs, renewing covering of centre plane and mainplanes, taping, doping, re-lettering, fuel flow tests, assembly, and rigging.
- Renewal of C of A for Avro Avian G-EBXY, involving dismantling, cleaning, installation of new cockpit decking, rubbing down, and respraying the whole aircraft, doping, lettering, reassembly, and rigging.
- Repairs and C of A renewal for Avro Avian G-ACGV, including insertion of new fabric panel on fuselage, re-spraying and painting.
- Repairs and overhaul for C of A of Avro 504N G-AEGW, including assembly, re-spraying, painting, and lettering.
- Collecting and dismantling D.H.60 Moth Major G-ADHE from crash site at Penkridge, Stafford.

Among other tasks he undertook were:

The pathetic sight of the front section of Avro 504K G-EASF after it had been dragged out of the hangar at Hooton on 13 March 1938, much to the amusement of onlookers at left.

- Recovering the mainplanes of D.H.82A Tiger Moth G-AELB.
- Collecting and dismantling Spartan G-ABWU and Spartan Arrow G-ABKL following a collision at Blackpool.
- Assembling and rigging D.H.60 Moth Major G-ACGX for Blackpool & Fylde Aero Club following repairs.
- Assisting with the C of A renewal of Airspeed Courier G-ACLF and for D.H.53 G-EBXN. Dismantling and packing Airspeed Oxford for shipment from Liverpool to New Zealand.
- Collecting BAC Drone G-AEEO from Speke for C of A, including repairing and re-covering, doping and painting. Carrying out repairs to rear bottom longerons of Avro 504K G-ABAA.

Apart from working on aircraft, there was plenty of opportunity for flying, and sometimes accompanying pilots test flying aircraft on which he had worked. E. J. R.'s log book records that on 15 August, he had a 15-minute flight in Avro 640 G-ACFT, flown by C. Williams from Hooton Park, with work colleague George Percival as co-passenger. A week later, there were three more very short flights in 'FT, this time with a new Utility Airways pilot who was practising take-offs and landings, interspersed with circuits flown at 150–200 feet. On 25 August, E. J. R. had a ride with E. D. Ward in Tipsy B G-AFEI from Hooton Park to RAF Sealand and back; the pilot allowed him to fly the Tipsy after take-off for the 6-minute flight.

When he completed his time with Martin Hearn in September 1938, E. J. R. was able, albeit briefly, to fulfil a boyhood dream of living and flying with barnstormers, with 'Pop' Rimmer taking him on as an engineer at his North British Aviation Company. During a few weeks touring the north-west, he was responsible for the maintenance and daily inspection of Avro 504N G-AEGW; he lived under canvas for much of the time.

It's the lunch hour at Martin Hearn's at Hooton in August 1938 and the lads are flying model aircraft. Left to right: Forester 'Tiddler' Lindsley, Eric Calland, George Atkinson, Maurice Mason, and Bill Williams. Would you find this kind of activity taking place during a meal break at aerospace companies today?

70 per cent of the Martin Hearn staff draped around Avro 504K G-ABAA at Hooton Park in August 1938. From left to right: Eric Calland, Forester Lindsley, George Nicholson (atop the Clerget rotary engine), Victor Thomas, and seated at the front, Doug Letford.

To his delight, there was again a lot more flying to be had, and his flying log book records the following, most of which were publicity flights over villages and towns that were visited:

- 10 September, 5-minute 'Bottle Flight' with L. J. Rimmer in Avro 504N G-AEGW from Tarvin.
- 13 September, 10-minute flight with Rimmer in 'GW from Tarvin, in formation with D.H.83 Fox Moth G-ACEY; stall turns and a falling leaf from 2,000 feet.
- 15 September, 10-minute publicity flight from Tarvin, 'shooting up' pubs at 100 feet with Flt Lt W. Hill in D.H.83 G-ACEY.
- 16 September, 'shooting up' Tarvin village in D.H.83 Fox Moth 'EY in formation with 504N 'GW with Flt Lt Hill.
- 17 September, beating up Hockenhull Farm and Tarvin village at 100 feet in Avro 640 G-ACFT from the field at Tarvin.
- 21 September, 20-minute flight with L. J. Rimmer in Avro 504N G-AEGW from Nantwich to Hooton Park.
- 24 September, 1-hour trip with Rimmer in 504N 'GW from Hooton to Walsall. Visibility was only 2,000 yards and roads had to be followed most of the way, flying at 500–800 feet.
- 25 September, 45-minute trip with Rimmer in 504N 'GW from Walsall to Wem (Buildings Farm) for joyriding at farm.
- 26 September, return trip from Wem to Hooton Park with Rimmer in 'GW, arriving after dark.
- 1 October, 35-minute trip from Hooton to Rochdale with Rimmer in 'GW, with Flt Lt Hill also a passenger.
- 5 October, 35-minute flight Rochdale to Barton with Flt Lt Hill in Avro 640 G-ACFT. Later the same day, Barton to Hooton Park via the Manchester Ship Canal and into a 40-mph headwind in 'FT with Hill.
- 9 October, 55-minute trip with Rimmer in Avro 504N G-AEGW from Rochdale (Milnrow) to Hooton Park via the north side of Barton and the Manchester Ship Canal in rain squalls and winds of 40 mph.

E. J. R. always believed that 'Pop' Rimmer was the very last exponent of the aerial barnstormer, and it was with a certain amount of sadness when his time spent with North British drew to a close. The last port of call for the tour was Runcorn on 16 October; E. J. R. flying there with Rimmer in G-AEGW from Hooton Park and back on the same day.

E. J. R. made two local flights with Rimmer in Monospar ST-25 G-AEDY on 13 October, consisting of take-offs and landings for a licence endorsement with co-pilot Flt Lt W. Hill. Three days later, he had two flights in Avro 504N G-AEGW with Rimmer from a joyriding field at the Warrington side of Runcorn. This was the final flight of the season, and soon after, E. J. R. left Rimmer and North British for pastures new.

AVRO 504K LOVE AFFAIR

Ever since his first flight in Avro 504K G-ABAA in May 1936, E. J. R. had a lasting affection for the old biplane. The following excerpts from letters he wrote to A. J. Jackson some years later give an idea of his passion for Avro 504Ks, and G-ABAA in particular:

The deafening, sizzling, spitting roar of a 110 Rhone, flapping fabric, juddering tailplanes, and the run, hop, and bump into the air and over the wall at the far end of the field.

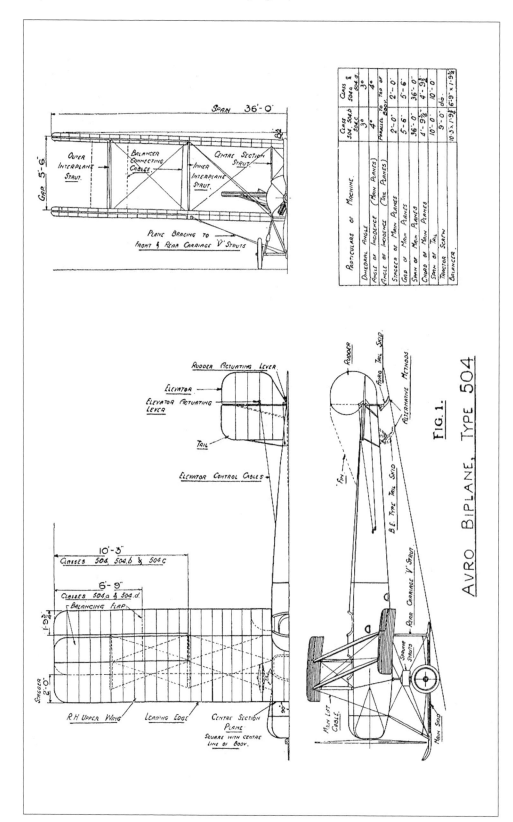

Particulars of Machine.	Class 504, 504.b & 504.c	Class 504.a & 504.d
Dihedral Angle	3°	3°
Angle of Incidence (Main Planes)	4°	4°
Angle of Incidence (Tail Planes)	Parallel to top of body.	
Stagger of Main Planes	2'-0"	2'-0"
Gap of Main Planes	5'-6"	5'-6"
Span of Main Planes	36'-0"	36'-0"
Chord of Main Planes	4'-9½"	4'-9½"
Span of Tail	10'-0"	10'-0"
Tractor Screw.	9'-0" dia.	
Balancer.	10-3 x 1-9½ 6'-9" x 1-9½	

Fig. 1.

AVRO BIPLANE, TYPE 504

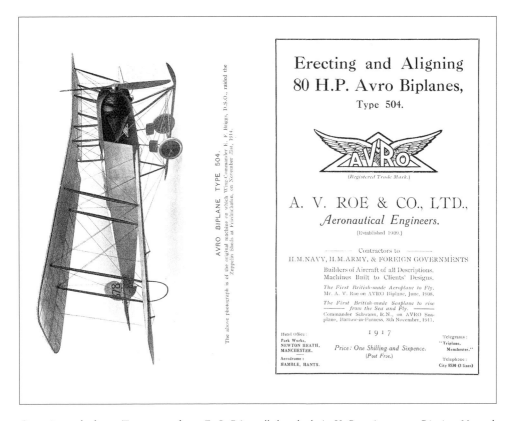

Erecting and Aligning
80 H.P. Avro Biplanes,
Type 504.

A. V. ROE & CO., LTD.,
Aeronautical Engineers.
(Established 1909.)

——— Contractors to ———
H.M.NAVY, H.M.ARMY, & FOREIGN GOVERNMENTS

Builders of Aircraft of all Descriptions.
Machines Built to Clients' Designs.

The First British-made Aeroplane to Fly.
Mr. A. V. Roe on AVRO Biplane, June, 1908.

The First British-made Seaplane to rise
——— *from the Sea and Fly.* ———
Commander Schwann, R.N., on AVRO Seaplane, Barrow-in-Furness, 8th November, 1911.

Head Office:
Park Works,
NEWTON HEATH,
MANCHESTER.

1917

Price: One Shilling and Sixpence.
(Post Free.)

Telegrams:
"Triplane,
Manchester."

Aerodrome:
HAMBLE, HANTS.

Telephone:
City 8530 (3 lines)

AVRO BIPLANE TYPE 504.

The above photograph is of the original machine on which Wing-Commander E. F. Briggs, D.S.O., raided the Zeppelin Sheds at Friedrichafen, on November 21st, 1914.

Opposite and above: Two pages from E. J. R.'s well-thumbed *A. V. Roe Avro 504 Rigging Manual,* published in 1917, price 1s 6d (8p) and still in use twenty years later.

I wonder what can equal the sensation of taking off in an Avro? The feeling as if you're forcing through the thick air with a Y503 (prop) milling round at 1,150 rpm in front of you, and a maize of wings, struts, and shrieking wires keeping you up there with the fat, comforting form of old 'Pop' a few inches in front, and his old battered helmet, that used to be white, sticking up above the coaming in front of you.

Yes, they were good old days at Hooton, and one of the last sights I'll never forget is the way those old Avros used to waddle up to the tarmac, swaying and bumping as their engines blipped and back-fired; test flights in 'SF and 'AA, the smell of castor and new dope, mixed with trodden grass, which only those in the joy-riding racket ever knew. Old Les Lewis and his beard, and how he got fired for crashing 'AA at Holmes Chapel on the first flight of the season ... Our motto in those days was, 'Never pay up unless you can help it.' Rimmer was the last bastion of the 504K.

A potted history of Avro 504K G-ABAA shows that it was built from spares, and featured an enlarged rear cockpit to accommodate two passengers. It was first registered in September 1930 to G & H Aviation Ltd at Stag Lane, North London. In March 1933, 'AA was acquired by Barnet Luffs Aviation Tours Ltd, and in May 1936, registered to Williams & Company and based at Squires Gate, Blackpool. In April 1938, 'AA overshot when landing at Holmes Chapel, and the bottom of the fuselage was torn out by a tree stump. For this indiscretion, pilot Les Lewis was fired. It was at this point that E. J. R. became involved with the 504, and he later wrote to A. J. Jackson:

I met G-ABAA for the first time at Rhos-on-Sea, and she came later to Hooton in October, where she became the 'oldest inhabitant' in 1938. I remember in her 1938 Certificate of Airworthiness renewal we used G-EASF's top planes, a port lower from G-ABHJ, and the starboard lower from 'AA. The fuselage had an RAF-stored rear end and G-AAEZ's fabric covering. It was a toss-up at first as to what we were going to call it, but unfortunately, Bill was broke at the time, so it had to be G-ABAA. He had another 'spare' fuselage with G-ABAA's number on it (blue with red letters). I heard that this machine was another three-pot job, but have never seen a photo of it.

After C of A renewal, G-ABAA was sold in September 1938 to a Flg Off Birch, before dismantling at Brooklands following its last flight on 16 October 1939. From this point, the aircraft's history is murky, to say the least. Some reports indicate that G-ABAA was acquired by collector Richard Nash. His collection of aircraft passed to the Royal Aeronautical Society, and the Avro allegedly resided at the RAF Museum's storage facility at RAF Henlow, disguised as H2311. In 1989, G-ABAA was acquired by the Greater Manchester Museum of Science & Technology, on loan from the Royal Aeronautical Society, and transported from RAF Henlow to the museum's workshops in Manchester. A thorough restoration of G-ABAA was put in hand and J. G. E. and the author assisted with photographs in order to reinstate the 504K to its 1938 configuration. On completion of the restoration, a ceremony was held at the museum on 25 June 1991 to mark the first public viewing of the aircraft. J. G. E. was there; if only E. J. R. had lived long enough to be reunited with his old love.

Opposite: One can almost smell the castor oil spewing from the Clerget rotary engine in this atmospheric photograph of Avro 504K G-ABAA being guided to the take-off area by a Martin Hearn employee hanging on to the lower starboard wing at Hooton Park in 1938. Avro 504s were not equipped with brakes or throttles.

Right: A fine study of 'Pop' Rimmer, about to set off from Hooton Park in Avro 504K G-ABAA in March 1938.

Below: Avro 504K G-ABAA was sold to a Flg Off Birch in September 1938, but before it was handed over, 'Pop' Rimmer gave the new owner some dual instruction. 'Pop' is seen flying the Avro from the front cockpit while Birch stands behind and watches, no doubt receiving a generous coating of Castor oil in the process!

Avro 504N G-AEGW undergoing a first engine run prior to the C of A renewal at Hooton Park on 25 August 1938. Listening to and watching the Mongoose IIIC engine are Vic Thomas, Maurice Mason, and George Atkinson. In March the following year, the National British Aviation Company advertised 'GW for sale as follows: 'One Avro 504N Aircraft: pilot and three passengers, fitted banner towing, Mongoose IIIC engine, C of A to August, excellent condition, price £300. Also numerous spares, axles, spare engine, etc. Apply, full details, Merseyside Air Park Co., Hooton, Cheshire'.

'Pop' Rimmer, with ever-present cigarette, having just flown Avro 504N G-AEGW *George William* at Nantwich in September 1938.

MARTIN HEARN LIMITED

DIRECTORS:
M. N. HEARN
M. G. SHERRARD

AERONAUTICAL ENGINEERS AND AIRCRAFT OPERATORS
ON THE AIR MINISTRY'S APPROVED LISTS

TELEPHONE
HOOTON 3147

TELEGRAMS
"AIRPARK"
LITTLE SUTTON

MERSEYSIDE AIR PARK
HOOTON, CHESHIRE

10th September 1938

To Whom it may concern

This is to state that Mr E.J.Riding has been employed by the above Company for the past six months as a Rigger, he is leaving through no fault of his own.

We found Mr Riding to be a very concientious and reliable workman, showing keeness in any job given him. He is very experienced in aircraft maintenance and overhaul. We also found him clean of manner and person.

We have no hesitation in recomending him.

For MARTIN HEARN LIMITED.

Director

E. J. R.'s letter of reference from Martin Hearn, dated 10 September 1938.

ESTABLISHED 1928.

NORTH-BRITISH AVIATION C⁰. L^TD.

DIRECTORS:—
L. J. RIMMER.
C. RIMMER.

PASSENGER FLYING.
AERIAL PHOTOGRAPHY.
AIR TAXIS.
BANNER FLYING.

(·REGD. OFFICE·) HOOTON AERODROME (·FLYING BASE·)

CHESHIRE

TELEGRAMS

TELEPHONE
HOOTON 243.

OUR REF.

YOUR REF.

DATE 8th November, 1938.

TO WHOM IT MAY CONCERN:

This is to certify that Edwin Riding worked as an aircraft engineer for the above firm and during the time that he was with us we found him satisfactory in every way.

L. J. Rimmer, Director

Letter of reference from North-British Aviation Co. Ltd's 'Pop' Rimmer, dated 8 November 1938.

A letter from 'Pop' Rimmer to E. J. R., also dated 8 November 1938, asking for the return of certain tools!

E. J. R. sitting in his favourite aeroplane – Avro 504K G-ABAA.

CHAPTER ELEVEN

On Tour with June Bug (1939)

I managed to visit seventy-four aerodromes before war started.

Letter from E. J. R. to A. J. Jackson in 1943

The first trip of the year was on 10 January to Meir Aerodrome, Stoke-on-Trent, home of the North Staffordshire Aero Club. Opened officially on 18 May 1934, it had been in operation since the end of 1931 under the management of National Flying Services, but at the time of E. J. R.'s visit, the aerodrome was being run by Stoke-on-Trent Corporation. It was a misty but sunny day, and E. J. R. and J. G. E. each took photographs of the other standing in front of Miles M.2Hs, belonging to the North Staffordshire Aero Club. In E. J. R.'s photograph album, both photographs bear the caption 'Hobos'.

Calling in at Woodford on 17 January, a line of pristine, N-serialled Avro Anson Is awaiting delivery to No. 6 ERFTS was photographed. On the same occasion, E. J. R. had his photograph taken with an RAF D.H.60M Moth and its attendant instructor.

A journey south to Croydon during the first week of February rewarded E. J. R. with pictures of both Short S.17L Scylla airliners G-ACJK *Scylla* and G-ACJK *Syrinx*. Standing not far away, and in complete contrast to the Scyllas, were British Airways' Lockheed 14 G-AFKE and Imperial Airways' Armstrong Whitworth A.W. 27 Ensign G-ADSR *Ensign*.

While E. J. R. was visiting Brooklands on 5 February, Alex Henshaw was speeding towards the Cape from Gravesend, hell bent on breaking the England–Cape Town–England record in his Percival Mew Gull G-AEXF, modified especially by Jack Cross of Essex Aero. Henshaw took 39 hours and 25 minutes for the outward journey. Amazingly, the return flight to Gravesend took just 11 minutes longer. E. J. R. called into Gravesend on 1 April and photographed the Gipsy-engined Comper Swift G-ABWW.

Like many aviation enthusiasts of the day, every month E. J. R. read W. E. Johns' *Popular Flying* magazine, subtitled *The National Aviation Journal*, though he may not have noticed that Johns' name was missing from the masthead of the May issue. The creator of that famous fictional airman 'Biggles' had been fired for his warmongering editorials. His place was taken by regular contributor, Maj. Oliver Stewart, the magazine becoming *Aeronautics* with the August 1939 issue. Stewart continued to edit the magazine until its closure in October 1961.

Birmingham's Elmdon Aerodrome was opened officially on 1 May; the city's municipal airport at Castle Bromwich had become inadequate.

On 7 May, E. J. R. had a 5-minute flight with Tom Brooke-Smith in Short Scion G-ACJN from Gatwick. When this colourful former test pilot for Shorts visited the author at the offices of *Aeroplane Monthly* many years later, he signed his name in the remarks column of E. J. R.'s flying log book! Another short flight was made by E. J. R. in the same aircraft a couple of days later, this time with Edward 'Bunny' Spratt as pilot. The same gentleman gave E. J. R. a trip in Miles M.3A Falcon Major G-ADFH from Gatwick on the same day.

Taylorcraft Model A G-AFJP at Meir on 10 January 1939. This two-seater was imported from the USA and first registered to Staffordshire Airplanes Ltd at Meir in August 1938. 'JP was withdrawn from use in September 1939, but restored to the register in May 1947. It crashed at Woodbridge on 3 October 1953 while owned by the Flying Tiger Cubs.

Looking like a plain clothes detective, J. G. E. stands with Miles M.2H Hawk Major G-ADBT at Meir on 10 January 1939. 'BT was registered first to Rosemary Rees, later to become a ferry pilot with the ATA, who flew the Hawk extensively around Europe. When this photograph was taken, it was owned by Stanley J. Hawley.

E. J. R. with another Miles M.2H Hawk Major at Meir on 10 January, this time all-silver G-AEEZ. Registered in March 1936, 'EZ was attached to the Phillips & Powis School of Flying before passing to the Reading Aero Club in January 1938. By the time this photograph was taken, the Hawk Major had moved north to the North Staffordshire Aero Club. On 8 March 1939, it was destroyed while landing in a gale at Barton.

Catastrophe occurred on 14 May when the prototype Short Stirling L7600 was destroyed on landing following a wheel brake seizure. On the same day, E. J. R. was attending the Royal Aeronautical Society's Garden Party at Fairey's Great West Aerodrome, where he photographed D.H.91 Albatross G-AFDJ *Falcon* with its smaller brethren D.H. 90 Moth Minor G-AFOM nestling under its port wing. Also present was the beautiful Fairey Firefly II, the exquisitely streamlined cowling of its Hispano-Suiza equalling the lines of those enshrouding the Gipsy Queen engines of the Albatross. For the man in the street, there was C. H. Latimer Needham's low-cost Luton Major, powered by a 62-hp Walter Mikron engine.

During Empire Air Day on 20 May, no fewer than seventy-eight aerodromes opened their gates, including sixty-three RAF stations; the largest number to have opened to the public before the war.

On 29 May, the AID posted E. J. R. to Fairey Aviation's works at Hayes. His work there involved detail-check inspections, and was followed by a period in the airscrew shop supervising Avro 652A Cheetah IX engines and propeller blades. He then moved on to monocoque fuselages for Fairey Albacores, supervising their removal from construction jigs and subsequent alignment. He also worked on Swordfish and Albacore centre-sections and fuel tanks, eventually becoming responsible for the final inspection of completed Albacores, including checking the installation of flying controls, engines, and miscellaneous equipment prior to aircraft being dispatched to Fairey's Great West Aerodrome for test flying. This involved many trips as 'observer' on first test flights.

The Military Training Act came into force on 3 June, and conscription and mandatory 6-month military training began for men aged twenty to twenty-one.

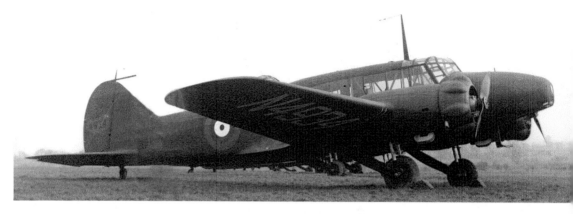

Avro Anson I N4934 at Woodford on 17 January 1939. First delivered to No. 6 ERFTS, it passed through various training units before being written off following a collision with Miles Master EM281 when taking off from Martins Farm, Longford, on 7 November 1943. At the time, it was on the strength of No. 5 Pilots Advance Flying Unit.

Avro Anson I N4934 with sister ships awaiting delivery from Woodford on 17 January 1939.

JUNE TO AUGUST

During the last weeks of peace, E. J. R. travelled throughout the UK, photographing as many aircraft as possible. By this time, the Riding family had moved south from Manchester to Wimborne, Dorset, although E. J. R. was living temporarily at Charlton, South London. He was still working in the AID department of Fairey Aviation, across London, in Hayes, Middlesex. His great friend and companion J. G. E. had remained up north with F. Hills & Son, first in Manchester, later in Stockton.

During late December 1937, E. J. R.'s Austin Seven *Busby* was retired, and another Seven was acquired for the princely sum of £9. Registered FU9165 in 1928, E. J. R. christened the 'new' car *June Bug*. At the time of purchase, the milometer recorded a mere 6,700 miles – probably a fraction of the true distance covered because the 'clock' returned to zero after 10,000 miles. By June 1939, E. J. R. had added a further 16,000 miles to *June Bug's* travels, and the old jalopy needed some attention. This necessitated two new front tyres (one for spare), shims for brake cams, rewiring of a side lamp, renewal of the front and rear bearings, repairing of three side screens and the rear window, and finally, scraping and repainting of the body. Road tax for six months set him back £1 1s 5d plus £1 8s for insurance. Petrol then cost £1s 5d per gallon, and oil 1s per quart! But that was a lot of money in those days, especially as E. J. R. was averaging 1,000 miles a month.

A photograph of curious perspective: E. J. R. at left and looking larger than life, standing with D.H.60M Moth K1894, complete with rear cockpit blind flying hood, at Woodford on 17 January 1939. This Moth was delivered to the RAF in 1931 and attached to No. 29 Squadron at RAF Duxford until May 1937 when it transferred to the Station Flight at RAF Northolt. After serving with several other units, K1894 was packed off to No. 27 M.U. at RAF Shawbury a month after this photograph was taken, and became 1306M.

During the latter half of the 1930s, Imperial Airways Ltd had two Short S.17L Scyllas flying European routes. It is difficult to believe that production ran to only two aircraft, although some cost must have been saved by using the same tail unit and superstructure of the Short S.17 Kent flying boat. Designed to carry thirty-nine passengers and powered initially by four 595-hp Bristol Jupiter XFBM engines, the two Scyllas poodled along at 100 mph and provided reliable service. The first, G-ACJJ, is seen at Croydon on 4 February 1939. Named *Scylla,* the airliner's flying career ended on 9 September 1940 when wrecked by a gale at Drem, Scotland.

G-ACJK was the second Short S.17L Scylla, and is also seen at Croydon on 4 February 1939. Named *Syrinx*, 'JK had her original engines exchanged in 1936 for four 660-hp Bristol Pegasus XC radials. The 113-foot-span aircraft was withdrawn from use in December 1939 and scrapped at Exeter the following year.

During June 1939, E. J. R. visited the following aerodromes: Henlow, Gatwick, Redhill, Hanworth, Croydon, Gravesend, Rochester, West Malling, Hooton Park, Speke (Liverpool), Southport, Barton (Manchester), Heston, and Brooklands.

On the way to West Malling on 24 June, E. J. R. popped into Hanworth and photographed Publicity Planes' Avro 504N G-AEMP standing in front of Exchange & Mart's very distinctive hangar. A wingless stable mate, 504N G-ACLV, owned by Aerial sites Ltd, stood forlornly nearby.

Arriving at West Malling, E. J. R. wangled a flight in D.H.60G Moth G-ABAM with pilot H. D. Williams. The 30-minute trip to Horton Kirby and back was made at 500 feet in pouring rain and a 20-mph wind. Sadly, no photographs were taken during the flight, but D.H.60G Moth G-AFTG, the last production example of this marque, was snapped. This aircraft had been exported originally to Switzerland as HB-OFL, returning to the land of its birth to take up British registry in November 1938, and subsequently in use by Malling Aviation Ltd. Three months after it was photographed at West Malling, the Moth was impressed into RAF service as X5054.

According to E. J. R.'s records the following day, 25 June, he called in at Southport and took photographs of D.H.83 Fox Moth G-ACCB, flying pleasure trips off the beach. Owned by Giro Aviation Ltd and operated from Southport beach since January 1936, 'CB ended its days following a ditching not far from its home on 25 September 1956.

During July, E. J. R. visited Brian Field's place at Kingswood Knoll in the depths of the Surrey countryside. Here he came across Hawker Tomtit G-AFVV, one of six Field had acquired from the Air Ministry and subsequently sold on the civil market. Built for the RAF as K1784, this aircraft had been registered to the Leicestershire Aero Club at Braunstone, operator of four Tomtits until the outbreak of war. Subsequently, 'VV was one of three Tomtits acquired by Alex Henshaw when he was chief test pilot with Vickers-Armstrongs at Castle Bromwich during the war.

With acquisition of its first Lockheed 14s, for use on particular European services, British Airways possessed the fastest aircraft of its class. Twenty-one Lockheed 14-F62s were turned out by Lockheed, all exported to Europe. Most famous of them was British Airways' flagship G-AFGN, in which Prime Minister Neville Chamberlain flew to Munich to meet Hitler, afterwards to wave that renowned piece of paper on his return. G-AFKE, named *Lothair*, was registered in November 1938 and seen at Croydon on 4 February 1939. In October 1943, it was transferred to the RAF to become HK982. During service with the Middle East Air Force, it was renumbered VF247 and struck off charge in 1945.

Though the four-engined Armstrong Whitworth A.W. 27 Ensign was ordered as early as 1935, it was not until January 1938 that the prototype made its first flight. First deliveries to Imperial Airways began later that year, but the Second World War resulted in many of the airline's dozen aircraft being camouflaged for a variety of duties, ranging from ferrying food and arms to France to operating BOAC's services in the Near East. Those Ensigns that survived the war were scrapped at Hamble in 1947. Pictured at Croydon on 4 February 1939 is the prototype and Imperial Airways' flagship G-ADSR *Ensign*, first registered in June 1938. 'SR was damaged in Lagos in September 1943 following an unintentional undercarriage retraction on the ground, and was subsequently scrapped.

D.H.60 Moth G-EBOI, seen at Brooklands on 5 February 1939 when it was owned by R. Boots, was first registered in July 1926 to the Hampshire Aeroplane Club and subsequently to several private owners, including gliding expert Phillip Wills. In March 1940, the Moth was impressed into the RAF and given maintenance serial 2061M.

G-ABWW was one of three Comper CLA.7 Swifts fitted with 130-hp de Havilland Gipsy Major engines, produced in 1932-33 purely for racing. It raced on behalf of the Prince of Wales when it achieved second place in the 1932 King's Cup air race. In the following year's Coupe Deutsch, held at Etampes, 'WW was hopelessly outclassed, although an average speed of 149 mph was impressive for a Comper Swift. Thereafter, successive owners tried to squeeze a few extra mph out of the Swift. Stan Lowe had the lift struts faired-in and 'WW was still sporting these at Gravesend on 1 April 1939 when owned by H. O. Winters. In 1943, the Swift was acquired by an ATC squadron at Maidstone, Kent.

There were not that many D.H.60 Moths still airworthy during the closing months of peace; one of the few was G-EBQX, seen at Gatwick outside Southern Aircraft's hangar on 6 May 1939. Delivered to the Norfolk & Norwich Aero Club in 1927, 'QX had several owners, and during the last months of 1939, was operated by Air Views Ltd at Castle Bromwich. In November, the Moth was put into storage at Gatwick and survived the war, only to be scrapped at Beddington in 1951.

From Kingswood Knoll it was a quick run down to Gatwick, where E. J. R. photographed Short Scion G-ACUV in its Air Touring-Gatwick livery. Delivered to Aberdeen Airways Ltd in July 1934, this Pobjoy Niagara-powered, five-passenger aircraft did not survive the war.

On 7 July, E. J. R. managed to find time to marry Marjorie Statham at Greenwich registry office.

A visit to Heston on 15 July was rewarded with the sight of a very rare bird indeed - American-built Fleet F.7C-2 G-AEJY, imported into Britain in mid-1938. Powered by a 135-hp Armstrong Siddeley Genet Major, 'JY passed through the hands of several private owners, survived the war, and was flying until put into storage at Kidlington, Oxford. It was moved to Ringway in 1958, and sadly was scrapped the following year.

Bristol Beaufighter prototype R2052 was first flown at Filton on 17 July, and eight days later, the prototype of the promising, twin-engined Avro Manchester L7246 made its first flight from Ringway in its original twin-fin configuration. A central fin was added later to aid stability, but the unreliability of its Rolls-Royce Vulture engines ultimately sealed the Manchester's fate. But from this inauspicious beginning, the four-engined bomber that became the Lancaster was born.

On 26 July, E. J. R. dropped into Yeadon and photographed Avro 640 Cadet G-ACPB; once a familiar sight with two other Cadets when used for formation aerobatics by Sir Alan Cobham's National Aviation Day displays, and later by C. W. A. Scott during 1933-36. By 1939, 'PB was owned by J. L. Bebb and kept at Croydon. Its flying career ending in the disastrous fire at Hooton Park on 8 July 1940. Also at Yeadon were D.H.60 Moths of the Yorkshire Aeroplane Club, including G-AAIA, destined for impressment and use as a decoy on a dummy airfield.

On 5 August, with war inevitable, Imperial Airways suspended its weekly transatlantic flights. During 8 to 11 August, the skies over the south-east and London area were filled with the sight and resonating sound of 1,300 aircraft taking part in one of the largest pre-war air and ground

These pages: By 1939, there were not many airworthy Avro 504Ks around; survivors were flown until C of A expiry, and were then either burnt or left in some dark corner to fall victim to the weather – or small boys. G-EBVL had been built by aircraft designer F. G. Miles from parts he had acquired from A. V. Roe, and he sold it to his associate Lionel Bellairs in 1927. After ownership by Southern Aircraft Ltd, the Avro passed to Francis C. Fisher and ended up in Christchurch, where it was abandoned in 1937. These three photographs were taken over a period of months, the last on 10 August 1939, recording the sad end to an historic aircraft.

defence exercises ever staged, including a foretaste of what was to come – a practice 'black-out' of the entire area.

During this excitement, on 5 August, E. J. R. and wife Marjorie set off from Charlton, South London, to Dorset for their delayed honeymoon. On reaching Wimborne, they met up with J. G. E. in his Austin Ten, in which the three of them made their way to Cornwall. The honeymoon did not interfere with visits to aerodromes on the way though, and on 9 August, they called in at Clyst Honiton, opened for flying in May 1937, now Exeter Airport. Here, they were rewarded with the sight of two very rare aeroplanes – Shapley Kittiwake Mk 2 G-AFRP and Surrey Flying Services' A.L.1 G-AALP. The former looked like a creation of Alfred Bestall, the artist who best illustrated the Rupert Bear annuals! The brainchild of E. S. Shapley, it was a side-by-side, two-seater, featuring a gull wing. The earlier Kittiwake Mk 1 G-AEZN was similar in design, but had an open cockpit. Fitted with a 50-hp Continental A50 engine, the Mk 1 was first flown in June 1937, but unsurprisingly, proved underpowered. Its successor, powered with a 90-hp Pobjoy Niagara, was first flown in 1938. The ungainly aircraft survived the war, but crashed near Exeter during spinning trials on 10 May 1946.

Lurking in the same hangar, the one-off Surrey Flying Services A.L.1 was an attractive little two-seat trainer, designed by genius Joe Bewsher of ANEC Missel Thrush fame. Built at Croydon in 1929, the A.L.1 loitered at its birthplace until moved to Exeter, where it was flown by new owner Bertram Arden until put into long-term storage. Tantalisingly, the aircraft is still extant!

Returning from Exeter the following day, E. J. R. called in at Christchurch, photographing the decaying and almost deceased Avro 504K G-EBVL. He had been taking pictures of the deteriorating biplane since it was abandoned at Christchurch after its Certificate of Airworthiness expired in March 1937. In a letter written to A. J. Jackson during the war, E. J. R. recalled:

The Percival Q. 6 was a five/six-seat, twin-engine monoplane powered by two 205-hp de Havilland Gipsy Six engines with either fixed or retractable undercarriage, although only four were equipped with the latter. First flown by Edgar Percival from Luton in September 1937, the Q.6 went into production the following year. Almost thirty were built and all but one was impressed into service during the Second World War, including G-AFIX, a retractable undercarriage version seen at Croydon in Western Airways livery on 6 May 1939. After being impressed as X9406, this Q. 6 acquired a fixed undercarriage following an accident at Bovingdon. After the war, it was restored to the British civil register and had several owners before ending up with Starways Ltd, at Speke, Liverpool. In May 1949, 'IX came to grief at Broomhall and was written off.

Aaah, why did you have to walk right in front of the Blenheim's serial number? Of course, this would not be a problem in this digital photography age, but in 1939... E. J. R.'s notes record the aircraft as Bristol Blenheim L6881 of No. 6 squadron, taxiing out at Gatwick on 6 May 1939. If the aircraft is L6881, it was newly-delivered to the squadron, but lost eventually when it flew into high ground during a sandstorm near El Daba, Egypt, in February 1941.

North American Harvard I N7001 at Heathrow on 14 May 1939. The second of a batch of 200 Harvard Is delivered from the USA from December 1938 onwards, this aircraft was evaluated by the A&AEE before going to No. 20 FTS. On 29 May 1942, it collided with Harvard I P5863 and crashed.

News of an Avro, to wit, G-EBVL, flying at Christchurch filtered through (the quality of Mersey is *not* strained) to Manchester, and we travelled day and night to Christchurch to photograph it, only to find it somewhat dilapidated by the ravages of weather and small boys. 'VL was tucked amongst the trees, and I remember walking for miles through the marshes and barbed wire to get to it. We also had some trouble with the 'management'. They had a 504N (Mongoose) G-AECS in fairly good condition, i.e. not very airworthy, parked to the left of the clubhouse. Bud Fisher was the bloke who chucked you out – he tried the same on us, but we were camping about 4 miles away and fooled him by getting up at 5 a.m. the next morning and getting a lovely brace of stopped-down exposures. Fisher and Clive-Smith were about the biggest rogues in the joy-riding racket, and I've met most of 'em! They were engaged on the old game of 'photograph your country seat from the air' at 50 guineas per time – perhaps. He got on swimmingly well until he photographed some MP's place without permission and questions were asked in Parliament. When he'd paid that lot off, he started the flying club and never looked back.

Visiting Portsmouth Aerodrome on 12 August, E. J. R. came across D.H.60 Moths G-AAIE of the Portsmouth Aero Club and G-EBZC of the Yapton Aero Club. After impressment as AW160, 'IE ended its days after a heavy landing at West Freugh in October 1942. Veteran 'ZC became AW158, but was struck off RAF charge at the end of 1940.

On calling at Hanworth on the way home, E. J. R. photographed Avro 504N G-AEMP, again with Aircraft Exchange & Mart's hangar as a backdrop. Operated latterly by Publicity Planes Ltd, 'MP was impressed into the RAF as BV208, but its service use has gone unrecorded. E. J. R. visited Hanworth the following day and grabbed a 10-minute flight with F. Brooks in Cirrus Minor-powered B.A. Swallow G-AFHM, operated by the London Air Park Flying Club. After the war, this Swallow defected to Ireland and became EI-AEC.

Above and below: How many people does it take to rig a 1911 Deperdussin? This Edwardian monoplane is still airworthy and can often be seen hopping around the Shuttleworth Collection's Old Warden airfield on windless summer evenings. Seen at the Royal Aeronautical Society's garden party at Heathrow on 14 May 1939, the same aircraft was active at Hendon before the First World War. After suffering damage, it was sold to A. E. Grimmer, repaired and sold again in 1935 to Richard Shuttleworth for further restoration at Old Warden, in time to fly at the 1939 RAeS garden party. The Dep was one of the stars of the 1965 film *Those Magnificent Men and Their Flying Machines*, and is believed to be the world's second-oldest airworthy aeroplane.

This Hungarian-registered Bucker Bu 131 Jungmann, powered by a Hirth HM 504 in-line engine, made an appearance at the Royal Aeronautical Society's garden party at Heathrow on 14 May 1939. First flown in May 1934, the Jungmann was a basic trainer with the German Luftwaffe for many years. The registration HA-LCA was re-used later on a Malev Tupolev Tu-154.

Two unique birds were seen at Gatwick on 20 August – Porterfield 35-70 G-AEOK and Hirtenberg HS 9A D-EDJH. Built at Hirtenberg, Austria, in 1937, as OE-DJH, the latter was a two-seater, powered by a 120-hp Gipsy Major engine. It was flown to England as D-EDJH a month before E. J. R. photographed it, and registered G-AGAK in November 1939. After surviving the war, this delightful aircraft was lost when it crashed in poor visibility at Butser Hill, near Petersfield, during a flight from Denham in April 1956.

The tandem two-seat Porterfield, built in the USA in 1936, was imported new by Surrey Flying Services, which operated it for instruction at Croydon. Stored during the war at Gatwick, it was unceremoniously put on the dump to rot in 1947.

E. J. R. returned to Hanworth on 25 August and received 12 minutes instruction from F. Brooks in BA Swallow G-AFHU. By this time, he had a total of sixty-nine flights recorded in his logbook, amounting to 19 hours aloft.

The next and last ports of call before war was declared the following week were during a foray into Essex, first to Broxbourne, home of the Herts & Essex Aero Club, and then to Maylands. It was 27 August. At Broxbourne, E. J. R. came across Dart Kitten II G-AEXT, built at Dunstable in 1937 and powered by a 36-hp Aeronca JAP J-99 engine. Its owner F. Dawson Paul kept it at Gatwick, and the history of this ultralight would fill a book. After many trials and tribulations, 'XT is still airworthy more than seventy-five years on. During the visit to Maylands, once the home of the Hillman's enterprise, E. J. R. came across one of that firm's early charter aircraft; D.H. 83 Fox Moth G-ABVI, owned by Maylands-based Essex Aero Ltd. The Fox went up in smoke on 2 February 1940 when the hangar in which it was residing was hit by a German bomb.

On 1 September, a blackout was imposed across Britain from sunset every evening, and the Army and RAF were officially mobilised. Following Germany's invasion of Poland, Britain declared war on Germany on 3 September and all civil flying came to a halt. National Service became compulsory for men aged eighteen to forty-one, unless they had reserved occupations. Working for the AID, E. J. R. continued his inspection duties at Fairey's Great West Aerodrome, before taking up similar posts with London Aircraft Production and later the de Havilland Aircraft Company at Leavesden Aerodrome, inspecting Handley Page Halifaxes and de Havilland Mosquitoes respectively.

And what became of trusty *June Bug*? The old Seven soldiered on until sold in March 1941 to a Mr H. R. Watson of Tilehurst, Berkshire, for £2 plus goodwill! During E. J. R.'s ownership, the little car had clocked up a further 29,500 miles. His next car, driven throughout the war, was a sporty little Austin '65', but as they say, that's another story.

Above: Parked next to D.H.91 Albatross G-AFJ at the Royal Aeronautical Society's garden party at Heathrow on 14 May is D.H.94 Moth Minor G-AFOM, with D.H.89A Dragon Rapide G-AEPW in the background. By this time, Moth Minor production was in full swing; aircraft were turned out at Hatfield at the rate of eight per week, the prototype having first flown in June 1937. Production was moved to Australia early in 1940 because space was required at Hatfield for war production. Powered by a 90-hp de Havilland Gipsy Minor engine, the Moth Minor proved very popular with flying clubs. 'OM was acquired by the London Aeroplane Club and based at Panshanger until shipped to Australia in March 1940, where it became VH-AED.

Opposite above: From nose to tail, the beautifully proportioned D.H.91 Albatross was an essay in streamlining. Even the cowlings of the four 525-hp de Havilland Gipsy Twelve engines were an incredible feat of engineering excellence. First flown in May 1937, the Albatross experienced a number of teething problems with undercarriage retraction and overload tests, and when the fuselage of the second prototype broke in two, subsequent aircraft had to be strengthened. Production aircraft also had a redesigned tailplane and accommodation for twenty-two passengers and four crew, the two prototypes being used for carrying mail. The five production aircraft flew on Imperial Airways' European routes for little more than a year before the Second World War intervened. Of the seven built, two were scrapped, while the five others were involved in accidents that ended their careers. By late 1943, none were airworthy. Seen with her Gipsy Twelves ticking over, Imperial Airways' D.H.91 G-AFDJ *Falcon* is taxiing out in the gloom for a demonstration flight at the Royal Aeronautical Society's garden party at Heathrow on 14 May 1939. 'DJ was scrapped in September 1943

Below: The curiously named, one-off Reid & Sigrist R.S.1 Snargasher G-AEOD was designed as a three-seat trainer and built at Desford shortly before the Second World War. Powered by two 205-hp de Havilland Gipsy Six engines, the aircraft's first public appearance was at the Royal Aeronautical Society garden party at Heathrow in May 1939. During the war, the Snargasher flew as the maker's communications aircraft until scrapped in 1944.

The Fairey Firefly II must rank as one of the most beautiful biplane fighters ever created. Seen at the Heathrow Royal Aeronautical Society garden party on 14 May is A.F. 5054, built by Avions Fairey as a Mk II, but later converted to Mk IV and fitted with a 785-hp Hispano-Suiza 12Xbrs engine. In late 1933, A.F.5054 was purchased by the parent company, and its performance was evaluated by Fairey test pilot Chris Staniland. With the Hispano-Suiza engine, it had a top speed of 220 mph at 20,000 feet.

The tongue-twistingly named Foster Wikner Wicko was the brainchild of Australian Geoffrey Wikner who had been designing aeroplanes since 1931. In an attempt to produce a cheap, two-seat cabin aeroplane, he came up with the Wicko. After experimenting with a variety of different engines, Wikner finally settled for the 130-hp de Havilland Gipsy Major. Nine Wicko G.M.1 production aircraft were built, one of which, G-AFKS, is seen at Heathrow on 14 May 1939. In June 1942, the aircraft was earmarked for impressment into the RAF as HM574, but never taken on RAF charge. Instead, it was used for communication duties by the manufacturer and eventually scrapped at Eastleigh in 1946.

Following in the slipstream of the Luton A.A4 Minor, so to speak, designer C. H. Latimer-Needham designed a cabin version powered by a 62-hp Walter Mikron II engine. The prototype was built by Luton Aircraft Ltd at Gerrards Cross in 1939 and registered G-AFMU. By the time of the 1939 Royal Aeronautical Society garden party at Heathrow, the two-seater had just received its Authorisation to Fly, having been test flown by Edward Mole on 12 March. Sadly, G-AFMU was burnt in the fire that destroyed the works in 1943. That was not the end of the Luton Major story however; Phoenix Aircraft Ltd acquired the design rights of the Major in 1958, and dozens of home-built L.A.5As have since given their owners enormous pleasure.

The Avro 640 Cadet three-seater, with the pilot occupying the rear cockpit, began appearing in 1933. Three of them – G-ACLU, G-ACOZ, and G-ACPB – all powered by Armstrong Siddeley Genet Majors, were used for joyriding and formation flying with Cobham's National Aviation Day displays. They were painted red, white, and blue, and later passed to C. W. A. Scott's Flying Display Ltd. When 'PB left the 'circus', it was acquired by J. L. Bebb and based at Hooton. The aircraft, seen at Yeadon, Leeds, on 26 July 1939, was another victim of the fire at Hooton in July 1940.

The H. G. Hawker Engineering Company concentrated on producing military aircraft, but the pretty little Hawker Tomtit was the exception to the rule. Although the majority of those built were supplied to the RAF during 1929-31 as trainers, a batch of five purely civil Tomtits was registered during 1930-31. In addition, during the latter half of the 1930s, RAF Tomtits came on to the civil market, taking the total British civil registered Tomtit population to fifteen. They were flown with a variety of engines ranging in power from 105 to 225 hp, but the most popular installation was the Armstrong Siddeley Mongoose. Seen at Brian Field's Kingswood field on 2 July 1939 is Tomtit G-AFVV, the penultimate Tomtit to be registered. Built as K1784, it became 'VV in July 1939, and was delivered to the Leicestershire Aero Club at Braunstone. During the war, it was registered to test pilot Alex Henshaw, who also owned G-AFTA and G-AGEF. The registration for 'VV was cancelled in 1945.

The Canadian Fleet F.7C Trainer was built in 1937 by Fleet Aircraft Ltd at Fort Erie, Ontario. Powered by a 135-hp Armstrong Siddeley Genet Major, the sole British example was imported in 1938 and registered G-AEJY in July, having been test flown at Gatwick. Seem at Heston on 15 July 1939, when owned by Heston-based Aero Industries Ltd, the Fleet survived the war, but received some damage after a bad landing at Kidlington, Oxford, in April 1946. Thereafter, it was stored and transferred to Ringway in 1958, only to be scrapped at Altringham in July 1959.

J. G. E. sorting out the plugs on his Austin Ten CNB 414 at Grampound, Cornwall, during the tour of the West Country in August 1939.

J. G. E. taking a breather as E. J. R.'s wife Madge rustles up a sandwich at Lyndhurst during the tour of the south-west of England in August 1939. Austin Seven FU9165 *June Bug* had an engine of 7.8-hp and was first registered in October 1928. It was acquired by E. J. R. in December 1937 for £9 with 6,760 miles on the clock, and sold in March 1941 for £2, plus goodwill. During E. J. R. 's ownership, the car accumulated a further 29,400 miles.

It's 9 August 1939, war is less than a month away, and two D.H.87B Hornet Moths of the Exeter Aero Club Ltd bask in the sun at Honiton Clyst, Exeter. G-ADKM, nearer the camera, was completed at Hatfield in 1935 and first went north to join the Tollerton Aero Club Ltd. G-AFMP was delivered to the Weston Aero Club Ltd at Weston-Super-Mare in January 1939. Both were impressed into the RAF. 'MP became W5782 and was used by No. 6 Coastal Patrol Flight on *Scarecrow* patrols. Following a heavy landing at RAF St Eval in February 1940, the Moth was taken off RAF charge. 'KM also went to No. 6 C.P.F., but spent most of the war being moved from one M.U. to another. It received a new C of A in May 1946 and was still airworthy at the time of writing.

Opposite below: One-off Surrey AL.1 G-AALP was a side-by-side trainer designed by Joe Bewsher and powered by a 95-hp Salmson A.C.7 radial engine. It was built by Surrey Flying Services at Croydon in 1929 and registered to F. J. Grant for a couple of years before returning to its maker. The biplane languished at Croydon for several years before being sold to Bertram Arden in May 1938 and kept at Honiton Clyst, where it was photographed on 9 August 1939. The aircraft still exists.

Above: Looking like something out of a Rupert Bear Annual, the first Shapley Kittiwake G-AEZN was an open-cockpit, side-by-side, two-seater, powered by a 50-hp Continental A. 50 engine. It was built by E. S. Shapley at Torquay in 1937 and first flown at Roborough, Plymouth. It received its Authorisation to Fly in June, but was dismantled soon after. In 1938, Shapley produced the Kittiwake Mk II, registered G-AFRP. It differed from the Mk I by having an enclosed cockpit and a bigger 90-hp Pobjoy Niagara engine. It too was first flown at Roborough in 1938, and after surviving the war in storage, crashed during spinning trials near Exeter on 10 May 1946. 'RP is seen at Honiton Clyst on 9 August 1939.

Next page above: The Austrian Hirtenberg HS.9A was built by the Hirtenberger Patronen Zundhutchen und Metallwarrenfabrik A. G. at Hirtenberg from 1932, and one was for British customer J. H. Davis. Registered in Austria as OE-DJH, it arrived in England as D-EDJH and is seen at Gatwick on 12 August 1939 before taking up British registration G-AGAK in November. During the war, 'AK was stored at Filton, Bristol, and had various private owners, the last being C. H. Cosmelli, who kept the aircraft at Denham from 1956. On 15 February that year, Cosmelli crashed the Hirtenberg in poor weather at Butser Hill, near Petersfield, and the aircraft was written off. Mr Cosmelli's misfortune continued, for on 31 January 1961, again flying from Denham, he crashed and wrote off his beautiful Aeromere F.8L Falco III G-APUO.

Spot the aeroplane. Avro 504N G-AEMP began life as J9017 with the RAF. First it was delivered to No. 2 FTS in July 1928, transferring later to No. 5 FTS before being demobbed in 1936 and sold to Air Travel Ltd that September. The same month, the Avro passed to Plane Advertising Ltd and was used for banner-towing from its Abridge base in Essex. In 1939, 'MP was acquired by Publicity Planes Ltd, in whose ownership it is seen at Hanworth on 12 August that year. In January 1941, 'MP went to war, having been impressed as BV208. Its military career is not recorded, although it may have been used as an airfield decoy.

The Porterfield 'Flyabout' 35-70 was a very popular, cheap to run, tandem-seater powered by a 70-hp Le Blond radial engine. Produced by the Porterfield Aircraft Corporation of Kansas City, the 35-70 was certificated in the USA in May 1935. Around 200 were built, one of which was imported into the UK in 1936. G-AEOK, seen at Gatwick on 20 August 1939, was imported by Surrey Flying Services Ltd and used for pilot training. It escaped RAF impressment during the war and was stored at Croydon for the duration, but having survived this far, was scrapped at Gatwick in 1947.

During 1936, A. R. Weyl, formerly a designer at Fokker, produced several interesting ultralight designs, all built by Dart Aircraft Ltd at Dunstable. The one-off Dart Flittermouse G-AELZ, powered by a pusher 25-hp Scott Squirrel, resembled a powered primary glider. The one-off Dart Pup was a pretty little high-wing, single-seat pusher, and lastly there was the Dart Kitten. The Dart Kitten Mk I was a low-wing, single-seater, powered by a 27-hp Ava 4a-oo engine. An improved Mk II version, G-AEXT, was powered by a 36-hp Aeronca JAP. J-99. Awarded an Authorisation to Fly in April 1937, the Kitten II passed through many owners and survived the war. However, a bad crash at Willindale in November 1964, in which the pilot was killed, was the end — or so it seemed. It was eventually rebuilt, restored to the register in 1976, and was still airworthy at the time of writing. This picture is of 'XT at Broxbourne on 27 August 1939.

Postscript

During the compilation of this book, I often wondered what had become of my father's home in Chorlton-cum-Hardy since he and his family moved south to Dorset in 1939, and so I wrote to the present occupier explaining my interest and enclosing some of the photographs reproduced in Chapter One. Almost by return of post, I received a very detailed letter from Russell Kirby, together with very recent photographs replicating those I had included with my letter. The changes to the house and the surrounding area are many, but some aspects are still recognisable. In a subsequent email, I explained my father's involvement with Avro 504K G-ABAA, and that it not only survives, but is exhibited at the nearby Greater Manchester Museum of Science and Technology. Less than a day later, I received this photograph from Russell, taken that day, standing with G-ABAA. Wonderful!

Appendices

E. J. R.'s FLIGHTS (1929-39)

Date	Aircraft Type	Reg.	Pilot	Journey	Time (minutes)
3 September 1929	Avro 504K	G-EBVW	A. N. Kingwell	Whitby Moor (local)	5
9 September 1930	Avro 504K	G-ABAV	E. W. Bonar	Holyhead (local)	5
17 September 1933	D.H.84 Dragon I	G-ACGU	J. Higgins	Squires Gate (local)	5
2 June 1934	Bellanca Pacemaker	G-ABNW	A. Weedon	Barton–Stockport return	13
23 June 1934	Bellanca Pacemaker	G-ABNW	A. Weedon	Barton–Woodford	12
23 June 1934	Bellanca Pacemaker	G-ABNW	A. Weedon	Woodford–Barton	14
27 July 1935	Avro 504N	G-ADBS	L. G. Anderson	Stretford (local)	4
27 July 1935	Avro 504N	G-ADBS	L. G. Anderson	Stretford (local)	4
14 September 1935	Avro 631 Cadet	G-ABYC	H. A. Crommelin	Woodford (test)	5
14 September 1935	Avro 594 Avian III	G-EBXD	H. A. Crommelin	Woodford (test)	5
27 July 1935	Avro 504N	G-ADBS	L. G. Anderson	Stretford (local)	4
27 July 1935	Avro 504N	G-ADBS	L. G. Anderson	Stretford (local)	4
14 September 1935	Avro 631 Cadet	G-ABYC	H. A. Crommelin	Woodford (test)	5
14 September 1935	Avro 594 Avian III	G-EBXD	H. A. Crommelin	Woodford (test)	5
12 February 1936	Avro 504K	G-EASF	W. Hobbs	Hooton Park (local)	4

19 April 1936	D.H.80A Puss Moth	G-ABLB	J. Woodman	Croydon (local)	15
23 May 1936	Avro 548A	G-EBIU	G. W. Haigh	Hooton Park (local)	3
23 May 1936	Avro 504K	G-ABAA	L. A. Lewis	Hooton Park (local)	3
23 May 1936	Avro 625 Avian	G-AAYV	J. S. Taylor	Hooton Park–Woodford	15
9 May 1937	D.H.84 Dragon I	G-ACIU	S. F. Woods	Croydon (local)	6
7 July 1937	D.H.83 Fox Moth	G-ACCB	S. N. Giroux	Southport (local)	9
8 July 1937	Avro 504K	G-ABAA	L. A. Lewis	Rhyl (local)	5
1 August 1937	D.H.80A Puss Moth	G-ABLB	P. Weiss	Croydon (local)	8
28 August 1937	Hillson Praga	G-AEUN	R. F. Graesser	Barton (instruction)	20
4 September 1937	Hillson Praga	G-AEUM	R. F. Graesser	Barton (instruction)	15
10 September 1937	Hillson Praga	G-AEUM	T. N. Winning	Barton (instruction)	15
18 September 1937	Hillson Praga	G-AEUK	T. N. Winning	Barton (instruction)	15
19 September 1937	Avro 504N	G-AEGW	L. J. Rimmer	Orford (Lancs)	4
1 October 1937	Hillson Praga	G-AEUM	T. N. Winning	Barton (instruction)	20
3 October 1937	Hillson Praga	G-AEPJ	R. F. Graesser	Barton (instruction)	35
5 October 1937	Hillson Praga	G-AEPJ	T. N. Winning	Barton (instruction)	30
6 October 1937	Hillson Praga	G-AEPJ	T. N. Winning	Barton (instruction)	35
30 October 1937	BA Swallow II	G-AEVZ	R. A. Caws	Hedon (local)	30
27 November 1937	BA Swallow II	G-AEVZ	R. A. Caws	Hedon (local)	45
19 December 1937	D.H.60X Moth	G-AAMS	R. A. Caws	Hedon (local)	30
1 January 1938	BA Swallow II	G-AEVZ	R. A. Caws	Hedon (local)	15
2 January 1938	BA Swallow II	G-AEVZ	R. A. Caws	Hedon (local)	20
2 January 1938	D.H.60X Moth	G-AAMS	R. A. Caws	Hedon (local)	35
12 April 1938	Avro 504K	G-ABAA	L. J. Rimmer	Hooton (test)	8

22 April 1938	Airspeed AS.5 Courier	G-ACLF	Leedham	Hedon (local)	9
23 April 1938	Avro 504K	G-ABAA	B. Prowse	Hedon (local)	5
25 June 1938	Avro 640 Cadet	G-ACFT	Miss Spiller	Hooton–Ringway	30
25 June 1938	Avro 640 Cadet	G-ACFT	Miss Spiller	Ringway–Hooton	35
15 August 1938	Avro 640 Cadet	G-ACFT	C. Williams	Hooton–Neston	15
23 August 1938	Avro 640 Cadet	G-ACFT	Flt Lt W. Hill	Hooton (local)	3
23 August 1938	Avro 640 Cadet	G-ACFT	Flt Lt W. Hill	Hooton (local)	3
23 August 1938	Avro 640 Cadet	G-ACFT	Flt Lt W. Hill	Hooton (local)	4
25 August 1938	Tipsy B	G-AFEI	E. D. Ward	Hooton–RAF Sealand	6
25 August 1938	Tipsy B	G-AFEI	E. D. Ward	RAF Sealand–Hooton	7
10 September 1938	Avro 504N	G-AEGW	L. J. Rimmer	Tarvin (local)	5
13 September 1938	Avro 504N	G-AEGW	L. J. Rimmer	Tarvin (local)	10
15 September 1938	D.H.83 Fox Moth	G-ACEY	Flt Lt W. Hill	Tarvin (local)	12
17 September 1938	D.H.83 Fox Moth	G-ACEY	Flt Lt W. Hill	Tarvin (local)	8
21 September 1938	Avro 504N	G-AEGW	L. J. Rimmer	Nantwich–Hooton	20
24 September 1938	Avro 504N	G-AEGW	L. J. Rimmer	Hooton–Walsall	60
25 September 1938	Avro 504N	G-AEGW	L. J. Rimmer	Walsall–Wem	45
29 September 1938	Avro 504N	G-AEGW	L. J. Rimmer	Wem–Hooton	25
1 October 1938	Avro 504N	G-AEGW	L. J. Rimmer	Hooton–Rochdale	35
5 October 1938	Avro 640 Cadet	G-ACFT	Flt Lt W. Hill	Rochdale–Barton	35
5 October 1938	Avro 640 Cadet	G-ACFT	Flt Lt W. Hill	Barton–Hooton	35
9 October 1938	Avro 504N	G-AEGW	L. J. Rimmer	Rochdale–Hooton	55
13 October 1938	Monospar ST.25	G-AEDY	L. J. Rimmer	Hooton (local)	5
13 October 1938	Monospar ST.25	G-AEDY	L. J. Rimmer	Hooton (local)	7

16 October 1938	Avro 504N	G-AEGW	L. J. Rimmer	Hooton–Runcorn	15
16 October 1938	Avro 504N	G-AEGW	L. J. Rimmer	Runcorn–Hooton	15
30 October 1938	D.H.87B Hornet Moth	G-ADMJ	C. Doodson	Woodford (local)	30
7 May 1939	Short S.16 Scion	G-ACUV	A. L. Brooke-Smith	Gatwick (local)	5
7 May 1939	Short S.16 Scion	G-ACUV	E. D. Spratt	Gatwick (local)	7
7 May 1939	Miles M.3A Falcon Major	G-ADFH	E. D. Spratt	Gatwick (local)	4
24 June 1939	BA Swallow II	G-AFHM	F. Brooks	Hanworth (instruction)	10
25 June 1939	BA Swallow II	G-AFHM	F. Brooks	Hanworth (instruction)	12

About 19 hours flying and 68 flights (1929-39).

J. G. E.'S FLIGHTS (1932-39)

Date	Aircraft Type	Reg.	Pilot	Journey	Time (minutes)
27 December 1932	Avro 504K	G-ABHK	J. Oliver	Edge House Farm	4
January 1933	Avro 504K	G-ABHK	J. Oliver	Edge House Farm	4
23 June 1934	Bellanca Pacemaker	G-ABNW	J. Weeden	Barton (local)	18
23 June 1934	Bellanca Pacemaker	G-ABNW	J. Weeden	Woodford (local)	17
2 June 1934	Bellanca Pacemaker	G-ABNW	J. Weeden	Barton (local)	25
27 July 1935	Avro 504N	G-ADBS	L. Anderson	Edge House Farm	4
27 July 1935	Avro 504N	G-ADBS	L. Anderson	Edge House Farm	4
2 February 1936	Avro 504K	G-EASF	E. Hobbs	Hooton Park	3
22 July 1936	Avro 548A	G-EBIU	L. Lewis	Kinmel Sands, Rhyl	8
13 August 1936	D.H.83 Fox Moth	G-ABUT		Croydon	7

21 May 1937	D.H.83 Fox Moth	G-ACCB	S. N. Giroux	Birkdale Sands	7
21 May 1937	D.H.83 Fox Moth	G-ACCB	S. N. Giroux	Birkdale Sands	7
21 May 1937	D.H.83 Fox Moth	G-ACCB	S. N. Giroux	Birkdale Sands	8
28 August 1937	Hillson Praga	G-AEUN	R. F. Graesser	Barton (instruction)	12
11 September 1937	Hillson Praga	G-AEUM	R. F. Graesser	Barton (instruction)	16
18 September 1937	Hillson Praga	G-AEUN	T. N. Winning	Barton (instruction)	18
2 October 1937	Hillson Praga	G-AEUK	T. N. Winning	Barton (instruction)	16
3 October 1937	Hillson Praga	G-AEPJ	R. F. Graesser	Barton (instruction)	15
8 October 1937	Hillson Praga	G-AEUM	R. F. Graesser	Barton (instruction)	45
11 June 1938	D.H.83 Fox Moth	G-ACCB	S.N. Giroux	Southport	5
30 October 1938	D.H.87B Hornet Moth	–	P. T. Eckersley	Woodford	28
25 January 1939	Hillson Praga	G-AEUN	Mickleson	Barton (instruction)	45
31 January 1939	Hillson Praga	G-AEOK	Imley	Barton (test flight)	5
6 February 1939	Hillson Praga	G-AEOM	Winning Jnr.	Barton (instruction)	30
24 February 1939	Hillson Praga	G-AEUS	T. N. Winning	Barton (instruction)	30
1 March 1939	Hillson Praga	G-AEUR	D. Winning	Barton (instruction)	30
20 March 1939	Hillson Praga	G-AEUR	W. Brown	Barton (instruction)	20
21 March 1939	Hillson Praga	G-AEUM	B. Winning	Barton (instruction)	30
20 April 1939	Hillson Praga	–	B. Winning	Barton (instruction)	30
7 May 1939	Hillson Praga	G-AEUM	B. Winning	Barton (instruction)	60
21 May 1939	Hillson Praga	G-AEUN	Gillespy	Barton (instruction)	25
22 May 1939	Hillson Praga	G-AEUS	Gillespy	Barton (instruction)	30
22 May 1939	Hillson Praga	G-AEUS	Gillespy	Barton (instruction)	30
23 May 1939	Hillson Praga	G-AEUS	Gillespy	Barton (instruction)	25
24 May 1939	Hillson Praga	G-AEUS	Gillespy	Barton (instruction)	25

11 July 1939	Hillson Praga	G-AEYK	Gillespy	Barton (instruction)	30
14 July 1939	Hillson Praga	G-AEYK	Gillespy	Barton (instruction)	30
14 July 1939	Hillson Praga	G-AEYK	Gillespy	Barton (instruction)	30
15 July 1939	Hillson Praga	G-AEYK	Gillespy	Barton (instruction)	30
19 July 1939	Hillson Praga	G-AEUM	Gillespy	Barton (instruction)	25
19 July 1939	Hillson Praga	G-AEUM	Gillespy	Barton (instruction)	30
21 July 1939	Hillson Praga	G-AEYK	Gillespy	Barton (instruction)	30
1 August 1939	Hillson Praga	G-AEYK	Gillespy	Barton (instruction)	25

About 16 hours flying in 45 flights (1932-39).

E. J. R. AND J. G. E. AERODROME VISITS (1930-39)

1930
Barton (Manchester)

1931
Woodford (Manchester)

1932
Barton (Manchester)
Woodford (Manchester)

1933
Barton (Manchester)
Blackpool (Squires Gate, Lancashire)
Hooton Park (Cheshire)
Maylands (Romford, Essex)
Woodford (Manchester)

1934
Barton (Manchester)
Blackpool (Stanley Park, Lancashire)
Brooklands (Surrey)
Croydon (Surrey)
Hooton Park (Cheshire)
Liverpool (Speke)

Lymm, (Manchester)
Reading (Woodley, Berkshire)
Southport Sands (Lancashire)
Woodford (Manchester)

1935
Barton (Manchester)
Blackpool (Stanley Park, Lancashire)
Blackpool (Squires Gate, Lancashire)
Brooklands (Surrey)
Castle Bromwich (Birmingham)
Croydon (Surrey)
Hanworth (Middlesex)
Hawkinge (RAF) (Kent)
Hendon (RAF) (Middlesex)
Heston (Middlesex)
Hooton Park (Cheshire)
Kenley (RAF) (London)
Leeds (Yeadon)
Lympne (Kent)
Manston (RAF) (Kent)
Sealand (RAF) (Cheshire)
Southport Sands (Lancashire)
Woodford (Manchester)

1936
Barton (Manchester)
Blackpool (Stanley Park, Lancashire)
Blackpool (Squires Gate, Lancashire)
Brooklands (Surrey)
Castle Bromwich (Birmingham)
Crownhill (Plymouth)
Croydon (Surrey)
Haldon (Teignmouth, Devon)
Hanworth (Middlesex)
Hendon (RAF) (Middlesex)
Heston (Middlesex)
Hooton Park (Cheshire)
Redhill (Surrey)
Rochester (Kent)
Southport Sands (Lancashire)
Walsall (Staffordshire)
West Malling (Kent)

1937
Barton (Manchester)
Bekesbourne (Kent)
Biggin Hill (RAF) (Kent)
Boscombe Down (RAF) (Wiltshire)
Bristol (Whitchurch, Gloucestershire)
Brough (Yorkshire)
Castle Bromwich (Birmingham)
Catfoss (RAF) (Humberside)
Croydon (Surrey)
Eastleigh (Hampshire)
Filton (Bristol)
Ford (Sussex)
Gatwick (Surrey)
Gravesend (Kent)
Hanworth (Middlesex)
Heath Row (Middlesex)
Hedon (Hull)
Heston (Middlesex)
High Post (Wiltshire)
Hooton Park (Cheshire)
Lympne (Kent)
Maylands (Romford, Essex)
Netheravon (RAF) (Wiltshire)
Old Sarum (Wiltshire)
Portsmouth (Hampshire)
Redhill (Surrey)
Rochester (Kent)
Sealand (RAF) (Cheshire)
Shoreham (Sussex)
Southport Sands (Lancashire)

Tangmere (RAF) (Sussex)
Upavon (RAF) (Wiltshire)
Witney (Oxfordshire)
Woodford (Manchester)
Worthy Down (RAF) (Hampshire)
Yatesbury (Wiltshire)

1938
Stanley Park (Blackpool, Lancashire)
Broxbourne (Essex)
Castle Bromwich (Birmingham)
Croydon (Surrey)
Driffield (RAF) (Humberside)
Finningley (RAF) (South Yorkshire)
Hanworth (Middlesex)
Hedon (Hull)
Heston (Middlesex)
Hooton Park (Cheshire)
Liverpool (Speke)(Lancashire)
Meir (Stoke-on-Trent)
Netherthorpe (Yorkshire)
Ringway (Manchester)
Sealand (RAF) (Cheshire)
Sherburn (Yorkshire)
Tern Hill (RAF) (Shropshire)
Woodford (Manchester)
Walsall (Staffordshire)
Woodford (Manchester)
Worthy Down(RAF) (Hampshire)

1939
Barton (Manchester)
Brooklands (Surrey)
Broxbourne (Hertfordshire)
Christchurch (Hampshire)
Croydon (Surrey)
Exeter (Devon)
Gatwick (Surrey)
Gravesend (Kent)
Haldon (Devon)
Hanworth (Middlesex)
Heath Row (Middlesex)
Henlow (Bedfordshire)
Heston (Middlesex)
High Post (Wiltshire)
Hooton Park (Cheshire)
Horton Kirby (Kent)
Leeds (Yeadon)
Liverpool (Speke, Lancashire)
Maylands (Romford, Essex)

Meir (Stoke-on-Trent)
Odiham (RAF) (Hampshire)
Old Sarum (Wiltshire)
Plymouth (Roborough, Devon)
Portsmouth (Hampshire)
Redhill (Surrey)

Ringway (Manchester)
Rochester (Kent)
Southport Sands (Lancashire)
West Malling (Kent)
Witney (Oxfordshire)

Bibliography

Amos, Peter *Miles Aircraft: The Early Years* (Air-Britain (Historians) Ltd, 2009)

Cruddas, Colin *Those Fabulous Flying Years: Joyriding and Flying Circuses Between the Wars* (Air-Britain (Historians) Ltd, 2003)

Halley, James, J. *The K File: The Royal Air Force of the 1930s* (Air-Britain Historians Ltd, 1995)

Halley, James, J. *Royal Air Force Aircraft L1000-N9999* (Air-Britain (Historians) Ltd, 1993)

Halley, James, J. *Royal Air Force Aircraft J1-J9999 and WW1 Survivors* (Air-Britain Historians) Ltd, 1987)

Hamlin, John, F. *Peaceful Fields: A Directory of Civil Airfields and Landing Grounds in the United Kingdom 1919-1939* (GMS Enterprises, 2007)

Her Majesty's Stationery Office *Report on the Progress of Civil Aviation 1932* (HMS Stationery Office, 1933)

Her Majesty's Stationery Office *Report on the Progress of Civil Aviation 1933* (HMS Stationery Office 1934)

Her Majesty's Stationery Office *Report on the Progress of Civil Aviation 1934* (HMS Stationery Office 1935)

Her Majesty's Stationery Office *Report on the Progress of Civil Aviation 1935* (HMS Stationery Office 1936)

Her Majesty's Stationery Office *Report on the Progress of Civil Aviation 1936* (HMS Stationery Office 1937)

Her Majesty's Stationery Office *Report on the Progress of Civil Aviation 1937* (HMS Stationery Office, 1938)

Her Majesty's Stationery Office *Report on the Progress of Civil Aviation 1938* (HMS Stationery Office, 1939)

Jackson, A. J. *British Civil Aircraft 1919-1972: Volume I* (Putnam, 1973)

Jackson, A. J. *British Civil aircraft 1919-1972: Volume II* (Putnam, 1973)

Jackson, A. J. *British Civil Aviation 1919-1972: Volume III* (Putnam, 1973)

Leeming, John, F. *Airdays* (George G. Harrap and Company Ltd, 1936)

Logan, Malcolm *The Civil Air Guard* (Nicholson & Watson, 1939)

Manning, W. O. & Preston, R. L. *A Register of Civilian Aircraft* (Sir Isaac Pitman & Sons Ltd)

Moss, Peter *Impressments Logs*, Vol 1-3 (Air-Britain, 1962)

Penrose, Harald *British Aviation: Widening Horizons 1930-1934* (Her Majesty's Stationery Office, 1979)

Penrose, Harald *British Aviation: Ominous Skies 1935-1939* (Her Majesty's Stationery Office, 1980)

Stroud, John *Annals of British and Commonwealth Air Transport* (Putnam, 1962)

Thetford, Owen *British Naval Aircraft 1912-1958* (Putnam, 1958)
Thetford, Owen *Aircraft of the Royal Air Force Since 1918* (Putnam, 1957)

UNPUBLISHED PERSONAL PAPERS AND RECORDS

Ellison, J. G. *Pilot's Flying Log Book* (Entries 1932-1939)
Riding, E. J. *Pilot's Log Book* (Entries 1929-1939)
Riding, E. J. *Newspaper Cuttings of UK Aircraft Crashes* (1929-1939)
Riding, E. J. *Correspondence from E. J. R. to A. J. Jackson* (1944-1950)
Riding, E. J. *Flight Logs and Aerodrome Visits* (1929-1939)